Staff
Management
in Library and
Information
Work

Staff Management in Library and Information Work

Noragh Jones · Peter Jordan

Gower   A Grafton Book

12481

Published by
Gower Publishing Company Limited
Gower House, Croft Road, Aldershot,
Hampshire GU11 3HR, England

Reprinted 1984

Distributed in the United States of America
by Lexington Books, D. C. Heath & Co.,
125 Spring Street, Lexington, Mass. 02173

Printed and bound in Great Britain by
Biddles Ltd, Guildford and King's Lynn

British Library Cataloguing in Publication Data

Jones, Noragh
Staff management in library and information work.
1. Library personnel management
I. Title   II. Jordon, Peter
025'.068'3   Z682

ISBN 0-566-03430-1

Contents

Preface

For a number of years we have taught library management to students ranging from those with no working experience at all to highly experienced senior librarians and we have been unable to find a satisfactory text covering personnel management for librarians. This is partly the result of past emphases on library administration rather than management and upon techniques and routines rather than people.

We hope that this book will provide a basis for taught courses in librarianship as well as a working guide for library managers. Although individual sections can be used to learn about particular techniques we believe that it is important for management to be viewed as a seamless web with a change in one part of the system affecting other parts. Thus many of the techniques should not be seen in isolation and out of the context within which they are to be applied. Much damage has been done by librarians applying techniques they have learned without properly appreciating the consequences for real people and real organizations. We have tried to present a management philosophy in the earlier parts of the book and refer to this in subsequent chapters. We believe that such a philosophy can be applied to all types of library and have endeavoured to make the text relevant to all types.

The practical nature of the book is demonstrated by the frequent examples including actual documents being used by libraries. At the end of most of the chapters there are work assignments. We have employed many of these successfully in our teaching and they can be used in training, in educational courses or individuals can test their understanding of chapters independently.

We are most grateful to all those libraries who allowed us to use documents produced by them:

City of London Polytechnic, Liverpool Polytechnic, Polytechnic of the South Bank, Brighton Polytechnic, Gwynned County, Bedfordshire County, Suffolk County, North Tyneside, City of Sheffield, Borough of Trafford, City of Bradford and City of Coventry. Our thanks are also due to Graham McKenna of Leeds Public Libraries for the use of his training questionnaire, to Charles Crossley of Bradford University Library for the use of 'Library subject specialisation at work' which was first published in the University of Bradford Newssheet on 16 October 1975, and to Clive Bingley Ltd. for the use of the mechanistic/organismic paradigm taken from p.126 of 'A reader in library management' edited by Ross Shimmon.

Peter Jordan
Noragh Jones

1   The working environment

Libraries and information units have become increasingly involved in management practices, as pressures from their parent institutions and from their user groups have impelled them to adapt to changing needs and resources. This has meant that many libraries are concerned to find answers to the following questions:

1. How can we evaluate our operations and services, so as to be able to justify our work to our paymasters, and to check that we are responding to user needs?
2. How can we improve our performance by making more effective use of funding, materials, accommodation and staff?
3. How can we create a positive approach to change among our staff?
4. How can we develop more systematic, cost-effective work methods?
5. How can we ensure that staff development and organizational development take place, even when there may be periods of stagnation or recession, with low staff turnover and limited funds?

Every one of these questions includes a reference to staff, which indicates the far-reaching effects that staff management, or lack of it, can have in a library or information unit.

Changes in the work-place

Library and information workers mediate between information and information-seekers. Their work has become increasingly complex with the rise of new technology, changing information needs, and the recognition that many groups need skilled help if they are to translate their latent information needs into articulate demands. The success of a service organization is dependent to a large extent on the knowledge, skills and attitudes of its staff, since they are the people the users meet, and it is their version of the library's objectives and their user-orientation (or lack of it) that is apparent to users in the everyday 'climate' of the library, irrespective of the official role of the library in the institution as 'learning resource centre', or 'on-line information unit' or 'community information service'.

Figure 1.1 summarizes the various layers in the academic library environment that influence, or indeed exert pressures upon, librarians in planning, organizing resources, motivating staff, and evaluating their achievements.

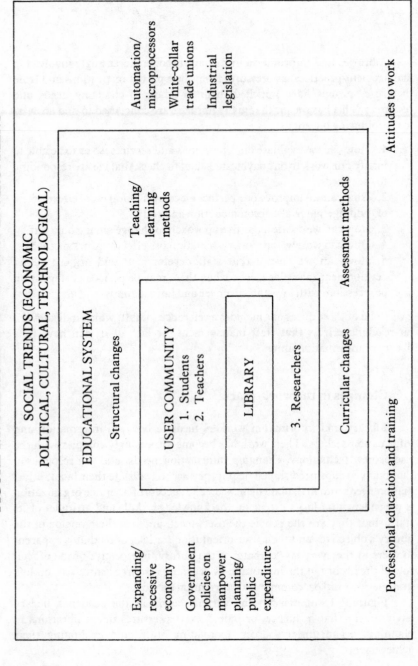

FIGURE 1.1. THE ACADEMIC LIBRARY ENVIRONMENT

SOCIAL TRENDS (ECONOMIC
POLITICAL, CULTURAL, TECHNOLOGICAL)

EDUCATIONAL SYSTEM

Structural changes

Teaching/
learning
methods

USER COMMUNITY

1. Students
2. Teachers

LIBRARY

3. Researchers

Curricular changes

Assessment methods

Automation/
microprocessors

White-collar
trade unions

Industrial
legislation

Attitudes to work

Expanding/
recessive
economy

Government
policies on
manpower
planning/
public
expenditure

Professional education and training

The diagram shows how the library's immediate environment, which is made up of groups of students, teachers and researchers, is affected by trends in the educational system. Library staff need to take account of teaching and learning methods, changes in curriculum and in assessment, when they plan and organize stock, information services, and user education. Beyond the institutional environment of a specific college or university lies the broad spectrum of socio-economic and political trends in the country. Finance for libraries expands or diminishes according to the economic state of health of the nation, and the political ideologies of the government in power. Staff numbers are affected not just by availability of finance, and the need for new services. Government manpower policies may have an impact on the numbers and levels of library staff trained and deployed. Encouragement of automation of library operations leads to reductions and restructuring of staff. The growth of white-collar unions and the spate of industrial legislation during the 1970s have had a major impact on relations between senior management and staff, and raise interesting questions about the nature of professionalism. Are staff loyalties moving more towards self-interest, and away from the traditional service ethic of the professions?

In British public libraries during the 1970s new demands were stimulated by external pressures from the Open University, and from the Adult Literacy scheme. More general social trends such as the increased proportion of old people in the population, and worsening unemployment in advanced industrial countries, have acted as further incentives to developing or extending services for particular groups such as the housebound, the institutionalized, and unemployed school leavers. To what extent are librarians to be trained as social workers?

In the special library field the economic recession of the early 1980s has meant ruthless pruning of those parts of industrial organizations that cannot justify their value to the firm. Information services are required to prove their cost-effectiveness and library staff have had to increase their knowledge of management techniques and management terminology in order to show clearly how their work contributes to the objectives of Research and Development. Another important emphasis in special libraries that necessitates retraining of staff is the rapid growth of on-line information services, which, in the initial stages at any rate, require skilled mediation between the system and the user.

These are some examples of the environmental changes which have caused library managers to reconsider their staff recruitment and training practices gradually during the 1970s and 1980s. Until then the pace of change was slower and more predictable. Staff worked in smaller libraries before local government reorganization in 1974, and before the higher education mergers of colleges (first to form polytechnics, and later to form institutes of higher education). Users did not have very high expectations of libraries, though generally considering them to be 'a good thing', so staff could grow comfortably into their jobs, and carry on for many years without any further training or retraining.

A great deal of this changed during the 1970s and into the 1980s. Libraries have become larger and more complex, which means that the methods of deploying staff need more thought.

Staffing Structures

What staffing structures can be devised to provide effective services, and give job satisfaction? What division is to be made between professional and non-professional staff, to make the most economical use of staff knowledge and skills in an era of frozen posts and public expenditure cuts? In trying to solve some of these staffing problems, librarians have devised a number of strategies, influenced by the new emphasis on user needs and the development of new services.

The team approach is perhaps the most significant, and is most common in public library systems. It makes more effective use of professional staff by giving them a range of duties involving a geographical responsibility for a number of service points, a specialist responsibility (such as information services, or work with children and young people), and often too a subject responsibility for stock in a particular Dewey class number. This means team members have a roving commission and plan their projects within a group of professional colleagues, rather than remaining isolated as branch librarians engaged often in routine clerical duties. Senior non-professionals are given the responsibility of the day-to-day running of the branches.

Another of the most significant changes in staffing structures has been the widespread deployment of subject specialists in academic libraries. The intention here is to provide user education and information services and stock management geared to a specific department or departments (e.g. engineering, business studies, biological sciences), so that professional staff can develop close connections with the faculty and base their services on a well-founded understanding of the subject and how it is taught and researched in their particular college. There seem to be a number of problems emerging from this mode of staff deployment, though it represents a healthily user-oriented approach. It is argued that while the small number of subject specialist librarians have an extremely interesting job, the remaining professional staff must make do with the less interesting work in technical services (acquisitions, cataloguing and classification, and circulation). It is further argued that subject specialists do not get enough practice in the supervision of staff or in management generally so that they may not have the experience useful for promotion to head of a section or to deputy librarian.

The third most striking change in staff deployment has been the deskilling of many library housekeeping jobs, due to the introduction of automated systems (in circulation and acquisitions and cataloguing). This is taken up later in this chapter under the heading of 'Technological innovation'.

Social changes and attitudes to work

Since the Second World War there has been a gradual rise in people's material expectations. A better standard of living, wider educational opportunities for one's children and more humane working conditions are widespread ambitions in advanced industrial societies. Whether this will continue to be so is another matter, as unemployment rises even among the professional classes, and the value of a university or polytechnic degree is no longer self-evident as a passport to a comfortable professional life. It is remarked that the Robbins era of expansion in higher education is dead, and stagnation and despondency are likely to result from the government's determined efforts to apply major cuts in education.

However this may be, people now at work in the 1980s have been moulded by higher expectations than the previous generation, and their attitudes at work are different. The deferential society has faded somewhat, under the influence of 'progressive' educational methods which emphasize child-centredness rather than teacher-centredness, and perhaps even more under the influence of youth subcultures (widely disseminated through the media) and alternative lifestyles. It is easy to exaggerate such influences, but combined with other social trends towards industrial democracy, towards increased unionization in the professions, and towards 'egalitarianism' in education, they are likely to mean different attitudes at work. Staff are less tolerant of working conditions marred by poor standards of health and safety, high levels of boredom, and authoritarian management styles. More staff are likely to want some say in the shaping of their working environment. They are less prepared to accept decisions made without consultation by management on such matters as staff structures and deployment, salary scales and working conditions.

Attitudes to work among library and information staff have been affected by this general background of social and educational change. The acceptance of librarianship as a graduate profession took place in the United States at the beginning of the century. In Britain it was still being resisted in the 1970s, but was finally agreed by the end of the decade. And yet many libraries did not know quite how to use their graduate professionals. The surveys on job satisfaction carried out by Roberts[1] and by Smith and Schofield[2] show that graduates working in academic libraries, for instance, felt that their qualifications were underused. There was too little opportunity for exercising subject knowledge and professional skills. The

Sheffield Manpower Project[3] further emphasized these problems of underutilising staff capability, and noted that methods of staff deployment could in many libraries lead to frustration and of course to services that were not exercising staff qualifications and so presumably were underdeveloped. Other problem areas identified were staff stress, resulting from changes in organizational structure and from technological change; poor communications between management and staff, and between staff and users. The question was raised of employing para-professionals for more of the housekeeping routines which were found by the Sheffield Survey to be carried out by professionals. The need for more highly developed social skills and communication skills was emphasized, reinforcing the trend towards user-orientation. Staff need to be adept at making effective contacts with user, and indeed also with colleagues, if they are to cope with more sophisticated information services and with new staffing structures, with the emphasis on teams and working parties and consultation.

Technological innovation

The automation of library housekeeping routines is widespread. Acquisitions and issue systems are the most obvious areas where computers have taken over the drudgery, but many libraries are now moving towards an integrated systems approach, where acquisitions, cataloguing and circulation of stock are based on computer manipulation of a common record or unit entry for each item of stock.

The other main area where automation has vastly changed the nature of library work is on-line information services. So far the output from these services has been mainly bibliographical citations, which the user must then go and locate in hard copy in conventional libraries. It is becoming clear, however, that the next stage of development will permit the user to have direct access to the text of the desired document, on screen or as a printout. Services such as Ceefax and Oracle offer information, for example, on a television screen in response to the user's progress through a set of branching questions, which should lead to the specific details wanted. But these services are limited by the number of spare lines available on conventional television channels, so their capacity to provide detailed information is restricted. They are not, moreover, interactive. These limitations do not apply to the Prestel information service, introduced into many libraries experimentally at the beginning of the 1980s. Here there is no limit to the amount of information which a user can access, beyond the important restrictions of cost, relevance of the material stored, and the efficiency of the indexing terms.

The implications of the microelectronics revolution for staffing library and information services are not yet clear, but certain tendencies are beginning to emerge. By automating library routines, one might expect to find reductions in the number of non-professional staff. An obvious example is computerized issue systems, where the time taken up in writing overdues as well as charging and discharging items under the old Browne system is much reduced. Whether staff freed in this way from routine duties are redeployed to other kinds of work, or lose their jobs, must depend on the financial situation and the personnel policies of the employing body.

The content of library jobs invariably changes with automation, and this may well affect job satisfaction. If, for example, cataloguing staff change from making their own decisions about cataloguing codes and class numbers, to simply checking computer printouts and manipulating centrally-produced records bought in from a cataloguing agency, this could be seen as job impoverishment. Though that will depend on the way in which they were previously deployed, and how much individual responsibility and specialization they were allocated.

A further problem which automation raises is whether to train existing staff in computerization, or to recruit specially qualified computer people from outside the profession. Many libraries have recruited systems analysts to plan their automation programmes; others have preferred consultation with experts. Whichever way it is done, the problem for existing staff is generally alleviated by setting up small working parties on which there is a balance between librarians and computer people, and by keeping staff informed about plans from an early stage. Inevitably there will be resistance, both thinking and unthinking, to technological innovation. The objectives should be to encourage the unthinking to think, and the thinking to participate in the planning and evaluation process.

Automation in libraries has been swift and widespread, so one of the problems is that education and training have in many cases not been updated. Librarians who received their professional education ten years ago will have received little if any grounding in the subject. The importance of continuing education tends to be overlooked, and staff are often eager to palm off all the responsibility for automation on to an individual whether specially appointed or designated from within. This can lead to many difficulties, since automation is quite justifiably an emotive activity, and staff should have a supportive framework within which they can express their worries and display their ignorance and learn new attitudes as well as new facts.

There are likely to be further major questions raised by microelectronics during the remaining years of the twentieth century. Anthony Smith[4] argues in his *Goodbye Gutenberg* that 'the computerization of print is truly a third revolution in communications of similar scale and importance [to the advent of writing and the invention of printing], in that it raises comparably fundamental issues concerning the social control of information, the nature of the individual creative function, the ways in which information interacts with human memory'. He interprets the information revolution of the 1980s and 1990s as a step towards a new Alexandria, in the sense that once again after two thousand years it makes feasible universal availability of a vast (computerized this time round) store of information. The role of the librarian, or as it is suggested 'the librarian's computerized successor', will be crucial, since it is the librarian who categorizes information and provides the codes through which it can be accessed. *Goodbye Gutenberg* asks some pertinent questions which may prove relevant to staffing information services in the coming microelectronics era:

> The librarian becomes, in a sense, the sentinel at the gateway of information and knowledge, and society may come to find itself demanding to see his credentials. What librarian ethic is the counterpart of the objectivity of a journalist or the scrupulousness of a judge? Who has made the computer-librarian lord and master over knowledge and how is his stewardship supervised and rendered accountable to society?[5]

His view then (doubtless seen as much dramatized by carefully balanced librarians) seems to be that the coming of information on-line means more than simply introducing new media to do the same old jobs more efficiently. The new communications technology is fundamentally changing the ways in which people use information and get access to information, and it is the librarian's responsibility to work out an appropriate ethic, as well as appropriate procedural frameworks.

Some of the questions which librarians will have to answer in relation to the new media are:

1. Should users have to pay for information which previously was 'free', just because it is the product of an on-line search?
2. What groups will be offered on-line searches, and which refused them?
3. Will there emerge a new information élite, and how will one qualify for it?
4. Will the evolution of 'electronic' print eventually lead to the demise of the hard-copy journal, and ultimately reduce the number of people who have access to journal contents?
5. How much pressure can users of on-line services put on suppliers, so that the needs of the users are properly taken into account?

Already librarians and information scientists have formed national and regional on-line user groups to monitor and influence the development of services. Areas of concern are education and training of library staff to develop the new skills needed; comparative costing and standards of individual on-line services; advance warning of future developments to keep users in touch with rapidly developing technology; and effective representation of users' views to the suppliers. The newsletters produced by the UK On-line User Group from 1978 onwards provide examples of the problems encountered and the skills needed by librarians who do on-line searching. For example *Newsletter No. 6*[6] describes strategies for conducting pre-search user interviews, so that the searcher's knowledge of the system combines with the user's subject knowledge to frame an effective enquiry. Databases can only be as good as their input, so the quality of citation and indexing must be high. *Newsletter No 7* refers to the problems of using databases, which could be overcome by using highly trained and competent information retrievalists at the indexing end. Databases may fail to deliver the goods by 'providing no references to a subject which might reasonably be expected to be covered, missing a crucial reference (found later by other means), or [giving out] a mass of irrelevant data as a result of unclear indexing'[7].

At the clerical level, the microelectronics revolution is already making inroads into the traditional spheres of office work, and this will clearly have a major impact on the mass of clerical work done in libraries. An Equal Opportunities Commission study by Bird[8] predicts that as a result of the introduction of word processors 21,000 typing and secretarial posts will be lost by 1985, and by 1990 170,000 or 17 per cent of the total will go. Although non-redundancy agreements may be negotiated with the unions, there must remain concern that jobs are being deskilled, that junior and trainee posts are being reduced, thus adding to youth unemployment, and that there may be health hazards for those making prolonged use of video display units. Manufacturers claim that one word-processing operator can do the job of two or three typists. It is estimated that shorthand skills are likely to become superfluous by the late 1980s when voice-activated word processors will be able to produce letters direct from dictation.

An example of the kind of staff savings which can be made is provided by Bradford Metropolitan Council, where in the Directorate of Development Services 44 staff have been reduced to 22 (a Nalgo agreement was made to redeploy the superfluous staff, rather than create redundancies), while productivity has risen by 20 per cent.[9] The Council continued to introduce microprocessors to other local government departments, as a result of their initial success, and the satisfactory (though belated) negotiations with Nalgo, the local government officers' union.

Role of white-collar trade unions

Until the 1970s there was little evidence of active trade unions in the library profession. It seems that library and information workers, like many other professionals seeking a voice in public affairs, thought it more appropriate to turn to their professional associations to speak where necessary on behalf of their members' welfare (in terms of status, and privileges very often), as well as the professional ethic and role in society.

There are many reasons why this situation gradually altered during the 1970s and why there has been a remarkable growth in membership of white-collar unions in Britain, such as Nalgo (in public libraries), Natfhe (in the public sector of higher and further education), and the AUT (in university libraries).

In a period of rising inflation professional workers sought ways of protecting their salaries from erosion. The multiplicity of salary scales and conditions of service for librarians in the UK means that it would scarcely be feasible for a professional association to safeguard the economic interests of all its members. Moreover professional associations are not generally recognized negotiators in the eyes of employers. Though they may be permitted to attend negotiations, their role is subsidiary to the recognized negotiators, who are the unions. Librarians therefore saw their unions as being likely to give more muscular protection to their salaries and status than the professional association could provide.

Between 1970 and 1975 the earnings differentials in Britain between white-collar and manual workers were eroded by 11 per cent.[10] This led to fears of lowered occupational status among middle-class professionals, and the response was increased membership of white-collar unions. On top of financial erosion, professional workers saw their traditional long-term job security being undermined in the late 1970s and early 1980s. Redundancies were no longer, it seemed, to be confined to manual workers. Teachers, architects, librarians, town planners and social workers were among those whose job security became rather shaky as local government, their main employers, were compelled to make a series of annual public spending cuts at the behest of the Conservative central government. The white collar unions could influence, indeed had the right to be consulted by the employers on redundancy agreements. So their power to influence the inevitable redundancies and early retirements, for the benefit (relatively speaking) of their members, was a further incentive to join.

In some cases they were instrumental also in 'unfreezing' library posts, by instructing their members not to carry out additional duties when asked to fill in for frozen posts. They could also draft policies restricting the employment of over-qualified librarians in junior posts on the grounds that this could give employers qualified labour on the cheap. But this could be two-edged, in that in a period of rising unemployment job applicants with professional qualifications could often expect to get a mere toe-hold (or non-professional post) for their first job, but this would place them in the running for jobs perhaps only advertised internally.

A further reason advanced for increased unionization of professional librarians resulted from the increasing size and complexity of both public and academic libraries throughout the 1970s. Local government reorganization on the one hand, and the various mergers in the public sector of higher education on the other, caused many librarians to sense a growing bureaucratization in their work place, a feeling of remoteness between the main body of staff and the decision makers at senior management level. Extra effort was required by managers if they were to be personally known to their new large staff. It involved crossing psychological as well as geographical boundaries, since amalgamations invariably leave a legacy of divided and partial loyalties. Knowing that communications problems existed did not necessarily help to alleviate them, for personnel management techniques were still not widely known among librarians, many of whom naturally still hankered after the informal 'seat of the pants' kind of management which had worked in the smaller 'all one family together' type of library.

In this situation the unions were the beneficiaries. Staff began to see the union as an important buffer between them and remote management. It could be a defence in times of stress, as when posts were frozen, and at all times it could provide an alternative focus for staff, a sense of group identity, in the face of, or fears of, bureaucratization. If the management climate proved a deterrent to developing a professional stance, then at least union intervention could preserve the material benefits of the job.

Closed shops for professional posts also began to make their appearance during the 1970s, through the conclusion of union membership agreements between unions and employers. A MORI poll in 1977 found that in the country at large 75 per cent of all voters, and 66 per cent of voters who were union members, believed the closed shop to be a 'threat to individual liberty'. And when the Leeds Polytechnic Natfhe Branch made a union membership agreement with the employers in September 1980, that all lecturers and professional librarians taking up post after that date should undertake to join the union as a condition of their employment, there was a furore of indignation. This led to accusations that union meetings were only attended by a small unrepresentative group of activists whose views were not those of the passive and inactive majority of members. In the end the decision taken by the Polytechnic Branch was reversed, but the incident proved instructive both on the power of the unions, and the need for more active membership by members as a whole, too many of whom perhaps see the union as a resort in crises only, whereas the white-collar unions (Natfhe and AUT) see themselves as taking a very wide interest in the furtherance of higher and further education generally. They have produced a series of instructive and valuable policy documents on such matters as continuing education, distance learning, and the role of educational technology.

A further reason for the growing influence of unions in the professions has been the changes in the legal framework surrounding trade unions which have been promulgated during the 1970s. Until the late 1960s union membership could even adversely affect the stated goals of the unions to improve salaries and working conditions. This was because people were reluctant to join unions where employers were hostile, and employers could punish union membership by actually holding back on improvements. During the 1970s, however, legislation favoured the unions, and consolidated and increased the rights of members. Employers now have clear obligations to recognize unions and their rights in the work place. Collective bargaining between employers and recognized unions is now fairly standard practice. Moreover there has been a spate of legislation which strengthens the rights of employees in the areas of health and safety at work, unfair dismissal and discrimination on grounds of race or sex. Employees who are union officials are also legally entitled to time off work for union business.

Why did the state intervene in this way after a century of government non-intervention in industrial relations? The stimulus was the realization that collective bargaining as it was in the 1960s was achieving very uneven results. The well-organized workers were getting unfairly ahead of the less-organized groups, in terms of earnings and conditions of service. Statutory recognition of unions will not of course remedy this situation, but it may alleviate it by giving all employees a framework of basic rights, and a standard mechanism (collective bargaining) for easing industrial conflict.

Employment legislation

By the 1970s the state had become the biggest employer of labour in the United Kingdom, and this was an added incentive to seek a legislative solution to the problems of personnel management stemming from poor industrial relations. The legal framework which has resulted is an official recognition that collective bargaining is the method by which industrial conflict may best be regulated, and that it is here to stay. The assumption behind the legislation is that industrial relations will improve if the security and status of individual employees are safeguarded by law. The Bullock Report (1977)[12] on industrial democracy noted the recognition by employers that they 'should develop effective systems of employee participation to channel the energies and abilities of the workforce...' This is of course partly a recognition of the reality of the increased and increasing influence of employees, through their trade unions, on company decision-making, but it is also an acceptance of the principle that a socially responsible company in a democratic society cannot operate without taking account of the interests of its employees.

Legislation

The major Acts of Parliament which became law during the 1970s and early 1980s which affect employees' and employers' rights and obligations at work are:

Trade Union and Labour Relations Act 1974
Health and Safety at Work Act 1974
Employment Protection Act 1975
Sex Discrimination Act 1975
Race Relations Act 1976
Employment Acts, 1978 & 1980

Since most libraries are part of a parent body (an academic institution, a local authority, an industrial firm) there will normally be a personnel section to formulate policies and procedures in accordance with the Acts. It is, however, very important that any librarian who is responsible for supervising staff (at whatever level) should have an outline knowledge of the provisions of the legislation, and the sort of situations which come under the employment laws, so that he or she does not unwittingly take action, or fail to take action, contrary to the spirit or letter of the law.

The following paragraphs set out to indicate the main kinds of situation covered by employment legislation. Any detailed interpretation of the law would be out of place here; that is the prerogative of the legal expert, to whom queries should always be addressed when there is any doubt as to the implications of action about to be taken on staffing matters.

Although this book is mainly aimed at those who are managing staff or learning how to manage staff, such people will also be interested in their position as subordinates with rights as well as duties. Most of the commentaries on the legal position take either a worker's stance like McMullen[13] or a manager's stance like Janner.[14] In order to gather evidence for this section, we interviewed a number of academic, public and special librarians and found that they have had to become familiar with some of the new legislation as situations arose which required such knowledge. In general the legislation has emphasized the need for the sort of systematic management practices prescribed in this book since poor practice can so easily result in librarians drifting into problems through failure to manage properly. Librarians do have to be aware of the main points made in the Acts and of the responsibilities and implications for managing staff.

Dismissal of staff

Legislation in Britain during the seventies tended to favour employees' rights but recently there has been a slight shift towards the employer with the 1980 Employment Act. The legislation serves to emphasize the need for managers to be very careful where dismissals are concerned and this is as it should be because dismissal is a serious matter. In particular managers must:

1. Ensure that staff are given every chance to succeed. This includes the provision of adequate communication, consultation, proper training and supervision. If this is not done the employees may have a case for

claiming constructive dismissal by which they can dismiss themselves. In Britain there is the Industrial Relations Code of Practice,[15] issued in 1972, to guide employers.

2. Be certain that they have acted fairly by ensuring that:

(a) The employee has been dismissed for a reason normally accepted as grounds for dismissal. British legislation lists the following: incapability; absence of appropriate qualifications; misconduct; redundancy; contravention of statutory requirements; refusal to join a specified union when a closed shop agreement is in force; or any other substantial reason sufficient to justify the particular dismissal.

(b) Proper procedures have been carried out and that such procedures are known to both management and staff. A written grievance procedure should normally be provided. The spirit of the ACAS code[16] should be followed and this includes: ensuring that immediate superiors do not normally have the power to dismiss without reference to senior management; giving the individual the right to be accompanied by a trade union representative or a fellow employee of his/her choice; ensuring that, except for gross misconduct, no employee is dismissed for a first breach of discipline; ensuring that disciplinary action is not taken until the case has been carefully investigated; ensuring that the individual is given an explanation for any penalty imposed; and providing a right of appeal.

(c) They are aware of which staff qualify for protection under employment law. Although good practice is essential for all categories of staff, it is useful to be clear about which categories are specifically protected. In Britain, for example, protection is given to those with at least fifty-two weeks' continuous service and who work sixteen hours per week or more, and are under retirement age.

3. They have a working knowledge of appeal procedures, since managers may be asked to provide evidence.

Redundancy

The Redundancy Payments Act 1965 defines redundancy in the following way:

An employee who is dismissed shall be taken to be dismissed by reason of redundancy if the dismissal is attributable wholly or mainly to:
(a) the fact that his employer has ceased, or intends to cease, to carry on the business for the purposes of which the employee was so employed, or
(b) the fact that the requirements of that business for employees to carry out work of a particular kind, or for employees to carry out work of a particular kind in the place where they were so employed, have ceased or diminished or are expected to cease or diminish.[17]

Redundancies are, of course, more prevalent at times of economic recession and the librarian may be involved with the redundancy of subordinates or as a redundant person. As managers, librarians should ensure that:

1. They know whether there is a redundancy policy in the organization and, if so, be aware of its contents and implications.
2. They follow the policy in the event of redundancies. If there is no policy they should ensure an adequate procedure is followed and in particular should keep within legal requirements. In Britain there is an Industrial Relations Code of Practice[18] and the Employment Protection (Consolidation) Act 1978 covers legal requirements. There should especially be consultation with the unions and individuals affected before final decisions are made, alternatives to redundancy should be sought and where necessary training provided. In some cases financial help can be obtained from Central Government.
3. They are familiar with scales of redundancy payments available or know how to find them out.

Health and Safety

Not only will the library managers be concerned with their own health and safety at work, but they also have responsibilities for the staff who work for them and the public who use the library.

In Britain these responsibilities are spelled out in the Health and Safety at Work Act, 1974. Library managers should first of all be aware of their organization's written safety policy and be prepared to contribute to it in respect of their own departments. This will require an identification of safety hazards such as those related to the storage and display of materials, electrical equipment, entrances and exits, steps and floors. Appropriate precautions will have to be devised to counter the hazards and people at risk must be made aware of the identified risks and the precautions they should follow.

The library should be represented on the organization's Safety Committee and there should be a recognized Safety Officer responsible for the library.

With the tightening-up of health and safety since 1974 it is clear that organizations need to keep comprehensive records and statistics to show the Health and Safety Executive Inspectors that they are taking their obligations seriously.

Discrimination

A management approach frequently prescribed is one which treats individuals equally according to merit. Burns' and Stalker's ideas,[19] discussed in Chapter 2, for example, are based on the belief that good ideas should be encouraged irrespective of their origin within the organization. In many countries certain kinds of discrimination have been declared illegal and this includes employment discrimination. In Britain, the Sex Discrimination Act 1975 and the Equal Pay Act 1970 cover discrimination on grounds of sex and the Race Relations Act 1976 prohibits discrimination on grounds of colour, race, nationality, ethnic or national origins.

The library manager is required to avoid direct discrimination, where a person is treated less favourably on grounds of race or sex than another person would be treated, and indirect discrimination, where a requirement is such that the proportion of one sex or racial group which can comply with it is considerably smaller than the proportion of the other sex or racial groups who can comply. An employer must show that the requirement is justified if it is not to be judged discriminatory.

The effect of these laws is that managers have to be extremely careful at all the stages of personnel management discussed in this book. In particular it is necessary for managers to be systematic in that they are clear about what they are trying to do, spell it out to all those involved, and monitor the results of their activities. This is neatly described by the Equal Opportunities Commission in its *Draft Code of Practice:*

> This Code advocates the use of consistent selection, training and promotion procedures and criteria which are known to all employees. This is in keeping with good employment practice and also helps to eliminate discrimination. Without this consistency, decisions can be subjective, which can lead to the most suitable person not being selected, and leave the way open for sex or marriage discrimination to occur.[20]

In recruiting staff job descriptions and specifications should be based on the qualifications and experience considered necessary for the job and should avoid asking for more qualifications than are necessary. Advertising should be clear and unambiguous and avoid anything, such as illustrations and wording, which is discriminatory. Advertisements should not be restricted to sources which can be seen only or mainly by certain groups. Staff giving verbal information about jobs should be careful not to indicate any bias. Application forms should be as simple as possible and cater for minorities. It is usual to ask for race and sex on application forms and the Institute of Personnel Management recommends this to be continued in order to furnish statistics on recruitment.[21] It is recommended that the application forms of rejected applicants be retained for about six months for this reason.

The selection interview should be unbiased. A code of practice issued by Camden Council in 1978 stresses the need for interviewers to prepare themselves fully by ensuring that 'the fullest possible information with regard to candidates is available and has been thoroughly read by those personnel involved in the interview process'. Camden also recommend that questions relating to marital status, occupation of spouse, number of children, family intentions, or domestic arrangements be avoided though the Institute of Personnel Management says that such matters should only be raised where there are certain special circumstances in the job and always the reason for such questions should be explained to the interviewee. It is important that systematic records are made of interviews so that a convincing case can be made to a tribunal if there is an appeal. In the same way records should be kept of staff appraisals since discrimination should be avoided in matters of promotion, transfers, training and grievance procedures.

Trade union activities at work

With the recognition of unions it has become common practice to allow staff time off to participate in union activities. Officials of unions recognized for collective bargaining purposes have a right in Britain to reasonable time off with or without pay during working hours for the purpose of taking part in the activities of their unions. The Advisory, Conciliation and Arbitration Service (ACAS) has produced a code of practice,[22] *Time off for trade union duties and activities* as a guide for employees. Library managers should therefore ensure they are familiar with the policy regarding time off so that they do not contravene employees' rights yet do not agree to time off which is not reasonable within the terms of the code.

Work Assignments

1. Ask a number of librarians to complete the attitude questionnaire below, or members of a training group can do so. The answers, when analysed, can be used to discuss:

(a) The conflict between professionalism and trade unionism.

(b) Reasons for the growth of trade unionism during the last decade.

(c) The relationship between library and information work and trade unions.

ATTITUDES TO TRADE UNIONS FOR LIBRARIANS

Please tick the appropriate column.

	Agree	Disagree	Undecided
1. Belonging to a union improves the economic prospects of library staff			
2. It would be unprofessional for me to join a trade union			
3. Unions are not competent to pronounce on professional matters (e.g. staffing structures, job rotation, professional development)			
4. Bigger and more complex library systems mean less community of interest among library managers and their staff, so unions are needed as intermediaries			
5. 'In most unions there is no place for the librarian as a professional, or for the development of the goals of any one profession... the individual librarian in a union becomes a member of a heterogeneous group and pursues only employee welfare for the whole group' (M. Boaz)			
6. A library supervisor who belongs to a trade union is likely to be involved in a conflict of interests			
7. As the labour market contracts, it becomes more important for librarians to join trade unions, if they want to secure satisfactory working conditions			
8. 'Successful unions limit the freedom of action of management in many areas... supervising librarians have to learn to live with the complicated consultation procedures and consequent delays in decision-making' (I. Winkworth)			
9. Active trade union membership is necessary, to ensure that unions represent librarians' interests and concerns more adequately			
10. There is basic conflict between unionism (which is there to foster the interests of library staff) and professionalism (which is about serving the needs of the users)			
11. Unions can achieve better staffing establishments than management (e.g. by fighting redundancies) and thus help to maintain services in recessionary times.			
12. A professional association is the best body for promoting librarians' interests.			

2. In each of the three examples below discuss whether there are grounds for appeal under current sex discrimination legislation. If so, describe how possible discrimination could have been avoided.

(a) You have worked as a part-time librarian for several years helping the librarian of a Research Association. You are a married woman of 29 and your competence and ability have never been questioned. You are well qualified and when the librarian leaves, you apply for his post but are not called for interview yet two men are, one an internal candidate and the other external.

(b) The post in question was advertised as one available to 'persons under 30 years of age' with relevant experience.

(c) You are granted an interview and you and two men are interviewed. You do not get the job but feel annoyed about a number of questions that were asked including:

'What is your husband's occupation?'
'What would you do if he moved his place of employment?'
'Are you planning to have children?'

2   Motivation at work

Figure 2.1 illustrates the place of motivating staff in the general management of a library or section of a library:

FIGURE 2.1. THE MANAGEMENT CYCLE

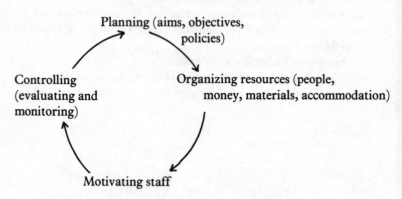

Motivating staff is a complex and delicate business, and pervades all phases of staff management from job analysis and description to staff selection, appraisal and training. Decisions, too, about organizational structures and staff deployment need to be made with some knowledge of motivation theories and their applications, to provide job satisfaction and alleviate dissatisfaction, as far as is consistent with getting the work done efficiently and effectively.

An individual's sense of job satisfaction (or lack of it) does not depend solely on his or her own motivation (since for example the individual alienated in the formal organization may find fulfilment in union activity or in the sociability of the informal work group). Nor does it depend only on the management styles and structures operating in the library. It is derived rather from the nature of the task to be carried out, the qualifications and skills and attitudes of the person responsible, the nature of the other people in the library, and the management climate (compounded from the values, styles and interests of those who do the managing). Environmental factors are also important, since the rate of change in organizations puts staff under stress and threatens existing job satisfaction.

Motivating staff depends on supervisors knowing what different groups of people need from their work. There have been a number of studies on job satisfaction carried out among librarians in Britain and the United States, which have shown that librarians are motivated by similar factors to other professionals (accountants, engineers, etc.) among whom surveys have been carried out in the process of building up theories of motivation.

For example, the Sheffield Manpower Project, which examined a sample of public, academic and special librarians in the 1970s, reported:

> Preference was expressed for greater responsibility of various kinds; more freedom of choice, less close supervision, and greater opportunity to improvise and act in a solo capacity. Work restructuring and job enlargement techniques should be considered in order to try and meet this desire . . . This applies at all levels, including the most junior. It especially applies in situations where duties have been rigidly divided into professional and non-professional categories.[1]

Lack of consultation and lack of information were pin-pointed as pervasive problems in staff management, and failure to deal with these was seen to result in lowered staff morale and staff performance. It was suggested that staff consultation might begin at a fairly simple level by involving staff in job design or redesign. This might enable staff to experience a sense of how their particular jobs fitted in with the work of the system as a whole, and also act as an incentive to improve the content of their jobs by the standard techniques of job enrichment and job enlargement. Any such exercise must take the temperature of trade union views, since job enrichment can be construed as making excessive demands on staff unless they are regraded and duly rewarded with higher salaries. Job enlargement, which means adding other tasks of the same level to a job in order to provide greater variety, can also come under attack, if it means that some of the tasks added are transferred from a frozen post.

Symptoms of poor motivation

The dangers of *not* applying some knowledge of motivation factors in staff deployment and staff supervision generally are that staff may suffer from endemic low morale. There will always be exceptions among the self-motivated and self-starters and the determinedly ambitious, but the warning signs to look out for among the rest of the staff are a high turnover, more than the average number of days off sick, persistent unpunctuality, and a tendency to identify with users' complaints about the library, rather than to identify with the library and take responsibility for remedying the problem behind the complaint.

There may well develop a defeatist spiral, whereby staff and user expectations of the library decline mutually towards a nadir of apathy and inertia. Rules and regulations are applied, but few staff know or care about the reasons that lie behind them, so readers are often fobbed off with bureaucratic excuses rather than explanations. If one tries to elicit from poorly-motivated library staff what they are trying to achieve, they will in all likelihood give an account of their routines and procedures, without any reference to purpose or justification. These are some of the symptoms of poor motivation that develop if the staff who operate a service do not have any part in the planning of it, if they are not asked to help in monitoring it, and if they cannot see beyond the small part of it which they have been given to do. Problems of consultation, communication and acknowledgement lie at the heart of motivation theory, but there are a number of difficulties in seeking universal panaceas for these problems.

First, different people want different things from their jobs. In a particular library or information unit there will be found a group of individuals whose degree of ambition varies, whose reason for working may be mainly for the money, mainly for the sociability of the work group, mainly for the opportunity of applying their professional skills and knowledge, or mainly for the chance of achieving responsibility and a position of authority. Confronted with such a variety of motives, how can motivation theorists help us to bring out the best in people at work? This leads to a second problem. What kind of 'best' do we really need? People who are, for example, overqualified for a particular job are likely to be frustrated, and spread despondency among other staff. So getting the right people in the right jobs, in terms of education, qualifications, experience and temperament, is an essential first step in having a well-motivated staff. Thirdly, the organizational climate of a library may range from the 'mechanistic' to the 'organismic',[2] and different people will feel more at home with one or the other tendency. (See later for the characteristics of these tendencies as displayed in organizations.) This will depend on the degree of need for security, self-expression, and openness in relations with others. Fourthly, the nature of library and information work is such that it almost invariably includes, even at senior levels, a proportion of routine, procedural duties that could no doubt be carried out by non-professional or para-professional staff. So it must be faced that parts of most library jobs will be dull, repetitive and routine, and this is frustrating for graduates especially, with their higher expectations.

Another source of frustration intrinsic to the nature of the work is the preponderance of technical services over readers' services. Many entrants to the profession want to work 'with books and people', they see librarianship as a service to users, and are disappointed to find that there are still so many techniques-oriented, rather than user-oriented jobs. In this case it could be argued that a knowledge of motivation theories might help, since it could encourage senior managers to try ways of deploying staff which would give more of them some contact with users.

A fifth area of difficulty in using motivation theories is that staff develop, both personally and professionally, in a supportive organization.

FIGURE 2.2 AN ADAPTATION OF BURNS' AND STALKER'S FRAMEWORK FOR ORGANIZATIONAL ANALYSIS

Mechanistic/organismic paradigm

Mechanistic		*Organismic*
Authority concentrated at 'the top'; little delegation. Low and localised; bureaucracy tends to take its place.	AUTHORITY	Dispersed; much delegation.
	PROFESSIONAL EXPERTISE	High and dispersed.
Hierarchical. Favours centralisation.	STRUCTURE	Network. Favours decentralisation.
Closely defined job description; sharp division of duties; fixed function of posts; emphasis on PROCESS (routine).	STAFF DEPLOYMENT	'Open-ended' job description; duties defined rather by purpose and staff interrelationships; team organisation; emphasis on PROJECT.
Little. One way, 'top' to 'bottom'.	COMMUNICATION – lines of;	Much. Multi-directional.
Mainly instructions, 'cut-and-dried' decisions.	– content;	Mainly information, advice, opinion-seeking.
Emphasis on written communication.	– format;	Oral, 'face-to-face' is important.
'Hygiene' factors important; reward and punishments.	JOB SATISFACTION	Herzberg's 'motivators' important. Opportunity for self-development and socially useful work.
Obedience and loyalty to an individual leader or/and a part of the organisation.	COMMITMENT	To the organisation as a whole, or, more likely, to professional goals, or, more likely, to a sense of social 'mission'.
Claims a relatively small share of the organisation's resources; confined to formal training in new skills and introduction of new knowledge.	STAFF DEVELOPMENT	Claims a relatively large share of the organisation's resources; employs a wide range of means to assist self-development; is concerned with attitude-change, as well as acquisition of knowledge and new skills.
Works best in relatively static environments, meeting predictable demands; inflexible, and unreliable under stress.	DEVELOPMENT CAPACITY OF THE ORGANISATION	Adapts readily to rapidly changing and unpredictable situations; flexible, and reliable under stress.

(*From* Ross Shimmon (ed.) *A reader in library management*. London, Bingley, 1976. p. 126.)

Their needs therefore can by no means be analysed once and for all and be prescribed for on the lines of one or other approaches to motivation. Rather must motivation of staff be seen as a continuous process, starting with selection, and considered again as an important factor in staff appraisal, training and promotion. It is known that the expectations librarians have of their jobs vary between the first job and the second (Sheffield[3] and Leeds[4] survey findings). In the first job after qualification colleagues are very important, since it seems a lot of importance is attached to the social needs at work, but by the second job, this factor diminishes, to be replaced by the need for self-expression at work (a chance to exercise some responsibility and apply a certain amount of professional expertise).

The contribution made by the different schools of management to understanding people's motivation at work can now be examined. What are the causes of satisfaction and dissatisfaction on the job? How can this knowledge help staff deployment? What is the relevance to staff selection, staff training and staff appraisal?

Scientific management and economic man

The scientific management school had its origins in the behavioural sciences in the early part of the twentieth century. Two of its major proponents were F. B. Gilbreth (1868–1924)[5] and F. W. Taylor (1856–1915).[6] They took the view that the average employee is motivated primarily by economic needs, so a pattern of status and financial rewards has to be built-in to the career path, to provide the main incentives. Employees are assumed to lack self-discipline, and so need a firm hierarchical structure within which their activities may be supervised and controlled. It is further assumed that employees tend to have little inclination to work, unless the 'carrot and stick' approach of incentives and punishments is used as a regulator.

The consequences of this position for personnel management are that all decisions are taken by the manager, without any consultation with employees, and that authority is concentrated at the top of a 'tall' hierarchy, with little delegation. It represents the 'mechanistic' approach (as outlined on page 23), since communication tends to be one way, from senior management down, by way of instructions and fixed decisions. The manager is seen somewhat as the fount of wisdom at the top of a clear-cut if fairly rigid hierarchy. He plans, controls, inspects and punishes as he sees necessary. Employees are expected to be obedient and loyal to the organization, or to their part of the organization, without looking more widely to professional goals or social commitment. They receive training in infrequent sessions, usually related to a new skill which must be acquired to keep up with their immediate job.

The scientific management school has influenced, and still does influence, the management style in libraries of all types. It may appear as the pervasive management style in most parts of a library, or it may coexist alongside other more 'people-centred' styles, operated in certain departments or by certain individuals on the senior staff. The findings of the Sheffield Project showed that it is more likely to occur in public libraries than in academic or special libraries; that is, if we take it that modes of consultation up and down the staff hierarchy are reliable indications of the management style in operation. When asked about consultation on work matters, 79 per cent of the academic librarians pronounced favourably on the situation in their libraries, and 81 per cent of the staff in special information units were satisfied. But only 59 per cent of public librarians expressed satisfaction about the way they were involved in consultation at work. It has been noted that the survey was carried out in 1976, only two years after local government reorganization, and this may have been a strong factor in influencing opinion about consultation.

Since that time it has been the turn of academic libraries to go through a series of mergers in the late 1960s and early 1970s, as colleges of education have been absorbed by polytechnics, or combined with other colleges in a locality to constitute the new institutes of higher education (for example Hull, or Doncaster). It may well be that it is now in the academic library sector where greatest dissatisfaction is felt about modes of consultation. The situation has been exacerbated by conflicts of loyalty and commitment, and by resistance to centralization. These changes have brought into sharp focus the need for sensitive and informed personnel management policies, in organizations which previously may have managed without. In environments which have lost their stable unchanging structure, and are subject to considerable changes over a period of years, the scientific or mechanistic management stance is less helpful. This has been the situation in the public sector of higher education during and since the mergers have taken place. Staff who felt secure in well-tried and familiar work have had to adapt to rapidly changing and unpredictable situations. The organizational loyalties have caused conflict, and problems of centralization or decentralization have heaped more difficulty on the staff of both the merging institutions. These problems have in many cases focused on communication and consultation (or perhaps it would be more accurate to say the absence of these, or the unsatisfactory form they have taken).

Where the emphasis has been on a scientific management approach, the weaknesses of this approach in a period of change have been evident. Authority concentrated at the top of the staff hierarchy, rather than dispersed, has led to feelings of alienation by staff lower down the hierarchy. Staff development and training that is confined to learning new technical skills alone does not solve the problems of interpersonal conflicts, since the introduction of new ideas and changes is ultimately dependent on the people

who will operate them. Stress within an organization is better borne by those who have been used to, or given training in, the management of change, rather than simply having change thrust upon them, as it were, from the top. In the Sheffield Survey public librarians expressed dissatisfaction with the management and organizational structure changes which had resulted from reorganization. Special librarians who at that time were beginning to feel the impact of 'on-line fever', the major technological change to affect their jobs in the last decades, made the following points about change:

> Staff resistance to change involving computers is less likely when systematic attention is paid to the need for consultation and keeping staff informed.
> It is important to ensure that, whatever their basic training, staff should be able to work together in a complementary fashion.[7]

Having drawn attention to some of the problems associated with the scientific management approach, especially in an era of rapid change for library and information work, it is now time to point out some of the old-fashioned virtues of this approach. This is especially important, as some organizations are tempted to reject scientific management ideas and techniques *in toto*, out of enthusiasm for the attractive-sounding tenets of 'organismic management'. It should be observed, however, that many activities in library work are fairly routine and procedural. Clear and straightforward instructions in written form may well be the most efficient way of getting through the work. Consultation is only necessary if problems arise, and then can most easily be sorted out by the supervisor on the spot. For this kind of work (and all the surveys which have been done on characteristics of library work and of staffing emphasise how high a proportion of work is of this kind), there is little opportunity or need for meetings, decision-making working parties, or other time-consuming gatherings.

A second point in favour of the scientific school of management is that it provides a great deal of security for the many staff who are not particularly ambitious, and who do not see themselves as management material. The Jones survey[8] of staff development in the mid-1970s indicated that in a preponderantly female profession like librarianship, women (whether from social conditioning or the stresses of the dual role of careerist and homemaker) are less likely to take part in developmental activities. Their chances of promotion are less, therefore, even if they do not have a break for childbearing at the crucial time in the late twenties when promotions are so important. This is indeed evident when considering the few women in senior management positions in libraries. For the less ambitious, and for those whose husbands' careers take precedence (and we cannot ignore these realities, whether we happen to subscribe to the role stereotyping they represent or not), library work is considered a pleasant, rather undemanding job, with, often, the advantages of amiable colleagues and a bookish environment. This group will not be too keen on responsibility, professional development, creative decision-making, and the other implications of 'organismic' management. They will be inclined to prefer a clearly-defined hierarchy with someone above them to take responsibility for when things go wrong, or where changes are needed.

Human relations school of management

There has been an observable trend away from scientific management towards 'human relations' management in recent years, which has affected libraries to a considerable extent. One social trend which underlies this change is the rise in educational levels which has caused more people to question the bases of power and authority. Educationalists have moreover emphasized different educational objectives over the last two decades, advocating the development of individual judgement and self-expression, rather than unquestioning acceptance of received truths. The secularization of society has strengthened this aversion to unquestioning social obedience to the establishment hierarchy, whether it be the family, or the bosses at work, or the forces of law and order.

A further incentive towards the human relations school of management has been the rise of the social commitment orientation in the professions, including librarianship. Taken to extremes this orientation regards professionalism as an obstacle to user-oriented services, following from Shaw's view that the professions are a conspiracy against the layman. In its more moderate form, social commitment in librarianship manifests itself in outreach philosophies, in community information services, in user surveys to analyse information needs, and in user education. Its impact on motivation and morale among library staff can be high, since enthusiasm and driving force at work is derived not so much from being socialized by the professional ethos in the work place, but from a wider sensitivity to information needs and deprivation in society at large, and in the local community in particular.

A further social trend which favours advance towards the human relations school of management has been the decline in job prospects for graduates in society as a whole. In the stagnant economy of the late 1970s and early 1980s, young people have been compelled to lower their expectations about employment, even if they are graduates and/or professionally qualified. First there is the hurdle of actually getting a start in the profession of their choice, and then there are the problems of lower job mobility and poorer promotion prospects. In these circumstances the traditional rewards of status and salary increases and regular promotions must diminish in importance, and it is not yet clear what will take their place. But it seems likely that greater emphasis will be placed on sharing decisions, being involved in work groups, and on the intrinsic interest of the job, rather than the job as a stepping-stone to the place you really want to be. It will become more important, if people are going to spend longer in the same job, or at least in the same institution, to provide opportunities for variety and enrichment and development, for those who need them. American managers have coined a phrase for it: 'The "now" orientation to career growth'.[9] This, roughly summarized, means that people at work want satisfaction in the present (not the deferred gratification which the professional classes used to accept as their lot); they want greater freedom, more immediate social and professional rewards from their work, and more consideration from their supervisors and bosses, in the form of different styles of management (more 'mutual influence' between supervisors and workers). These are not new desires, but have begun to gain strength and significance, in the light of the economic recession. They can be traced back to the 1920s, when the human relations school of management began to gain ground in the United States.

Mayo and the 'Hawthorne Effect'

Some of the early experiments which led to a realization of the limits of the scientific management approach were carried out by Elton Mayo[10] in the United States. Although his studies took place in the Hawthorne Works of the Western Electric Company, his findings are quite relevant to any organization concerned about staff management. One of his most significant discoveries was the importance of the 'informal organization', which exists in any workplace and which often subverts the official formal organization existing alongside it in the form of the traditional formal organization chart, or staff structure. He identified the need of employees to have a stable social relationship at work, thus questioning the validity of the 'rabble hypothesis', which held that each individual pursues his own rational self-interest irrespective of the work group. He argued that people at work need to be provided with a secure base for 'spontaneous co-operation'. This need can be met by deploying people in a team or work group with which they can identify, and have some sense of belonging. Such an approach will, he argued, diminish the occurrence of conflict and disagreement, and enable individuals to commit themselves through the group to the aims of the organization.

The experiments carried out by Mayo at the Hawthorne Works have been immortalised in subsequent management literature, through the concept of the 'Hawthorne Effect'. Participant observers found that there was in this case no correlation between material working conditions and productivity. There was however a high correlation between the employers taking an interest and productivity. It turned out to be the fact that employers were concerned to change conditions for the better, and were prepared to consult the workers about it, which improved productivity. This was an unexpected result, since it had been assumed that by tinkering with material working conditions such as tea-breaks, work output would rise. This was the old 'carrot and stick' approach of the scientific school, and it appeared in this case to ignore important principles of consultation and communication. The incentive that employees feel as a result of management taking an interest, consulting them and acting upon some of their suggestions, is now known as the 'Hawthorne Effect'.

In the Bank Wiring Room experiments, Mayo observed that employees have a way of setting out to control their work activities by their own methods, irrespective of the official management controls. The group of workers observed in this study had its own informal social structure and code of behaviour, which in fact clashed with that of management. They had a standard for output which no individual would exceed, and they were indifferent to the company's financial incentive scheme. Too much work would be 'rate-busting'; too little would be 'chiselling'. The company assigned formal roles to the workers, but the really influential roles were the informal ones developed within the group by the employees themselves. The same applies to libraries.

The significance of Mayo's findings is that they demonstrated the importance of the human factor in the work place, whereas previously the scientific school of management tended to assume that material incentives were primary. In particular he showed that the work group is a major determinant of employee behaviour. He also identified communications as a problem area, and related it to the need for a communications system which makes provision for communication up the hierarchy as well as downwards. Traditionally it had been assumed that the only necessary channel was from management down to workers.

Maslow's hierarchy of needs

After the Second World War, the work of A. H. Maslow[11] was very influential in the development of the human relations school of management. This influence has continued to the present time, and the Maslowian hierarchy has been widely used to analyse people's needs at work. The assumption is that if we want people to give of their best we must respond to their needs, wants, aspirations, thoughts and fears. The first step in creating a work environment which will be conducive to high output and high morale is to understand the kinds of needs people experience. Only then can the manager create the conditions necessary to achieve that environment. Maslow's hierarchy, (Figure 2.3), applies not only to people's needs at work, it has been used to form the basis of a 'whole-life' programme of self-development, as well as for more limited professional development at work.

In Maslow's view, people are not able to progress to satisfying their higher needs (such as social needs and esteem needs) until they have first

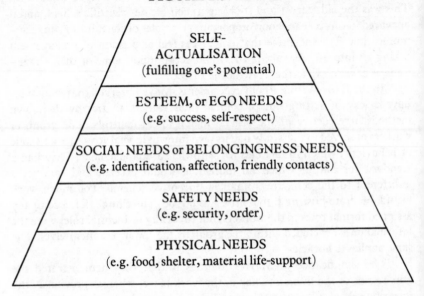

FIGURE 2.3. MASLOW'S HIERACHY

SELF-
ACTUALISATION
(fulfilling one's potential)

ESTEEM, or EGO NEEDS
(e.g. success, self-respect)

SOCIAL NEEDS or BELONGINGNESS NEEDS
(e.g. identification, affection, friendly contacts)

SAFETY NEEDS
(e.g. security, order)

PHYSICAL NEEDS
(e.g. food, shelter, material life-support)

satisfied the more humble needs (those which appear lower down in the hierarchy, such as safety needs). However, in western societies most workers earn enough to take care of the basic material comforts of food, clothing and shelter. Once this level of need is met, people aspire to the next level, which is the need for safety and security. In this area is included not just security of income and tenure, though these are becoming increasingly important to job-holders as the unemployment figures rise. Also included is the need for information, for this is an important source of security for employees. They need to know where the organization is going, what its future is likely to be, and how this will affect their jobs. This is why house magazines, staff magazines, bulletin boards and other simple devices are so important. Equally important is the communication climate in an organization, the ease with which important developments get passed on, formally and/or informally. Another source of security is adequate training for the job one is required to do. In periods of rapid technological and structural change in libraries, staff are made to feel insecure if they see their jobs changing, and no provision is made to train them or retrain them in how to cope. This applies not only to technical skills (automation, for example), but also to interpersonal skills (adapting to the team method of working in public libraries, for example). In special libraries the rapid growth of on-line searching involves staff not just in new technological know-how, but in more sophisticated intermediary work to interpret the user's needs accurately and precisely, so interpersonal skills become more important than before.

When the needs for material comforts and security are adequately met,

Maslow argues that people then aspire to the next level of need up the hierarchy, that is, to social or 'belongingness' needs. Once staff have reasonable working conditions, reasonable salaries, and a certain level of security, they will still not be positively motivated, because their needs are more complex than was assumed by classical management theorists. This is not to say, of course, that these lower needs are not important. It is to emphasize that by themselves they will not spur staff on to permanent contentment and high achievement. There will always be employees whose expectations of work remain at a fairly basic level of need, and this will apply to libraries as to other organizations. Nonetheless a large proportion of the staff will be concerned to aspire at least to the level of social needs, as shown in Maslow's hierarchy. We have seen how Elton Mayo's experiments outlined the value that staff attach to the work group, and to the sense of belonging which comes from membership of such a group, whether it is formally structured by management or informally arranged by the employees. We can see examples of both kinds of group in the world of librarianship.

Public librarians are much more likely to be part of a professional team responsible for all the service points within an area, since the team structure has been gaining favour to combat isolation of branch librarians, and raise the level of professionals' work. In addition public librarians may belong to working parties of an *ad hoc* nature, when, for example, automation schemes are being introduced. There are also in some authorities groups of 'Young Professionals' to bring together people with ideas which might not otherwise find expression. In some public library systems a matrix management system operates, which may involve the same individual in area team meetings, in subject specialist meetings, and in, say, specialist meetings county-wide of childrens' librarians, or information services' librarians. By contrast, in the university sector, meetings tend to be more unstructured and informal. Subject specialists may meet as need arises to co-ordinate their approaches to, for example, user instruction or information bulletins, or they may indeed abstain from such meetings to concentrate on their individual approaches. However informal the structure in academic libraries, the number of librarians working as isolated individuals appears to be decreasing, and it could be argued that even if there are fewer formal meetings than in public libraries, a sense of identity, of belonging to a work group, is almost universal. The categories that appear to suffer most from isolation in this respect are school librarians and librarians in the smallest special libraries and information units. The usual answer to this problem is that they should develop contacts with other people in similar positions, and attend as many meetings and short courses as possible, but this is often made impossible just because they are isolated and have no-one to stand in for them while they are away.

The message which the Maslowian hierarchy has for managers about social needs is that a sense of identity is a prerequisite for job satisfaction, and if the deployment of staff does not provide this, workers are likely to form their own informal groups, which may or may not be pursuing the same objectives as senior management (but more likely not). There are many notorious examples of the flouting of this principle in the work place. The open-plan office, for example, diminishes the sense of identity and undermines the need to belong to a group with some common purpose. The buying-in of centralized services (cataloguing data, for example) may de-skill the previously demanding cataloguing activities in many libraries, undermining morale, and instilling a sense of futility, as the work is reduced to complex but inherently clerical levels. There is no indication that the moves towards larger and more centralized libraries will ever be reversed, so it is essential to provide for employees within these large organizations the kind of small work groups with which they can identify, and within which the level of work they do is enriched rather than impoverished, by careful planning and attention to work needs. It is the 'primary group' (that is the group which one meets 'face-to-face' in one's daily contacts) that matters to people, rather than the 'secondary group' (consisting of the more formal official forums within the organization). Social psychologists argue that the ideal size of the primary group is between eight and twelve (beyond this figure subdivision is likely to take place). The primary group at work is the one which regulates people's opinions, goals and ideals. If there is conflict between these and the secondary group or organization's goals, the primary group is likely to prove stronger, and no amount of senior management propaganda will change things. The only possibility is that some agreement might be reached by starting with the primary group and, working from there, involving them in planning their own work, or in small *ad hoc* working parties to work on problems.

The two highest levels in the Maslowian hierarchy are concerned with people's needs for achievement, challenge, self-expression and self-fulfilment. Many people at work have had their needs for these things unsatisfied for so long that they have ceased to want them, or even to know that it might be nice to have them. Others have perhaps decided that the workplace is not the arena they would choose for the higher satisfactions. However that may be, a lot of the bloody-mindedness, resentment, absenteeism and apathy, which one finds no less in libraries than in other work places, stems from the inability of the organization to make some attempt to satisfy these needs, particularly among their professionally qualified staff. The surveys carried out by Roberts (1973)[12], by Smith and Schofield (1973)[13] and by Jones and Jordan (1975)[14] on job satisfaction among recently qualified graduates in libraries, all reported frustration and disappointment caused by the following factors:

1. Lack of opportunity to exercise one's professional expertise.
2. Lack of opportunity to exercise responsibility.

3. Dull and repetitive routine work, rather than a chance to use the skills acquired during one's professional education.

4. Insufficient contact with users (staff deployed in technical services, and non-professional staff had more contact with users than professional staff), so sense of achievement missing.

It may be that to a certain extent, librarianship does contain more than its fair share of dull and repetitive routines, and librarians must expect to take their turn. It may be that the proportion of professionals to non-professionals or para-professionals is too high, and so the professional work is spread very thinly. However, there is little doubt that many librarians could be more creative in their jobs, could be more user-oriented, could experience a greater sense of achievement if the work were structured differently, to take account of the higher needs in the Maslowian hierarchy. Is automation an opportunity to change direction? It is supposed to cope with the dull and dreary routines, the chores which were associated with circulation and acquisitions work in particular, and indeed with the production and filing of catalogues. Is there, then, a corresponding diversion of effort by professionals towards the kind of work with books and users which is so often the reason why they chose librarianship as a occupation? Or will economic difficulties cause library staff to revert to purely housekeeping routines once more, after the brave moves during the 1970s towards outreach, community analysis, and extended information services in all three kinds of library, public, academic and special?

Herzberg's Satisfiers and Dissatisfiers

Herzberg is well-known for the studies he carried out on groups of engineers and accountants, to elicit their attitudes to work. A number of studies have since been done, based on his original pattern, and these include a study of American librarians by Plate and Stone (1974)[15] and what causes them satisfaction and dissatisfaction at work. It is Herzberg's view that:

> the factors involved in producing job satisfaction (and motivation) are separate and distinct from the factors that lead to job dissatisfaction. Since separate factors need to be considered ... it follows that these two feelings are not opposites of each other. The opposite of job satisfaction is not job dissatisfaction, but rather, *no* job satisfaction; and similarly the opposite of job dissatisfaction is not job satisfaction, but *no* job dissatisfaction.[16]

In other words, it is not an adequate solution to remove certain causes of dissatisfaction, such as raising pay, or improving supervision, or providing more security. This will not in itself provide satisfaction; it will merely remove dissatisfaction. In order to provide satisfaction, Herzberg continues, it is necessary to bring into play the factors which he calls motivators. These are reminiscent of the needs from the higher levels of the Maslowian hierarchy. They include achievement, recognition, responsibility, advancement, the nature of the work itself. The motivators, then, provide satisfaction, and relate more to the content of the job, than to contextual factors. The contextual factors, external to the work itself, which he calls hygiene factors, include pay, security, status, technical supervision, company policy and administration, and interpersonal relationships. These hygiene factors are potential dissatisfiers. He uses the medical analogy of hygiene factors to show that by paying attention to these factors an organization may *prevent* dissatisfaction, without however providing positive motivation. Nonetheless the removal of dissatisfiers is important, just as hygiene factors in the medical situation are important, since it clears the way for the benefits that may be obtained from the positive motivators.

The nature of motivators, Herzberg argues, is that they have a much longer-term effect on employees' attitudes than the hygiene factors. If, therefore, more time, effort and money were to be applied to job enrichment, which is based on knowledge and understanding of the motivators, rather than on tinkering with the hygiene factors, the results would be striking. Herzberg sums up the argument for job enrichment as follows:

> If you have someone on a job, use him. If you can't use him on the job, get rid of him, either via automation or by selecting someone with lesser ability. If you can't use him and you can't get rid of him, you will have a motivation problem.[17]

This motivation problem may be alleviated by the job enrichment strategies which Herzberg advocates. He notes the importance of looking at jobs with the conviction that they can be changed. There is a habit among low-motivated employees and indeed their line managers of assuming that the job content is inviolate, and it is the people who need changing. The next step is to draw up a list of enrichment ideas for the specific job, and eliminate from it hygiene-based suggestions, to leave only motivator-based suggestions. Next cross out, or refine, vague generalities like 'give them more responsibility', since unless this is translated into specific deeds it will mean nothing. Herzberg warns against singing the good old anthems containing the sacred words 'achievement', 'challenge', 'growth', 'responsibility', without actually clothing the form with the substance. His views are that the people whose jobs are involved should be consulted in advance, but not directly involved in the exercise of planning their job enrichment, since they are to be motivated by the content of the new job, not by the challenge of redesigning the job. This is very arguable, arising as it does from his view that interpersonal relationships are a hygiene factor, rather than a positive motivator. In an occupation like library and information work, it is probable that the 'people factor' is seen as very much part of the job content, rather than the job context.

Plate and Stone used Herzberg's theories on job motivation to examine factors affecting job satisfaction among 162 American and 75 Canadian librarians from all types of library. The results confirmed Herzberg's views that certain factors are positive 'motivators' in the work-place, while others are merely 'hygiene factors', which will cause dissatisfaction if absent, but not positive motivation. The study found that 'of all the factors named by librarians as contributing to job satisfaction, 99 per cent were motivators and were related to job content. Of all the factors contributing to their dissatisfaction at work, 81 per cent involved hygiene factors found in the work environment (context factors)'. The following were found to be *positive motivators:*

Achievement (generally taken to mean the feeling of having completed some difficult task rather well).

Recognition (by the public, by superiors, or subordinates one is responsible for).

Intrinsic nature of the work, or 'the work itself'.

Responsibility (as a result of participative management, for example).

Advancement (recommendations and promotions).

Professional or personal growth (often hard to differentiate from achievement and responsibility).

The *hygiene factors* identified were as follows:

Institution policy and administration (management factors/style).
Supervision.

Interpersonal relationships (with public and colleagues).

Working conditions (such as lack of clerical and technical help).
Status.
Salary.
Security.

Note, in conclusion, that Herzberg's hygiene factors are closely linked with the lower levels of the Maslowian hierarchy, which represent people's physical needs, safety or security needs, and social needs. The motivators, on the other hand, are linked with the two highest levels of the hierarchy, representing people's needs for esteem and for self-fulfilment or self-actualization, as Maslow expresses it.

McGregor's Theory X and Theory Y[18]

Douglas McGregor built on Maslow's ideas, and pointed out that the 'hard approach' to staff management of the scientific school satisfied people's physical needs and security or safety needs, but frustrated their social needs, their esteem or ego needs, and their need for self-fulfilment. He encapsulated the two major positions which managers could take up, and called them 'Theory X' (roughly representing the scientific school) and 'Theory Y' (roughly representing the human relations school). Note that in a real-life situation in any organization one rarely finds such clear-cut positions, and very often different departments or sections are characterized by different approaches. A cataloguing or acquisitions department in a large library might be managed along Theory X lines, while in the same library a team of subject specialists or a team of area librarians might be operating along Theory Y lines. Theory X and Theory Y stances should be seen not so much as extremes which never meet, but rather as opposite ends of a continuum. Then individual libraries or parts of libraries can be placed at the appropriate point on the continuum, if one is analyzing their staff management policies, with a view to improving morale and performance.

Theory X. Employees are on the whole indolent. They lack ambition and are resistant to change. They are inherently self-centred and indifferent to the organization's needs. Without the active intervention of management people would be either passive or even resistant to the organization's goals. It follows that management must impose firm direction and control on its staff, and attempt to modify their behaviour to fit in with the goals of the organization. There can be both a 'hard' and a 'soft' approach by management who take up the Theory X stance.

The hard approach involves very tight inspection, checking and control. A certain amount of threat and coercion is usually implicit, though often concealed. There is little communication except downwards from seniors to juniors, and what there is tends to be rather formal (nearly always printed words, rather than face-to-face explanations). This approach is likely to provoke responses in employees that tend to counteract the whole aim of the exercise. The experience of industry over the last fifty years indicates that in these circumstances workers will respond in fairly predictable ways. They will restrict their output, engage in militant trade unionism, and subtly undermine the objectives of senior management.

The soft approach involves management in speaking softly, but still using the 'carrot and stick' approach. Staff normally take advantage of a soft approach, and their performance gets worse. Harmony of a superficial kind may be achieved, but at the cost of output and commitment.

McGregor argues that in many work-places observation might appear to confirm many of the tenets of Theory X, about people's laziness, lack of commitment and passivity. However, this, he says, is a consequence of management policies and practices, rather than the inevitable outcome of man's and woman's natures. He is indebted to Maslow for his views on people's needs at work, and he emphasizes that in many work-places only the lower level needs are satisfied. This leads to the frustration and anomie which causes people to behave in a lazy, uncommitted, irresponsible manner. Therefore we need an alternative theory based on more adequate assumptions about human nature. This, he argues, is provided in the set of propositions which he calls Theory Y.

Theory Y. Employees are capable of assuming responsibility, and of supporting the goals of the organization. It is the responsibility of management to provide the right conditions in which people can fulfil themselves, and satisfy their higher level needs for esteem, recognition and achievement. By being given more say in their work operation, people will not only achieve their own goals better, but will contribute more to the goals of the organization.

It sounds rather Utopian, and McGregor admits that there are problems. After people have been treated as passive and irresponsible for some time, they are not likely to be able to switch to being mature, self-activating beings very easily, just because there has been a change in direction by their managers. People who are used to being directed closely and strictly controlled at work are likely to turn to other spheres of their life for satisfaction of the higher level needs, and offer only a minimal commitment to their job. Also, it must be faced, a lot of jobs are not worth more than a minimal commitment, and this is indeed a problem in librarianship, where employees in all kinds of libraries complain of the high level of dull, routine procedural work. Nonetheless, there are clearly areas for improvement, even if progress must be gradual, in most organizations. It is a stance which has undeniable appeal in humanist terms, with its emphasis on individual responsibility, self-starters, and the dignity of man and woman *vis-à-vis* their superiors. McGregor is anxious to point out that the Theory Y approach to management need not be 'soft', that it can lead to high performance levels as well as a more satisfied staff. People's will to work is strengthened and they may commit themselves more genuinely to the service aims of the organization. This may, unfortunately, be offset by a certain anarchy and reluctance to carry out the duller work with competence and discipline.

Rensis Likert and participative management

The human relations school of management, (to which Maslow, Herzberg and McGregor subscribe) places much emphasis on drawing out staff potential, and on creating conditions at work in which staff can make greater use of their capabilities. This, it is hoped, leads both to greater self-fulfilment and to improvements in the services of the organization. One of the fundamental ways of achieving this is participative management. This is often seen in contrast to mechanistic management, which is associated with the scientific school of management. McGregor's Theory X is a good starting point for understanding what is meant by mechanistic management, and his

Theory Y implies participative management. Another term associated closely with participative management is 'organismic' management, implying that the library or other organization should be regarded as a complex living organism, rather than as a machine. Participative management is a range of attitudes and techniques intended to carry into practice the theories of the human relations or human resources school, based on the Maslowian hierarchy of human needs.

Rensis Likert is one of the leading proponents of participative management. His view is that the majority of people at work prefer this approach, and that it results in better performance. Figure 2.4 is a summary of his views on the range of management styles which may be practised:[19]

FIGURE 2.4

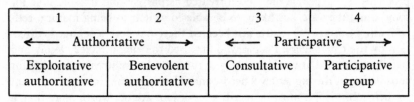

1	2	3	4
← Authoritative →		← Participative →	
Exploitative authoritative	Benevolent authoritative	Consultative	Participative group

Writers distinguish between immediate participation and distant participation. Immediate participation refers to employee involvement in matters concerning their everyday work, typically, if we think of the library situation, through informal interaction (or just reaction) from their immediate superiors. Attempts may be made to involve staff in taking decisions either through their supervisors asking for their opinions (stage 3 in the diagram) or through actual participation in the decisions (the work group decides, rather than the supervisor on his own, with or without consultation). The genuine participative decision is shown as stage 4 on the diagram. In the authoritative model, stages 1 and 2 on the diagram, decisions are taken by managers without reference to employees, though there may be some distant participation. This means that staff representatives sit on company boards, or in the case of libraries, on senior management teams, library committees, etc. 'The exploitative authoritative' style of management assumes that 'buying a man's time gives the employer control over the employee's behaviour', and that 'the organisation must put direct hierarchical pressure upon its employees to produce at specified levels'. There is little or none of this management style evident in libraries, but stage 2, the 'benevolent authoritative' can be found. This is marked by the more distant kinds of participation, by some show of representation, but the important decisions are still made by the people at the top. Thus authority remains concentrated among a few, with little delegation of decision-making. The organization structure is likely to be tall and narrow, favouring centralized decision-making, and with the emphasis on downward communication, rather than lateral and upward communication.

Likert's research studies indicate that in American industry the highest-performing managers have a 'supportive orientation' toward other members of the organization. The extent of this support can be gauged by asking their *subordinates* the following questions:[20]

1. To what extent does your supervisor try to understand your problems at work, and your personal and family difficulties?
2. Is he interested in helping you get the training which will help you in your present and future jobs?
3. How much confidence and trust do you have in your supervisor, and how much does he have in you, do you feel?
4. Does he ask your opinion when a problem comes up which involves your work? Following this, does he attach any value to your ideas, and try to use them?

Likert also argues that the highest-producing managers make more use of work-groups in decision-making, as well as involving individuals in work-related discussion. An important aspect of high performance also appears to be that the model acts as an incentive for other workers, particularly if there is a lot of group working. But it apparently takes quite a time to develop co-operation rather than competition in groups, though in the end it may be rewarding both for the people and for the organization. There seems to be a basis here for better staff management in libraries, since the team structure is becoming more common, and can provide opportunities for the kinds of participation Likert advocates.

Blake and Mouton's managerial grid[21]

The managerial grid is a device for managers to plot, by means of self-scoring questionnaires, the extent to which their management style shows concern for output and concern for people. Blake and Mouton show how production through people may be achieved by different theories about management, all of which take up a different position on the 'concern for people' continuum, and the 'concern for production' continuum. They present nine different theories, and suggest that the most satisfactory is team management (represented on the grid in the 9.9 position). They recommend that once managers have identified their own style and its position on the grid, they can then think about training techniques that will enable them to move towards a desired style. For Blake and Mouton the desired style is the 9.9 position, high on concern for people and high on concern for output.

Using this grid with a group of librarians on a part-time course at Leeds School of Librarianship has led to some interesting results. The tendency was to place libraries at the 9.1 position, which represents high concern for

FIGURE 2.5. THE MANAGERIAL GRID BASED ON THE RESEARCH OF BLAKE AND MOUTON

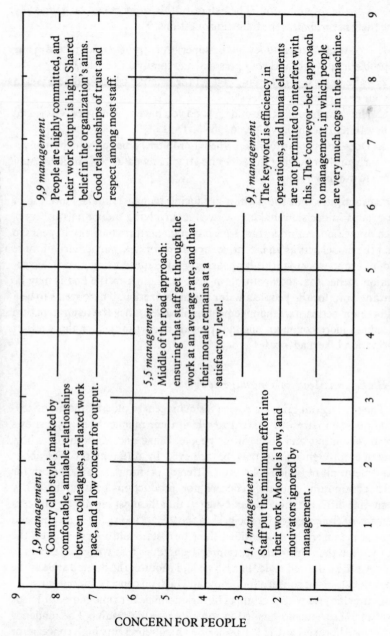

CONCERN FOR PEOPLE

CONCERN FOR PRODUCTION

1,9 management
'Country club style', marked by comfortable, amiable relationships between colleagues, a relaxed work pace, and a low concern for output.

9,9 management
People are highly committed, and their work output is high. Shared belief in the organization's aims. Good relationships of trust and respect among most staff.

5,5 management
Middle of the road approach: ensuring that staff get through the work at an average rate, and that their morale remains at a satisfactory level.

1,1 management
Staff put the minimum effort into their work. Morale is low, and motivators ignored by management.

9,1 management
The keyword is efficiency in operations, and human elements are not permitted to interfere with this. The 'conveyor-belt' approach to management, in which people are very much cogs in the machine.

40

output and low concern for people. This is perhaps surprising, since outside observers would tend to place libraries rather in the 1.9 position, representing low concern for output and high concern for people. Many libraries appear to have the fairly comfortable relaxed work tempo and friendly atmosphere among staff, which is only possible in uncompetitive, non-profit-making concerns. McGregor would characterize this approach as 'soft management', and is concerned to show that concern for people in management need *not* be soft. Blake and Mouton say that the 9.9 position of team participation 'is not for social purposes or to maintain morale as an end in itself, nor does the team concept provide a cloak of anonymity within which inadequate performance can be buried or hidden. Rather, sound interpersonal relations are seen as the *best* way to achieve or to maintain production at peak levels'.[22] The 9.9 position enables, moreover, conflict to be 'worked through', rather than avoided, as in the 1.9 position, or punished, as in the 9.1 position.

There are clearly many limitations in applying the grid to library situations. There can be wide swings within a library from time to time (for example there might be support for aiming at 9.1 during term-time and 1.9 during vacations in an academic library). Countervailing positions may be taken up by staff at different levels (for example 9.1 by line managers, 1.9 by a personnel officer, 9.9 by the chief librarian and/or his deputy). Then again, there are tasks to be got through, limitations of resources, and people who may resist any kind of 'team-socialization', and these factors may in a number of cases militate against 9.9 as a practicable goal.

The grid theory is interesting in that it encapsulates much of the behavioural sciences research findings of the 1960s and 1970s on what kind of conditions are effective in providing people with job satisfaction *and* in keeping up output. It emphasizes many of the earlier factors we have looked at, while summarizing the work of Maslow, Herzberg and McGregor, and Rensis Likert.

To recap, the techniques advised are dispersal of authority, by more delegation; making communication multi-directional, rather than downwards only; encouraging commitment through teams and groups agreeing on their actions and goals; providing positive motivators (achievement, recognition, responsibility) rather than solely hygiene factors (pay, status, security), in order to meet the higher-level needs as well as the lower-level needs in the Maslowian hierarchy.

The most recent theorists in personnel management have tried to evolve more complex models of the work situation. Vroom[23] for example stresses individual differences in work motivation, and Fiedler[24] has proposed a theory of leadership which tries to integrate a concern for differences in the situation with concern for differences between individual leaders. He believes that effective management depends on a complex matching up of the supervisor's management style with the organizational climate and the varying situations he or she has to face. The 'complex systems' approach is outlined in for example the work of Schein, who usefully summarizes the research findings on what makes an organization effective. He emphasizes that any organization consists of a number of subsystems (in a library these would include the technical, social and environmental systems), and argues that the interplay of these subsystems is as important, if not more important, than the behaviour of individuals. Staff can be motivated or demotivated as much by the work group to which they belong, or the roles and norms of their professional colleagues, as by their individual needs for self-identity, self-fulfilment, etc. Someone who is alienated in one library or section of a library may be motivated by moving to another post, or may find self-expression through union activities, while remaining inert and repressed on the job:

> Ultimate satisfaction and the ultimate effectiveness of the organization depends only in part on the nature of his motivation. The nature of the task to be performed, and the abilities and experience of the person on the job, and the nature of the other people in the organization all interact to produce a certain pattern of work and feelings. For example a highly skilled but poorly motivated worker may be as effective *and satisfied* as a very unskilled but highly motivated worker.[25]

Pirandello says that truth in a particular situation is a collection of what each person in the situation sees. If, in addition, everyone is wearing a *commedia del organizatione* mask (deputy dawg, scapegoat, joker, token woman manager) whatever is the poor personnel manager to do?

Plate and Stone, in their survey of job satisfaction among American librarians, say:

> Libraries, despite their apparent homogeneity, differ considerably with regard to their organizational history, leadership climate, and even goals and objectives. Library procedures vary from library to library and so must personnel practices and supervisory styles... Library managers must therefore be skilled in the adaptation of existing principles of motivation to local requirements.[26]

Applications of motivation theories in libraries (human relations school)

The work of Maslow, McGregor, Herzberg and other proponents of this approach to motivation theory provides a whole range of useful background information on the factors underlying people's attitudes and behaviour at work. This is a valuable start in analysing staff needs at work, and in attempting to take these needs into account in staff deployment, in the allocation of duties, and in job design (shaping the set of tasks and responsibilities which go to make up the job of any one individual).

Motivation theory can also prove useful in helping to solve specific staff problems. The initial step is analysing the problem and very often motivation and morale lie at the heart of the matter. In approaching a solution, the techniques which stem from the human relations school of theorists may be relevant. Can the job be enriched or enlarged to increase the job-holder's need for esteem and recognition? Can a larger element of professional work be injected into an 'impoverished' (by automation, for example) job content? Can staff be restructured into small work groups, to enhance the sense of identity and diminish isolation? Can initiative be encouraged rather than stifled by delegating more responsibility, or by providing more opportunities for staff to use their particular gifts, capacities, specialisms and enthusiasms?

There may well be a conflict between the aims of employers and the aims of employees, and this is a very obvious constraint in the business of trying to achieve a healthy balance between concern for output and concern for people:

Aims of employer	*Aims of employee*
Work specificity	Work flexibility
Output	Input
Uniformity	Individuality
Performance (what one does)	Personal qualities (what one is)

The transition from Theory X to Theory Y is justified, however difficult, it is argued, because of the extra energies released for work.

Participative management and the human relations school of motivation

Motivation theorists of the human relations school place great emphasis on participative management, as a method of satisfying a greater proportion of people's needs at work. The characteristics of participative management are considered to be conducive to high staff morale and motivation. They include more delegation, or pushing decision-making down the staff hierarchy; communication of a face-to-face kind, through group and team and working party meetings, rather than written memos from above. Other features are the involvement of staff in setting their own objectives on an annual basis, and in evaluation of their performance, usually also on an annual basis. Emphasis is attached to 'self-starting' attributes, or the capacity of staff to develop their jobs, and to 'grow' professionally. It can be seen that these characteristics of participative management are directly derived from the human relations school of motivation theorists. They follow from the view that the higher levels of the Maslowian hierarchy of needs should be satisfied by the content and context of professional work. They fit well with Herzberg's theory that the hygiene factors (pay, security and working conditions, for example) are not sufficient in themselves to motivate professional staff, but must be supplemented by the positive motivators (recognition and sense of achievement, for example). For library managers with motivation problems arising perhaps from unsatisfactory staffing structures, participative management ideas may suggest some solutions.

The most obvious example of this is the widespread introduction of the area team structure in public libraries since local government reorganization in 1974 led to the existence of larger, more complex, systems. The area team usually consists of six to twelve professionals, responsible for all the service points in a geographical area, each with a specialism, such as information services or children's work. In addition to a geographical responsibility, and a specialist responsibility, the member of staff may belong to a system-wide working party (on training or collection-building in a subject field). Compared with the previous fixed function posts, this team system displays at least the promise of participative management. Responsibility is delegated from headquarters to the area teams. Individual professionals enjoy greater autonomy in shaping their work, and developing their jobs (within the guidelines of overall aims and objectives, of course). There is more face-to-face communication, through area team meetings, and the attendance of the area librarian at senior management meetings. Members with specialist responsibilities may also attend meetings with their opposite numbers throughout the system (children's librarians for example, or community information people). Thus more decision-making takes place lower down the staff hierarchy, and there is less 'authoritarian' management by memo from the senior management team at HQ. In a number of systems where some kind of management by objectives has been introduced, professional staff are moreover involved in setting their targets for the coming year, and thus taking responsibility for developing their job, and measuring their own achievements, as opposed to carrying out orders from above, or maintaining traditional routines inherited from a predecessor.

Dutton provides an interesting example of participative management in an ICI information unit. The main features were that individual staff adopted their own individual targets; and having defined their own objectives, they were encouraged to attend relevant meetings and courses to get training, and feed back their increased expertise to the unit. All jobs, including counter work, were subject to 'self-examination'. (What is the borrowing success rate for inter-library loans from different sources? Standard practice was reversed as a result of the small study done on this.) Dutton also emphasizes the importance of openness in dealing with problems, and the involvement of staff who will be the operators of a new system, at the planning stage. He found that a more participative structure led to the elimination of excessive control and checking of minor matters. This led to economies in the use of time, besides encouraging staff at all times to differentiate between the essential and the trivial.

Dutton sums up the value of motivation studies as follows:

> These studies [Maslow and Herzberg] suggest that in developing staff we need to recognise two fundamentally different types of effect on motivation relating, respectively, to hygiene factors and to motivation factors. Further, whilst the hygiene factors must be considered first, it is only necessary to ensure that these do not get out of line. The only practicable method for doing this is through comparison with similar units. It is not profitable to become continually preoccupied with improving these aspects... Rather we must concentrate on trying to improve the motivation factors through the better organization of work, and experience points to staff participation as a highly effective means for doing this.[27]

In the academic library sector, Ashworth notes that with the development of multi-site polytechnic libraries from the 1960s, the old hierarchical staffing structures with strong central control and little delegation from centre to periphery proved inadequate:

> For example, a local academic librarian can be faced with demands from a Board of Studies which conflict with total library policy, and an embarrassing division of loyalties ensues. If the secondary centres take independent action, the whole model fails.[28]

And if it does not take independent action, the usual complaint of every centre-branch conflict is made, that the centre is out of touch with branch needs, that it is slow to act, and unreceptive to communications from the branch. Ashworth argues that library management must move towards the 'organic' model, away from the traditional hierarchical or 'mechanistic' model, if these problems are to be solved. The organic (or 'organismic', as the Americans call it) model derives from the human relations school of motivation theory. Behind its assumptions about human nature in the work-place lies the Maslowian hierarchy of needs, with its emphasis on social needs, need for esteem and recognition, and the need to fulfil one's potential. The organic model is based on McGregor's Theory Y, the optimistic image of employees, which sees them as capable of assuming responsibility, and of supporting the aims of the organization, if given the right context of participative management.

Likert also argues strongly for the organic approach to staff management, on the grounds that the genuinely participative work group, where decisions are reached by immediate involvement of staff and supervisor working together, (rather than supervisor occasionally asking staff for their opinions), produces better results and higher performance from staff. Herzberg's positive motivators, as opposed to the hygiene factors, are built into the organic model, which emphasizes staff development and commitment and self-motivation. Ashworth selects certain features of the organic structure, which he sees as specially relevant to the problems of academic library management.

First, the chief's role changes from omniscient being, to pilot of a team, all of whom may be more professionally expert in their own specialisms than he can be. Secondly, staff are expected to take part in setting their own work goals, and evaluating their achievements as a matter of course. The emphasis is on filling out the details of a rather open-ended job description, by encouraging staff 'to stretch themselves and set their own reach for the stars standards'. Thirdly a good communications network is an essential characteristic of the organic model. This can begin, suggests Ashworth, with inter-branch working parties to make recommendations about standardizing as many routines as possible, to remove low-level causes of friction. These working parties should be drawn from all strata, and will form the basis for building up networks which can be used later for more important matters such as designing new services. To reduce the amount of time spent in round-table discussions, the 'network' idea is to use wherever possible 'nodal' individuals who have emerged from group discussions as the people who will most efficiently facilitate specific developments or activities. This kind of communications network is more informal, *ad hoc*, and decentralized, than the traditional hierarchical structure, which emphasizes one way, top-to-bottom written communication, consisting mainly of cut-and-dried decisions. This makes it appropriate for the multi-site library (and all our public and most of our academic libraries are now multi-site), at least within certain areas of work. However, the question is raised as to what areas of work are appropriate for the organic model, and what areas benefit from the mechanistic model. Just as the organic model derives from the humans relations school of motivation theory, so the mechanistic model derives from the scientific school of motivation theory.

Applications of motivation theories in libraries (scientific school)

The advantages of centralized decision-making and fixed-function posts are that they provide staff with security and clearly-defined duties, and that the day-to-day routines get carried out reasonably well without questioning. Supporters of the mechanistic model argue that the majority of the staff are not really interested in responsibility or creativity at work. They further argue that there are not many areas in library work which require the exercise of much creativity. The smooth running of the acquisitions section, the streamlining of inter-library lending, the cataloguing of a special collection of nineteenth-century French literature – these are more typical of library work than designing a community information service, or an on-line information service for chemists. The qualities required are skill rather than imagination, efficiency rather than originality, endurance rather than flair and insight.

The nature of job satisfaction in the mechanistic model is confined mainly to the lower levels of the Maslowian hierarchy. In other words people's needs at work are met mainly in the areas of material reward and security. Herzberg's hygiene factors are normally present to prevent dissatisfaction (pay, working conditions), but the positive motivators are often lacking. Does it matter?

An examination of Tables 2.1 and 2.2, showing the findings of the Sheffield Manpower Project on what librarians consider to be the best and worst features of their jobs, goes some way to providing an answer. Hygiene factors, (such as 'job opportunities', 'colleagues', 'atmosphere' and 'pay'), get a number of mentions among the 'best features'. But overwhelmingly more important are the positive motivators (such as 'involvement with users', 'intellectually satisfying', 'variety of work', 'service aspects'). Routine was seen as the greatest scourge of library work, and in public libraries hours of work and physical demands were common causes of dissatisfaction.

Job enlargement, job enrichment and job rotation

Since there is a large element of routine in library work, both at professional and non-professional staff levels, and since variety of work turns out to be one of the features most appreciated by librarians, job rotation can be used on an hourly, daily, weekly, monthly or even annual basis. It is more often applied to humble jobs of a clerical nature in British libraries, though in the United States it is fairly common for headships of libraries and library schools to rotate.

Job enlargement means adding other tasks of the same level to a person's job, usually to prevent boredom (though it often means adding one boring job to another). Job enrichment on the other hand implies the addition of tasks of a more interesting or demanding nature. In library work at professional level this often means providing opportunities for staff to use specialist expertise, of a subject or professional kind. It may be achieved by subject specialization structures in academic libraries, and by area team structures in public libraries.

Selection, appraisal and training systems

These activities are significantly influenced by the management philosophies and techniques of the specific library, and/or its parent organization. For example, at ICI Dutton reports that the company initiated a staff development scheme which involved the application and understanding of Herzberg's hygiene factors and positive motivators. This meant that the library staff as part of company staff were encouraged to explore the applications of Herzberg's thinking to staff development:

> To encourage the widest sharing of experience, in addition to homogeneous work groups, representative groups comprising staff of different grade levels

Table 2.1 – Summary of 'best' features of library and information work

	Public	Academic	Special	Total
Work-centred factors:				
Variety	194	75	98	367
Involvement with users	231	77	80	388
Service	136	68	58	262
Social worth	30	10	8	48
Intellectually satisfying	92	49	73	214
Personal development	57	31	35	123
Books, library material etc.	75	3	6	84
Tangible end product	1	1	2	4
Opportunity for initiative	11	8	11	30
Particular tasks itemized	10	–	–	10
The work itself	21	4	4	29
	858	326	375	1,559
	(82.0%)	(83.6%)	(88.2%)	(83.8%)
Working conditions:				
Colleagues	31	6	3	40
Atmosphere	24	13	4	41
Stress free	13	6	3	22
Work style	7	7	10	24
Responsibility	3	–	4	7
Teamwork	5	1	3	9
Status	3	1	1	5
Physical aspects	4	2	2	8
Working conditions	5	–	1	6
	95	36	31	162
	(9.1%)	(9.2%)	(7.3%	(8.7%)
Terms and conditions of service:				
Job opportunities	25	9	9	43
Promotion; career prospects	6	5	2	13
Job security	13	4	1	18
Pension	1	–	–	1
Pay	20	5	1	26
Hours of work	16	1	–	17
Holidays	1	1	–	2
Sex equality	3	–	–	3
Training	2	–	–	2
Terms/conditions of employment	3	–	–	3
	90	25	13	128
	(8.6%)	(6.4%)	(3.1%)	(6.9%)
Miscellaneous	3	3	6	12
Total	1,046	390	425	1,861
	(100%)	(100%)	(100%)	(100%)

(Figures refer to the number of times each feature is mentioned.)
(*From* R. Sergean, *Librarianship and information work: job characteristics and staffing needs*. British Library, 1976.)

Table 2.2 – Summary of 'worst' features of library and information work

	Public	Academic	Special	Total
Work-centred factors:				
Routine	174	95	113	382
Involvement with users	78	15	16	109
Inability to provide service	5	6	5	16
No intellectual demand	3	4	6	13
No end product	1	1	3	5
Physical demand	115	22	13	150
	376	143	156	675
	(46.2%)	(51.6%)	(54.4%)	(49.0%)
Working conditions:				
Colleagues	5	3	3	11
Management and organization	42	12	4	58
The profession and professional librarians	7	3	2	12
Pressure of work	18	2	21	41
Rush/slack periods	5	1	2	8
Interruptions	5	2	5	12
Quiet; isolated	1	3	1	5
Status	30	21	31	82
Undermanned	10	6	2	18
Underfinanced	14	2	3	19
Physical aspects	22	1	10	33
Working conditions	2	–	–	2
	161	56	84	301
	(19.8%)	(20.2%)	(29.3%	(21.9%)
Terms and conditions of service:				
People/jobs ratio	2	3	7	12
Promotion; career prospects	30	14	10	54
Job insecurity	–	1	2	3
Overqualification	4	–	2	6
Pay	31	11	11	53
Hours of work	199	42	6	247
Holidays	3	2	–	5
Training	–	1	2	3
Terms/conditions of employment	1	–	–	1
	270	74	40	384
	(33.2%)	(26.7%)	(13.9%)	(27.9%)
Miscellaneous	6	4	7	17
Total	813	277	287	1,377
	(100%)	(100%)	(100%)	(100%)

(Figures refer to the number of times each feature is mentioned.)
(*From R. Sergean, Librarianship and information work: job characteristics and staffing needs. British Library, 1976.*)

and in different disciplines also explored common problems. As anticipated, hygiene factors predominated initially, but a constructive approach to these moved attention to motivational factors. Thus individual staff from the most junior began to analyse and discuss their individual jobs, in the light of library operations; to single out and express the important elements and existing shortcomings, and to suggest methods for improvement. A number of such operations, previously spread over several individuals, were reconstituted and total responsibility allotted to one person.[29]

In the following chapters of this book, dealing with job analysis and description, selection, appraisal and training, the significance of different management approaches derived from the scientific or classical school of motivation, and from the human relations school, will be taken up and further illustrated.

Summary of factors causing satisfaction and dissatisfaction in library work

Table 2.3 gives a brief summary of the main factors relevant to job satisfaction. The studies which the table draws on are the two surveys of British university library staff done by Roberts[30] and by Smith and Schofield[31] in the early 1970s; the Sheffield Manpower Project[32] which surveyed a representative sample of British public, academic and special librarians in the mid-1970s; and the Plate and Stone[33] survey of American and Canadian public, academic and special librarians. The purpose of grouping staff needs in this oversimplified way is to provide those concerned with managing staff with a basic tool-kit for approaching staffing problems. It could be used, for example, as a basis for taking action along the lines suggested in Table 2.4.

It should be added that a combination of strategies and actions is often necessary to effect improvement of staffing problems. A motivation problem with counter staff, for example, might be improved by experimenting with job enlargement and job rotation, by providing some interpersonal skills training, and by attempting to formulate a policy of improved rewards for non-professional staff.

Problems in the application of motivation theories and techniques

Cultural bias

Much of the research into motivation originated in the United States, and the results, it is argued, may not always be replicable in a British situation. It may be that the 'achievement ethic' is not as highly developed in

Table 2.3 – What motivates librarians? Summary of satisfaction and dissatisfaction in library work

	JOB CONTENT (intrinsic factors)	JOB CONTEXT (extrinsic factors)
S A T I S F Y I N G	Variety Involvement with users Satisfaction with books/ library materials Service orientation Personal/professional growth Intellectual satisfaction/use of professional expertise	Colleagues Atmosphere/work climate
D I S S A T I S F Y I N G	Routine Physical demands	Management and organization (staffing structures, supervision) Working conditions (physical aspects, unsocial hours of work) Status Undermanning Pressure of work Salary Career prospects

INTERACTION NEEDS OF LIBRARIANS AT WORK

To give and receive recognition for work done

To feel a sense of achievement

To have opportunities for feedback about their work

To experience positive supervision ('affective' as well as task-oriented)

To identify with the system through a work group or team

To participate in decision-making about their own work and related areas

Table 2.4 – Staff needs and management action

	Staff needs	Action
JOB CONTENT	Variety	1. Job enlargement, job rotation
	Removal of unnecessary routine	2. Systems analysis, organization and methods (O & M)
	Involvement with users	3. Modify staffing structure, to provide a mix of technical and reader services in a higher proportion of jobs
	Personal/professional growth	4. An objectives approach (*not* a rigid version of MbO) which involves staff in developing their own area of work, and monitoring progress each term or year
		5. Appraisal and training programme
		6. Supportive staff structure e.g. teams, work groups, *ad hoc* working parties
	Use of professional expertise/intellectual satisfaction	7. Increased delegation, job enrichment (plus 3-6 above)
	Satisfaction with books	8. Recruit staff who *read; use* their subject knowledge

Britain, particularly as Britain declines in power, prestige and prosperity *vis-à-vis* other advanced industrial nations. Furthermore the achievement ethic is becoming unacceptable to many young professionals, and is being replaced by a social commitment stance, based not on 'Where am I going in my professional career?', but 'What can I do in my occupation to help the information-deprived?' Achievement is also sometimes unobtainable and the late twentieth century is one of those times, with endemic recession and unemployment spreading into the graduate professions.

For these reasons the Maslowian concept of 'self-actualisation', or fulfilling one's potential at the higher levels, may be condemned through association with the achievement ethic, though that is probably unfair to Maslow's concept, which is complex and deserves more consideration. Whatever the reason Maslow appears to provoke an angry response or sheer bafflement among British librarians who attend short courses where his ideas are introduced. Letters to staff magazines indignantly attack the perpetrators of such workshops, so that one is moved to the conclusion that the human relations school of motivation is all very well for the New World, but that it may not do at all for Europeans. It is all very well for Americans to be concerned and articulate about self-analysis and self-expression, but for many Europeans openness is agony, or just plain bad form. This situation is probably changing as the influence of the American encounter movement and the Rogerian approach to interpersonal skills gain ground in Britain. Their views are beginning to take effect in the spheres of educational methods (emphasis on discussion groups, role-play, communications skills) and management (work-groups, with more meetings and discussion and expression of ideas) as well as in popular psychology (EST movement and the like).

Having noted the problems that British pragmatists have in accepting conceptual frameworks like Maslow's on motivation, it should be observed that if 'self-actualization' and 'identity needs' are translated into everyday terms like 'a sense of achievement at work', 'using one's intellectual and/or professional capacities to the full', then librarians on both sides of the Atlantic agree largely on what motivates people at work. An interesting difference between surveys of librarians and of other professionals (working in industry) is that exercising responsibility ranks lower with librarians as a source of job satisfaction. It is not clear whether this is because the nature of the work is such that not much responsibility comes the way of many staff, or because of staff structures that do not delegate much responsibility, or because many librarians do not have the personal thrust towards responsibility found in professionals working in industry.

Closed system approach

Work is only one aspect of an individual's life, and his or her work is affected to a greater or lesser degree by other aspects such as personal relationships, personal interests and leisure pursuits. Yet on reading some of the human relations school of motivation theorists, the impression is sometimes conveyed that the work situation is a world in itself, a closed system not much affected by the varying states of all the people who operate within it. For a large number of people the various levels of need (for self-identity and social recognition, for esteem or sense of achievement) may be met by situations and activities outside work, correspondingly reducing in some cases their needs at work. It could be argued that the human relations school of management has a tendency to idealize the satisfactions to be had from work, and that for the majority of people the expectations they have about work remain justifiably low, as a result of their past experience.

In times of economic recession, which diminishes choice, promotion prospects and job mobility, many people are forced to lower their expectations of a professional career even further, settle for a fairly routine job, and turn to other spheres of activity for the higher satisfactions.

Concern for people versus concern for output

Herzberg argues that for most of the twentieth century people have been tied to jobs which do not make enough demands on their capabilities, and have actually deterred them from developing any sense of responsibility. The 'carrot and stick' approach of classical management encourages workers to become passive and indifferent to what is often rather dull, meaningless work. They do not therefore subscribe to the same goals as management, and improved output can only be achieved by reward (pay, holidays, working conditions, 'perks') and punishment (docking wages, reprimanding, putting people on awkward shifts). Herzberg, on the contrary, argues that by treating people as self-starting mature adults rather than naughty and irresponsible children, managers will encourage staff to identify more with the aims of the organization, and output is likely to improve. Human relations theorists believe that a lot of extra energy can be released if staff become better motivated, and so more work will be achieved from 'Theory Y' people.

Herzberg admits, however, that it can be extremely difficult to transform 'Theory X' staff into 'Theory Y' staff, and that includes managers as well as those they manage. Progress can usually only take place in small slow stages, and sometimes by the use of cunning stratagems, as when Sears Roebuck was trying to encourage their managers to delegate more. In the case of one authoritarian manager this was only achieved by gradually increasing the number of staff reporting to him until he could no longer control the numbers in his traditional autocratic way (taking all the decisions himself), and was forced to delegate. The company was trying to get classical managers off people's backs, so that more staff would be free to plan and organize their own work in line with the company's objectives.

It is often assumed, but almost impossible to prove (especially in libraries, where the output is qualitative as much as quantitative) that satisfied workers are more effective workers. The human relations school is perhaps open to criticism on the grounds that it is too people-centred, and insufficiently concerned with technology, cost efficiency and cost-effectiveness.

Simplistic view of people?

Both the scientific or classical school of management and the human relations school imply a rather greater degree of consensus in the work-place than experience suggests is feasible. Motivation often looks very different from a management viewpoint, staff viewpoints, and trade union viewpoint. Trade unionists naturally feel compelled to look sceptically at job enrichment schemes, to see if the employers are trying to get higher levels of work done on the cheap. Many managers resent attempts to persuade them to delegate more, to give their subordinates more participation in the decisions they have hitherto taken. So they find ways of keeping up the appearance of participative management (meetings are held and bits of paper kept circulating), but in fact retain the decisions that really matter, and sometimes important matters get 'accidentally' left off the agenda of meetings, so that the manager deals with them himself (often with the excuse that there was not time for consultation – a paper had to be rushed through). Other managers simply do not know how to delegate, or to provide a framework for participation, and so a massive amount of training is needed, to change attitudes and skills. It seems that this can be successful:

> Man is capable of learning new motives through his organizational experiences, hence ultimately his pattern of motivation and the psychological contract which he establishes with the organization is the result of a complex interaction between initial needs and organizational experiences.[34]

Work content and motivation

It is a sad fact that attention to work which is neither enjoyable nor unpredictable is for most people extraordinarily difficult to retain. There is only so much that can be done to enlarge and/or enrich the more lowly routines of library work. And if the manager tries to alleviate the dullness by putting the staff in a congenial work group, the old problem arises of concern for output versus concern for people. However it should be noted that much of the interesting training material produced by libraries in the last decade has been directed at non-professionals, and in public libraries in particular new staff structures have led to job enrichment for them. In academic libraries and in special libraries non-professionals have traditionally had as much or more contact with the users than the professionals in such day-to-day matters as giving help and advice as far as lies within their expertise.

Are some aspects of motivation theories untestable, therefore unproven?

Maslow's concept of 'self-actualization' is difficult to test, though reading his writings brings to most people a strong recognition that in at least some area of their life, whether work or not, they have experienced this sense of richness in themselves, of 'having a strong true purpose' for once.

In the 1970s librarians began to be interested in techniques for improving job satisfaction, and there are now sufficient surveys published to confirm that the basic findings of the motivation theorists are replicable in librarianship.

Over-emphasis on participative management?

Participative management may appear to be offered as the universal panacea by many motivation theorists, and librarians seem to be moving cautiously in this direction, as shown by new staff structures and frameworks of consultation. In doing so they have encountered a number of common problems. First, participation is very time-consuming, and the thought occurs that, if it continues at the present rate of increase, by the year 2000 library work will consist entirely of meetings. Secondly a fair number of librarians are either openly against participative management, or they have received no education or training in the skills it requires, so are very bad at it. Even if a participative framework is set up by senior management, it will most likely produce effective participation only where the individuals involved are in favour, or at least prepared to be interested. Attitudes are involved, and these are themselves a product of organizational experiences, as well as cultural influences from home, education and society at large.

In a study on attitudes to change in organizations, Bowey[35] found that different types of organizational structure lead to different capacities for adapting to change. Change is more difficult and more stressful where staff see the organization as 'essentially hierarchical, with rules and procedures to be conformed with, and with authority vested in senior positions', compared with staff who see the organization as 'an interdependent system of parts, all making their essential contribution to the development and survival of the organization in its environment (characterized by threats and opportunities)'. The problem is that although human relations management is 'inherently or culturally appealing... people are forced to depart from it in their working lives... It is possible that the classical and pluralist models are so pervasive and strongly held in the work force that people who enter the work force with different perspectives find themselves being socialised into adopting these approaches.'

A related problem is that among those who work in libraries, there are very often differences of values, styles and interests (as much as between managers and workers), and conflicts based on values and stances tend to be disguised as technical problems. Effective staff management depends on the very complex interplay of values, organizational structures, and technology.

Many of the problems of participative management stem from inadequate skills in communication, one-to-one, and in groups. Interpersonal skills training is beginning to find a place in the education and training of librarians. Ken Jones, for example, has produced a series of useful strategies aimed at making one-to-one discussions and team meetings and committee work more productive and satisfying.[36]

Work assignments

1. Questionnaire: What do you expect from your job?
2. Case study: *Problems at Brightford*
3. Case study: *The difficult member of staff*

Assignment 1

(Use with a group of students or librarians)

WHAT DO YOU EXPECT FROM YOUR JOB?

1. To earn as much money as possible.
2. To work for as few hours as possible.
3. To be on good terms with your supervisor.
4. To be kept in the picture about what is happening in the organization.
5. To be on good terms with colleagues.
6. To have an interesting job.
7. To have good working conditions.
8. To receive full appreciation for work done.
9. To have a secure job.
10. To have chances of promotion and growth within the organization.
11. To experience a feeling of achievement.

A. Read the list of expectations carefully.
B. Each one is numbered.
C. In the top box on the right of this sheet write the number of the 'expectation' you consider to be most important, e.g. if you consider that: 'To have a secure job' is most important write '9' in the top box.
D. Write the number of the next most important expectation in the second box, and so on, until all the boxes are filled.

When the members of the group have filled in their table of preferences, the scores can be totted up, and each factor can be ranked in order of preference to indicate the factors which contribute most to job satisfaction in the group.

The tutor or trainer can then draw comparisons between the group's views and the findings of surveys on job satisfaction referred to in Chapter 2.

Assignment 2

Case study: *Problems at Brightford*

Read through the description below of the staffing situation in Brightford Area Library, and try to answer the following questions:

1. What levels of need (using the Maslowian hierarchy) are the different members of staff aiming, consciously or unconsciously, to satisfy in their jobs?

2. What are the causes of satisfaction and dissatisfaction for each member of staff? Use Herzberg's list of hygiene factors and motivators to help you answer this question, and/or McGregor's Theory X and Theory Y.

3. Where on the Blake and Mouton Grid would you place each member of staff who occupies a managerial role, i.e. Mr Easy, Mr Drive, Mr Lax, Miss Saintly and Mrs Fineman?

4. To what extent would you say the management style is authoritative or participative, according to Rensis Likert's chart and the explanations accompanying it?

Brightford Area Library serves a prosperous, lively town of 65,000. There is much science-based industry in the locality and an extensive commercial and business community serving the surrounding countryside. The Area Library is an attractive modern (and generally adequate) building, with a bookstock of 60,000. The staff comprise the Area Librarian (Senior Officer grade), the Lending Librarian, Reference Librarian, Readers' Adviser and Childrens' Librarian (all on AP 4). The Lending Librarian has two assistants (on AP 2/3), the Reference Librarian has one assistant (on AP 2/3). There are in addition two full-time service points, or 'neighbourhood' branch libraries each in the charge of a professionally qualified Branch Librarian (on AP 4). The larger branch has a qualified assistant (on AP 2/3). As well as the qualified staff, there is an adequate number of junior staff, some school-leavers, some older women part-timers.

The Branch Librarians are responsible for selection and management of adult fiction and popular non-fiction at their branches. The remaining stock is managed by the Lending and Reference Librarians, the Readers' Adviser, and the Childrens' Librarian, who divide up the responsibility on a subject basis. The Area Librarian exercises overall control. The service is quite well regarded in the town, since the bookstock is kept at a reasonable standard, and individual staff show various professional talents. However, staff morale is low. There is a high turnover of junior staff, much 'sickness' leave, poor work output, and a symptomatic untidiness and negligence in various sections.

The staff and their activities

Area Librarian: Mr Easy. Distinguished-looking, charming, kind and warm-hearted, but lacks confidence. He was appointed Area Librarian after many years in charge of various Branch Libraries. He took up the post some time after the rest of the senior staff had established themselves. He is inclined to indolence, keeps gentlemanly hours, and expects the library to run itself. He is unwilling to take decisions and procrastinates but will occasionally lash out by written memo, rather than face what he sees as time-wasting and tedious discussion with his staff. The memos are broadly phrased, invariably procedural in content, and often require precise interpretation by his senior staff (who often see them for the first time when their juniors come to complain). Mr Easy is given to sarcasm rather than direct reprimand, but tends to give way quickly when faced with resistance from strong personalities. He is, informal gossip has it, henpecked by his wife, whom he has recently installed in a small part-time branch in a Community Association building. Mystified by the 'Higher Bibliography' in which he finds the more egregious of his staff engaged, Mr Easy exercises his own penchant for exhibitions and display work by maintaining a series of highly-thought-of exhibitions on hobbies, crafts and sport in the foyer of the Library. These have won him a number of friends among the local community, and he tends to spend his leisure time with them, rather than with anyone from the library.

Reference Librarian: Arthur Drive. An able, energetic librarian who attempts to jolly along Mr Easy, in order to get things moving a bit. He has extended the scope of his ill-defined duties to include much promotional work, has built up and well publicised a local studies collection, has reorganized stock management procedures and undertaken other ongoing if more minor developments (with, for example, local schools in connection with the local studies collection). Some colleagues suspect him of empire-building, and remain cool in the face of his endless flow of initiatives and/or ideas. Besides his dynamism inside the library, he is active in the town, in local politics and as a Governor of one of the secondary schools. He is looking for another post, and in the meantime is collecting material for an M.Phil. thesis on 'Promoting the public library: philosophies and practices'.

Lending Librarian: Jack Lax. Experienced within a familiar range of duties, but unlikely to favour new approaches, partly because he likes undemanding routine, and is happy enough in his present situation, in charge, though not being very supportive, of his juniors. He is sometimes matey, sometimes a real disciplinarian with them. He himself has been 'bawled out' by the Area Librarian on a few occasions, in front of his staff, for work lapses which could really only be attributed to his general idleness. However, he is genial and affable with his equals, lunches in the local hostelries, rarely on his own, and looks like he is settled where he is for the rest of his career (he is in his early forties). A year or two ago he submitted an ALA bibliography which was turned back to him for further work. But he seems to have given up any idea of going on with it, and instead has been increasing his social activities, especially since he married a second time last year, and his new wife, a private secretary in one of the local industrial plants, has brought him into a new social circle.

Readers' Adviser: Julia Fineman. An able woman, with high levels of professional competence, who lacks confidence, and looks battered by frustration at work and at home. She is bringing up a couple of kids on her own, and although they are both now in secondary school, she worries about them, and even more about her work, if she has to take the occasional day off to solve problems they have at school, or if her child-minder fails to turn up during school holidays. In fact she has fewer absences than most of the other professional staff, in an average year. She fills at work a lot of the vacuum created by Mr Lax in the Lending Library, and keeps things going on the Adviser Desk and on the requests side where she liaises with Mr Drive in Reference. They work well together, since she appreciates his ideas, and finds the enthusiasm a nice change from Mr Lax's amiable apathy. She does not get much appreciation for her hard work, except from Mr Drive, but she keeps going, and gets away to professional meetings and conferences from time to time, partly for the social side, partly because she needs the stimulus of papers and discussion, as she is really quite keen on her career, but does not get much mental excitement from her work-group in the Lending Library.

Children's Librarian: Janet Saintly. Quiet, reserved, unimaginative but endlessly conscientious. None of the others takes any interest in her work, and she in any case easily becomes resentful at what she calls 'outside interference', on the rare occasions when they do. Like Mr Easy and Mr Lax, she is likely to be here for the rest of her working life (she is in her late forties, unmarried, but with a settled circle of friends in the town, with whom she plays bridge, attends the local cultural events, and goes on trips to London for opera and ballet). Her interest in childrens' librarianship is genuine, but she is suspicious of new approaches and firmly believes that if anyone needs the service they can come and get it. She does story hours on Saturdays from time to time, but the kids are a little wary, because her manner is a bit authoritarian. Her relations with colleagues are very formal; she invariably sends written memos to Mr Easy, rather than popping in to see him about estimates, accommodation problems or other matters.

The Branches. Both branch libraries have steadily lost business in recent years to the Central Library. They have been in the charge of senior staff considered unsuitable for central library responsibilities, and have been run in a routine and barely competent fashion. The staff are happy enough in their isolation from Central, since they have fixed ideas about procedures, and are hostile to any changes that might be imposed if Central 'interfered more'. Their view of librarianship is very much the 'Higher Clerical' one, and they do not see that there is much to it, except common sense (*their* common sense). They would try to get out of any staff meetings that were held, but Mr Easy does not believe in meetings anyway, so their contacts with Central are minimal.

Central Library Assistant Librarians. The two in the Lending Library (recently out of library school) are used mainly for enquiries and bibliographical tracing, under the direction of either Jack Lax or Julia Fineman. They feel 'unsettled' and would like work of greater professional scope and variety. There is apparently no time to give them any in-service training (even induction training), so they do not know much about the objectives of the service or how their work fits in. It all seems pretty boring and a bit of a let-down after library school. They are rather envious of the Reference Librarian's Assistant, who is the same age as them, because her work obviously provides much more satisfaction. She gets a lot of interesting enquiries, and has more things explained to her by Mr Drive, who communicates his enthusiasm, and actually discusses with her things like project kits on local studies, which some local teachers are getting together with the help of the library. He is also planning to publish, in order to raise funds for the library, some reproductions of old photographs of the area with commentary, and she is delegated the job of sifting through the illustrations for specific examples of various themes.

Central Library junior staff. The two who work in Children's are keen and hard-working, though they do not always strike the right note with Janet Saintly. She does not expect them to make suggestions, and would prefer them just to do what she instructs them to do. She sometimes fails to explain things clearly, and has a tendency to blame them if they get it wrong. The remainder of the juniors are on counter or workroom duties. Control is by daily work sheet, plus erratic oral supervision from the Area Librarian, the Lending Librarian or the Readers' Adviser. On occasions, when the senior staff decide to have a blitz on lateness or untidiness or poor attitudes to the public, the discipline can be harsh. It usually passes over fairly quickly, though, and nothing happens (no real training even) till the next time.

Assignment 3

CASE STUDY: THE DIFFICULT MEMBER OF STAFF

The problem: Two character sketches are provided of Miss Ellen Foy and Mr Geoffrey Marr, two problem members of staff. You are invited to assume the role of a senior assistant librarian responsible for supervising Miss Foy and Mr Marr. Using your knowledge of motivation theories, try to 1) analyse problem symptoms, 2) consider how you would become aware of problems by filling in the grid at the bottom of 'Consciousness raising', 3) make notes on what action you would take to discover the causes of the problems, and 4) suggest some solutions.

Role-play. Where possible, trainees should have the opportunity of playing the role of both a difficult member of staff, and, in turn, the supervisor conducting an interview with the problem member. Others in the group should act as observers, and give their comments on the effectiveness of the interview, in terms of getting at the causes of the problem, and/or moving towards solution or alleviation of the problem. Each interview should last fifteen to twenty minutes. When a number of interviews have been role-played, and observers have made their comments after each one, it is useful for the tutor or trainer to draw together the conclusions in a summarising discussion. The tutor should comment on the extent to which students or trainees used motivation theory in their analysis and solutions, since the temptation in some trainees is to use 'off the cuff' responses and not think the problem through with reference to what they have learned about motivation.

General notes on the case study (pp 65-6). These should not be consulted until the trainees have tried to arrive at solutions of their own. They consist of four headings:

Recognizing a problem exists
Deciding to act
Taking action
Solving the problem

They may be used after the role-playing sessions as a basis for the concluding discussion, or simply as a check-list by which trainees can measure their own suggestions.

The difficult member of Staff: Character sketches

Miss Ellen Foy. Age 18. Non-professional assistant, one of two employed in the section. Often arrives late, though she only lives a short bus ride from the library. Works hard when she finds the work interesting, but is slow and inaccurate on routine jobs (which form the bulk of her tasks). This leads to friction with Betty Martin, the other assistant, who is quite conscientious, but feels it is unfair that she has to do more of the dull work to make up for Ellen's deficiencies. Ellen is popular with users, since she has a bright chatty manner and likes passing the time, is sociable, sometimes to the further detriment of her routine duties. This also leads to Betty, a quieter type, having to take on an obviously bigger share of the work than Ellen. Ellen was expected to do better at A levels last summer than in fact she did. She got one A level in French (D grade), but failed her English. However she was not keen on going on to college, because she had had, she says, enough of that sort of thing at school. She took the job in the library because it would be meeting people, and she didn't want to become just a typist in a dull office, like some of her school friends. She has now been in the library about five months, and her standard of work is not improving with time, though she has her ups as well as her downs, and is sometimes slapdash, but at other times shows she is quite capable of competent work. It seems to depend, the impression is, on the state of her social life.

Mr Geoff Marr. Age 34. A professionally qualified librarian, who has worked in this library since he finished his library school course ten years ago. He is overconscientious in all he does, taking a great deal more time than you think necessary to complete jobs. He has been found to continue to keep records which are no longer needed, in your opinion, and from time to time he puts in for extra office equipment which he says is needed for more efficient record-keeping. He is rather possessive about his work, and unwilling to explain or delegate any of it to anyone else, even when he is on holiday. He is never off ill, and seems quite satisfied with the work he is doing (even if you are not). He does not seem to have any ambition to move either to another library, or even to other jobs in this library. In fact even minor changes in the policies and procedures of the department make him turn very defensive about his work, and automatically resist anything new, though he is more quietly stubborn than openly resistant. He is really intended to act as your general helper and assistant, as well as carrying on with his own specific duties, but he is unwilling to stand in for you if you are away, and tells enquirers when you will be back, rather than attempting to handle their queries himself. This of course irritates any users who naturally expect there to be someone on the spot to help them, but Geoff (to whom you have spoken previously about this) insists that he has no time left from his own work to cope with these extras. The two non-professionals tend not to take him seriously, and look to you to sort out any queries they have. This suits him, anyway, as he is very much a loner, and restricts his conversation with the juniors (and you too quite a lot of the time) to formal good-mornings and leave-takings, as far as possible.

Consciousness raising

How would you react to the problem staff members?
How would you know there was a problem?
Fill in the grid at the end considering the following statements in two ways:

A. Is this the way you tend to act?

B. Is this the way you would recommend a person to act?

1. Whenever I am working with the other staff I am watching out for problem symptoms.

2. I have trained myself to look round my staff for problem symptoms at least twice per day.

3. I don't specifically look for symptoms but I like to think that my general interest in the staff and my approachability cause me to notice when there is anything wrong or I am told there is.

4. As soon as I notice a problem symptom I step in because I think it is wrong to let problems build up.

5. With some staff and some problems it is best to step in quickly but with others it is better not to.

6. I am the sort of person who cannot rest unless I sort out a problem when I see it. If I don't I worry about it.

7. Some staff are always trying to get away with things and I sort them out pretty quickly; others are very trustworthy and I know their mistakes are really oversights so I don't say anything.

8. Some staff, quite frankly, scare me so I try to keep out of their way. If I have to do anything I usually ask my senior assistant to talk to them.

9. I prefer to reprimand staff in front of others. I somehow feel less exposed that way.

10. I think over problems a lot before I decide to act, then I look for opportunities during the day.

11. I rehearse over and over again what I am going to say but I have great difficulty in saying it so that days can go by when I kick myself for not having the courage to say something. Somehow the problem always seems worse when I think about it at home than it does when I meet the problem person next day.

12. I worry all the time that I might be the cause of the problem.

Record your reactions to the statements by ticking the appropriate boxes.

Self		1	2	3	4	5	6	7	8	9	10	11	12
	Yes												
	No												
Recommendation													
	Yes												
	No												

Comments:

If you find a number of inconsistencies between A and B, when you have recorded your answers in the grid, take careful note of the fact. It may be that when you recommend that some action be taken, even if you wouldn't take it yourself, this is due partly to your own personality, partly to ignorance of some possible strategies, and partly to your socialization at work ('people don't do that sort of thing in our place'). Think about these explanations, and ask yourself to what extent they are relevant in explaining discrepancies in how you filled in the grid.

General notes on the case study

It is suggested that there are several stages which the person trying to solve the problem is likely to go through (whether or not he is conscious of it). Analysis of these stages is useful for discussion purposes and as a checklist.

Stage 1. RECOGNIZING A PROBLEM EXISTS
Requires two processes:

(a) *Observation* on the part of the supervisor enabling the symptom to be recognized. This is closely associated with several of the principles of good personnel management derived from the workroom juniors exercise, e.g. genuine interest in the people you work with and an empathy with them.

(b) *Awareness of symptoms or indicators.* These can be communicated by the problem staff member and/or by others. A useful categorization or 'things to look out for' might be:

Personal non-verbal:	Facial expression, way the person moves about, dress, general appearance.
Personal verbal:	Things said by the person to you or to others.
Work performance:	Quality of work: speed, accuracy.
Absence from work:	Absenteeism, illness, bad timekeeping, taking longer over coffee breaks, etc.
General:	e.g. lack of willingness, general disposition, attitude, lack of initiative or interest.

With existing staff it may often be *change* in behaviour that is noticed.

Stage 2. DECIDING TO ACT
The decision whether to do anything about the observed symptom or not. Clearly the only reason for stepping in should be the belief that this will improve the situation but there may be other reasons.

Stage 3. TAKING ACTION
Within work

(a) Discussion with others: staff of library, previous colleagues.

(b) Interview: where? when? how? – authoritarian-benevolent/task-people orientations.

(c) Passing matter to others: chief librarian, staffing officers, welfare officers, etc.

Outside work

Contacting others outside the organization for information, opinions: other employers, family, relatives, friends.

Recording

What should be written down and retained in personal files? How confidential should the information be?

This stage should discover the problem. The most likely causes of problems:

(a) *Work problems* (based on Herzberg)

Lack of achievement in work.

Lack of recognition for work done.

Disinterest in work itself.

Lack of responsibility.

Lack of promotion or prospects of it.

Not getting on with superiors.

Not getting on with other members of staff.

Dissatisfaction with salary.

Dissatisfaction with working conditions e.g. hours of work, holidays, physical conditions at work.

(b) *Personality problems*

Many of the above may result from personality, e.g. values and attitudes to work which may result from social background or age group, inability to concentrate, lack of intelligence or ability.

(c) *Problems outside work*

Whole variety of domestic problems with relatives and friends.

(d) *Physical and mental illness*

Stage 4.   SOLVING THE PROBLEM

Not just for the good of the individual but bearing in mind the effect on others. Note the continuing nature of problems and that each person and situation is in some sense different from any other.

Work-centred problems

It is important to use a thorough knowledge of motivation theories in analysing the problem. What levels of need is the staff member hoping to satisfy at work, and are these being met? Is there a conflict between satisfying the individual's work needs (for sociability, say) and keeping up the output of work that the department requires? Is the person's job design appropriate to the departmental objectives? Maybe the job description could be re-done, in consultation. Note all the standard techniques (summed up in Table 2.4), which are recommended for increasing motivation. To what extent are these relevant in the present case study? Note that in the case of interpersonal problems a new understanding or new attitudes may be necessary. This is partly of course a matter of personality but interpersonal skills training may help.

Problems outside work

Great care is necessary here, as the member of staff, relatives and friends may (singly or together) believe it is no business of yours. It is best to enter this area very carefully, and get out of it as soon as there is any opposition. But very often staff *do* want someone to know about their problems (domestic, health, financial, personal relationships), and sometimes it is the supervisor who wants to keep everything neatly compartmentalized and is not prepared to listen to what are seen as non-work area 'excuses'. In terms of motivation theory, of course, security needs, social needs and esteem needs are all relevant to work, and the extent to which one is trying to 'self-actualize' at work often depends on relative satisfactions in other parts of one's life. Some training in non-directive counselling might be helpful, but is not likely to be common except for those who, like training officers, are much involved with staff welfare. In most cases of personal problems, however, many may get relief simply through talking it all through, even if they ultimately have to find their own answers.

Physical and mental illness

Many of the above remarks are apposite here, but knowledge of where help can be obtained from outside professional and support services is most appropriate.

3 Manpower planning

Manpower planning covers a range of activities designed to ensure a balance between the supply and demand for library and information workers, in both quantitative and qualitative terms. It is concerned with the kind of people needed to run libraries, as much as with the numbers of staff needed at each level, from library assistants to senior management.

The first step in manpower planning is to analyse the existing situation: number of staff at present employed, their qualifications in relation to the work they do, and 'job characteristics', or an analysis of the tasks and responsibilities carried out by staff, in terms of intellectual, physical and social demands. Do the jobs require someone with a degree? Do staff work in backroom isolation, or do they have a fair amount of contact with others, either colleagues (as in a team staffing structure) or users? Do the jobs require stamina to cope with periods of intense pressure, or is the work easy-going and lacking in stress situations?

Having analysed the existing situation systematically, so that all jobs and the staff in those jobs have been covered, the second step in manpower planning is to calculate likely wastage rates for the period (say five years) over which the plan is likely to be used as a guideline for staff recruitment, training and development. This involves working out the pattern of job mobility and resignations that may be expected on the basis of past experience. But social trends have an important influence which may upset predictions in this area. Married women, for example, may work longer before resigning to have a family, because of pressures on young couples to maintain two incomes to meet mortgage payments. Women's liberation has moreover had the effect (even on the not particularly committed) of making it more normal for women to keep up their career as well as having a family, or sometimes instead of having a family. Gavron's[1] book on the captive graduate housewife and her problems of lack of fulfilment has been one of many which have raised women's expectations of work as a means of achieving independence and self-identity (even if this is sometimes shattered by the actual work experience they achieve, which under-uses their talents and training). Since librarianship is predominantly a female profession, these social factors have an impact on wastage rates, in addition to the usual factors of normal age of retirement, and premature retirement, due to illness or (increasingly, as cuts in public expenditure occur) special schemes whereby the over-fifties may retire early with a lump sum and a pension proportionate to their years of service.

Socio-economic factors clearly affect wastage rates, and in the early

1980s there has been an upsurge in unemployment as a result of stagnant economies in advanced industrial countries. The reaction of many governments has been to make public expenditure cuts, by reducing the number of jobs in the public sector, both at central government level and in local government. Schemes for early retirement and voluntary redundancy have been devised to achieve reductions in jobs. Other methods include delays in filling empty posts, or freezing posts indefinitely. Since library jobs are almost entirely in the public sector (academic and public and many special libraries are financed by central or local government) the effects of economic recession are severe. Information workers in industry are also likely to feel the icy winds of recession, since their parent bodies have shown themselves rather ready to look to the information unit as a place where staffing economies can be made.

The third stage in manpower planning is the calculation of the likely demand for staff during the period under review (usually the next five years). This too is affected by socio-economic considerations, since plans for expansion of existing services or the creation of new services all depend on the money being available. It is also influenced by automation, which seems more likely to reduce the number of clerical staff needed rather than the number of professional staff. Trends in librarianship, such as outreach services in public libraries, expansion of information services in academic libraries, and the on-line revolution in special libraries, all affect the number and quality of staff needed.

The fourth stage is the production of an actual manpower plan. This is in theory done by matching the supply and demand findings, as outlined above, and coming to decisions about the number and nature (qualifications, experience, personal attributes) of staff who will be needed to man the service over the period covered by the plan. In practice it is by no means straightforward, since social and economic trends are notoriously difficult to predict accurately over long periods; as are developments in technology, and changes in information needs within the country at large. Similarly unpredictable are the priorities which paymasters may hammer out, as they devise ways of controlling public expenditure while at the same time trying to convince the electorate that public services such as housing, education and libraries are not really suffering a decline in standards.

The four phases which make up the manpower-planning cycle may be applied either within an individual library system, or to a particular sector of the library world (academic libraries, or school libraries, for example), or to the profession as a whole, nationwide. The Institute of Information Scientists, for instance, modifies its entry requirements and its approval of information science courses in Britain, by taking account of manpower trends, such as the growing need for social science specialists in information work, where previously the emphasis was almost entirely on science and technology.

Reasons for manpower planning

Before examining some of the major surveys of manpower planning, it is important to be clear about the uses of manpower analysis and prediction of needs. Broome[2] usefully summarizes the ways in which manpower planning can help staff management.

1. It helps to determine recruitment levels on a rational basis, rather than waiting for problems of oversupply or undersupply to become apparent, before taking action.
2. It helps in determining training needs in relation to required skills and specialisms. Without it, training may become a somewhat piecemeal, haphazard activity, insufficiently related to the actual needs of a developing service.
3. It enables costing of labour to be carried out rationally, when new projects are being planned or contemplated.
4. It encourages organizations to plan their future staffing structures, to take account of changes in services and in technology, rather than making *ad hoc* arrangements as problems arise (such as jobs fading away, or new jobs emerging, as a result of automation).

Surveys on supply and demand in librarianship

Arguments about manpower planning in librarianship have been concerned mainly with the quantitative aspects, and in particular recruitment to the library schools (the supply side of the formula) in relation to the number of jobs in libraries (the demand side of the formula). The Department of Education is active in monitoring output from the schools and success rates in finding jobs in the period immediately following library school. These figures are collected and published at regular intervals in the *Library Association Record:*[3] (see Tables 3.1–3.5).

Jessop Report 1968. The first attempt to monitor supply and demand on a national basis, with a view to predicting manpower requirements in libraries over the following ten-year period, was the Jessop Report, produced by the Library Advisory Councils for England and Wales in 1968. The general conclusions of this report were:

Although it is recognised that the estimates of total demand (see below) are extremely tentative, these output figures (also given below) are so far ahead of those estimates as to give some cause for concern. It is possible that, if the staff are available, employers will be willing to develop their services more rapidly than has been envisaged, and there is ample evidence that such development is needed. It is probably unrealistic however to expect the profession to absorb for many years numbers of newly qualified librarians very far in excess of those suggested.... These estimates therefore suggest that no further expansion of schools of librarianship, leading to increased output of librarians is

Table 3.1 – Students surveyed,[1] replying and professionally employed (PE) with percentages – 1969-1977

Academic Year	Number		% Response	Number		% PE
	Surveyed[1]	Responding[1]		Responding[1]	With PE	
1969-70	1381	1193	86	1220	1005	90
1970-71	1477	1242	84	1183	1023	86
1971-72	1329	1119	84	1066	894	84
1972-73	1502	1213	81	1166	965	83
1973-74	1395	1141	82	1122	991	88
1974-75	1409	1139	81	1093	859	79
1975-76	1465	1125	77	1093	754	69
1976-77	1420	1148	81	1088	635	58

Table 3.2 – Students surveyed,[1] with response percentages for each type of course – 1970-71, 1972-73, 1974-75, 1976-77

Academic Year	Two-year		First Degree		Postgraduate		Master's	
	Number Surveyed	% Response	Number Surveyed	% Response	Number Surveyed	% Response	Number Surveyed	% Response
1970-71	842	82	83	90	479	86	73	89
1972-73	739	81	154	83	544	79	58	89
1974-75	470	80	218	88	637	81	84	89
1976-77	276	84	376	84	634	79	134	78

Table 3.3 – Students replying,[2] with professional employment (PE) percentage, for each type of course – 1970-71, 1972-73, 1974-75, 1976-77

Academic Year	Two-Year		First Degree		Postgraduate		Master's	
	Number Responding	% PE	Number Responding	% PE	Number Responding	% PE	Number Responding	% PE
1970-71	661	89	75	64	387	87	60	83
1972-73	573	84	128	71	409	85	56	80
1974-75	348	83	181	65	493	80	71	79
1976-77	219	48	303	49	477	65	89	80

(1) Includes overseas.
(2) Excludes overseas.

Table 3.4 – Studies in professional employment, for each type of course and destination,[3] as percentages – 1970-71, 1972-73, 1974-75, 1976-77

Academic Year	Two-Year			First Degree			Postgraduate			Master's			All Courses		
	P	A	S	P	A	S	P	A	S	P	A	S	P	A	S
1970-71	72	15	13	35	29	35	46	34	20	12	40	48	59	23	18
1972-73	73	15	11	43	26	31	44	30	26	13	31	56	57	22	21
1974-75	77	13	10	54	30	16	52	28	20	16	30	54	58	23	19
1976-77	73	8	20	50	14	36	42	23	36	21	21	58	46	18	36

(3) P, Public; A, Academic; S, Special.

Table 3.5 – Students without professional employment (PE) by type of course and intentions, percentages and totals in two-year periods

| Academic Period and type of course | | Still Seeking Library Work | | | | Full-time work | Still Student | Non-professional Library work (1977 only) | Other | All without PE | |
| | | Working | | Not Working | | | | | | No. | % |
		Other limits	Geographical limits	Geographical limits	Other limits						
Two-year	1970-72	2	20	27	23	13	7	–	6	138	11
	1975-77	6	4	20	27	6	1	24(43)[4]	13[4]	178	20
First degree	1970-72	5	7	21	11	21	32	–	3	57	30
	1975-77	4	6	21	22	5	8	12(22)[4]	22[4]	280	42
Postgraduate	1970-72	4	3	34	22	14	7	–	16	119	16
	1975-77	2	4	24	27	4	3	11(25)[4]	23	293	23
Master's	1970-72	6	6	17	17	33	11	–	11	18	15
	1975-77	2	2	20	20	7	17	2 (6)[4]	29	41	25
All courses	1970-72	4	11	28	20	16	11	–	10	332	14
	1975-77	4	5	22	25	5	5	14(27)[4]	21	792	26

(4) Based on those lacking professional employment in Summer 1977, 409.

likely to be justified in the immediate future. It is desirable however that both output and demand should be kept continuously under review.[4]

The conclusions of the Jessop report contain the seeds of most of the arguments that have been advanced for or against manpower planning in the last decade. Estimates of future demand remain tentative because there are so many imponderables. To what extent will the British economy recover from the recession of the late 1970s and early 1980s? Information is a growth area; it is becoming big business (computer databases of bibliographical citations, and data banks of actual information). Will this lead to more jobs for library and information workers (if they can establish themselves in these new areas) or fewer jobs (if they fail to find a role in the developing areas, due perhaps to conservative attitudes or failures in education and training)?

While the major library systems are unlikely to grow further (unlike during the 1960s, when the post-Robbins era saw a vast expansion in higher education and libraries to support it; or the early and mid-1970s, when public libraries after local government reorganization (intended to achieve economies of scale) increased and developed their services and their staffing establishments), there has been a noticeable expansion in the number of small specialized information and advice centres. Some of these are government supported; others are the work of people on the receiving end of government activities, who have set up their own information networks, in many cases to fight or to attempt to modify government plans and policies. Will qualified librarians find a role in these organizations, where the work demands the same kinds of skills needed in library work (the management of resources – materials, people and money, to provide information services to defined groups of users and non-users)?

The DES censuses 1972 and 1976. Perhaps the major problem in assessing demand is in predicting growth or stagnation in the economy of the

Table 3.6. Jessop Report estimate of total demand for qualified librarians 1968-1969

Year	Graduates	Nongraduates	Total
1968	403	697	1100
1969	405	702	1107
1970	417	721	1138
1971	445	776	1221
1972	457	794	1251
1973	469	812	1281
1974	480	832	1312
1975	482	842	1324
1976	442	825	1267
1977	460	850	1310
1978	470	867	1337
1979	480	885	1365
1980	496	912	1408
1981	513	971	1484
1982	514	969	1483
1983	490	858	1348
1984	497	867	1364
1985	504	875	1379
1986	511	885	1396
1987	517	896	1413
1988	501	836	1337

Table 3.7. Jessop Report estimate of output figures from schools of librarianship

1967	No. of students likely to successfully complete courses	c.1000
1968	do.	c.1200
1971	do.	c.1400

These estimates were based on information from the schools about numbers of students enrolled.

country at large. A further difficulty arises in attempting to carry out censuses of the number of librarians in employment, since this is often equated with the number of jobs in libraries and information units (the traditional public, academic and special library sectors), but this does not take account of the kind of information centres described above. In 1972 and

73

in 1976 the Department of Education and Science carried out censuses of the numbers of staff, qualified and unqualified, employed in libraries and information units in the United Kingdom. So far, with only two censuses to go on, it is difficult to extrapolate trends in the market or demand side. Note also that the DES censuses identify posts occupied by unqualified staff, which when they fall vacant might provide additional jobs for qualified librarians. The censuses also identify qualified librarians in non-professional posts, who are really in the category of 'actively unemployed', rather than 'employed', since they are presumed to be looking for qualified posts, and to be using non-professional work as a stopgap only.

Tables 3.8 and 3.9 show the findings of the 1972[5] and 1976[6] DES censuses of the number of posts in the main types of library, indicating where decrease or increase in number has taken place.

Table 3.8. Comparison of DES 1972 and 1976 censuses of qualified librarians in post

	1972	1976
Qualified staff in qualified posts (full-time)	10,873	12,756
Non-qualified staff in qualified posts	4,872	3,677
Part-time staff in qualified posts	1,256	872
Total staff occupying qualified posts	* 17,001	17,305
Vacant posts	816	695
Total potential posts	17,817	18,000

* Possible error: may be 289 less, due to calculations for public library posts.

Allowing for the error discovered in the computation of public library results, it can be seen that the overall increase in professional posts for the years 1972 to 1976 lies somewhere between 2.6 per cent and 4.2 per cent. The number of jobs therefore had continued to increase into the second half of the 1970s. However the overall figure conceals varied trends in the main types of library. Public library posts increased by 5.9 per cent, and school library jobs doubled. But academic libraries saw little or no increase in the number of posts, and special libraries suffered a definite decrease in professional posts, somewhere between 2.6 per cent and 5 per cent.

Barnes Report 1977. In 1976 the Library Association set up a Commis-

Table 3.9. Comparison of numbers of full-time and part-time established posts in public academic and special libraries, 1972* and 1976

	1972	1976	% increase or decrease
Public library professional posts: occupied and vacant	8,277	8,762	+5.9
Academic library professional posts: occupied and vacant	4,276 (4,137)	4,224	−0.8 (+2.6)
Special library professional posts: occupied and vacant	5,264 (5,124)	4,994	−5.2 (−2.6)
School library professional posts: occupied and vacant	297(est)	594	+ 100
Total number of professional posts: occupied and vacant	18,114 (17,835)	18,594	+2.6 (+4.2)

* Possible error: figures given in brackets for 1972 academic and special libraries allow for the excess public library posts. ('Unfortunately a small error has been found in the 1972 figures for public libraries. It has therefore been necessary to provide two figures, one including the 289 posts in other categories, the second . . . assuming the total is 289 less.' Barnes, 1977)

(*From* L. A. Commission on the supply and demand for qualified librarians. *Report*. London, Library Association, 1977. (Barnes Report))

sion on the Supply of and Demand for Qualified Librarians. Its terms of reference were:

> To review the current situation, and developments in recent years, of the employment of qualified librarians....
> To examine the effects... of the current economic position of the UK on employment prospects for librarians.
> To examine the future prospects in the light of the planned or expected production of librarians and anticipated trends in demand in the light of economic and other developments.[7]

The Commission included information scientists within the term 'librarian'.

The results of the Commission's deliberations were published in 1977, and caused considerable controversy within the profession, since there appeared to be little general agreement about the validity of some of the arguments used in support of the conclusion that: '... by 1981 there will be an over-supply of qualified librarians amounting to between 4,606 and 3,106.[8]'

This conclusion was based on estimated figures of supply and demand, using the formulae:

$$D = x - y$$

where D = demand; x = total no. of established posts; y = posts frozen or held vacant.

$$S2 = S1 + c - e - f - h$$

where $S2$ = supply in 1981; $S1$ = supply in 1976; c = projected output of library schools; e = loss through death; f = loss through retirement; h = net wastage, based on leaving and re-entry figures.

In estimating future demand, the Commission concluded that in public libraries the growth in the number of professional posts between 1976 and 1981 would be in the range from nil to 1.5 per cent. In academic libraries they estimated the change in the number of posts between 1976 and 1981 to be in the range from minus 0.5 per cent to plus 0.5 per cent. In other words the number of professional posts might actually fall from 4,244 to 4,223, if the more pessimistic forecast proved to be accurate. In the special library sector, and in industrial libraries in particular, it was felt that the very substantial reduction in jobs between 1972 and 1976 (as shown from the DES censuses) meant that the 1977 situation should be fairly stable, and nil growth was predicted. School library posts, which saw 100 per cent increase between the two censuses, were estimated to have left only a very small capacity for growth between 1976 and 1981, due to falling school populations and teacher unemployment. The Commission put the likely growth in the range of nil to thirty new posts, or from nil to 5 per cent.

Taking these estimates together, the overall demand for qualified librarians in 1981 was estimated to be within the range of 18,666 to 18,870. Should these estimates prove accurate, the Commission argued that the supply of librarians coming out of the schools of librarianship between 1976 and 1981 should be in the range of 829 to 929 annually. This would be adequate in their view to meet the market demand. If the present trends in supply continued, however, the output of students would be in the range of 1,500 to 1,750 per annum, and this would constitute serious overproduction in a static market.

The arguments about the validity of the Barnes Report have centred around the factors, social and political, which influence market demand, and which affect output from higher education institutions. These factors not only affect the librarianship and information science profession, but clearly have an impact on graduate employment in general, and on professional education, whatever the subject area. The Barnes Commission took these background factors into account, but their interpretation did not always coincide with their critics' interpretation.

The first and primary factor is levels of public expenditure, by central government and by local government. Over 50 per cent of library budgets is spent on staff salaries, so clearly there will be an effort made in periods of economic recession to curtail growth in numbers of posts. Indeed there are likely to be cut-backs. These may be achieved by allowing a time lag between staff leaving and new staff being appointed, thus saving perhaps half a year's salary; or by 'freezing' posts for an indefinite period, so that although posts remain on the establishment, they may lie vacant for one, two or three years depending on the state of the budget, and the policy of the employing institution. A closer examination of job content by Organization and Methods teams (which happens more often when economies are required by paymasters) may lead to the merging of jobs, or regrading (non-professional rather than professional) or even to the removal of some posts from the establishment.

In all these matters unions will exert pressure on behalf of their members. In Birmingham Public Library in 1980, for example, Nalgo organized industrial action (in the form of withdrawal of labour) in protest against the high number of frozen posts which was proposed for the library system due to the latest round of local government spending cuts. Ultimately the level of public expenditure depends on the political philosophies of the government in power, though made of course in the light of trends in the economy (growth, stagnation or recession), and it is a tricky business forecasting changes in government over the next five or ten-year period, so the amount of money that will become available for library development must remain obscure.

This leads to a second area of argument, concerned with standards of service which should be aimed at, and which might be achieved were sufficient funds available. Critics of the Barnes Report take the view that library services in Great Britain are very uneven, and that there is room for improvement in a number of areas of specialist service, in different parts of the country. For example, in the public library sector some systems have achieved high standards of service to disadvantaged groups, such as people in hospitals, prisons, ethnic minorities, and the housebound, but other systems need developing, or could be developed, along these lines. In academic libraries there is similarly an unevenness of achievement in the evolution of information services, and in user education which is geared to the curriculum and teaching methods. So it is argued that more jobs are required to improve standards. The development of school libraries and resource centres has remained patchy, and in many parts of the country (outside the Inner London Education Authority, which is developed to high standards) there are no professional librarians working in large comprehensives, the work still being done in the small amount of spare time which the English Department may allot. In the industrial library sector, the 'on-line revolution', may lead to more jobs for librarians or information scientists, since this mode of accessing information requires more mediation than the traditional manual search. While the members of the Barnes Commission and their critics both seem to accept the *need* for higher standards of provision, they differ in their degrees of optimism (or pessimism) on the *achievement* of higher standards over the next five year period. And it is not possible to resolve this question, without once again crystal-gazing to divine the future of the economy and of public spending.

Another relevant factor in assessing manpower needs is automation. There appears to be a dearth of hard facts about how automation in libraries has affected staff establishments, but comments by librarians suggest that the main savings might be in non-professional staff, who are relieved of some routine housekeeping activities by computerized issue systems, acquisitions systems and others. Barnes comments that senior non-professional staff:

> ... could, it is increasingly argued, carry out much of the work normally undertaken by junior professional staff, especially now that automated issue and reservation systems are providing opportunities for their redeployment. The graded series of certificates for library assistants, proposed by the LA Working Party on the future of professional qualifications, would be a positive forward step in recognising the important role of the senior non-professional... and if they can carry out work previously regarded as professional and do it more cheaply, there could eventually be a reduction in demand for newly qualified librarians.[9]

There have already been reductions in the number of professional posts in public library systems which have introduced team structures for professional staff, and replaced professional branch librarians by senior non-professionals, on the grounds that the day-to-day running of a branch library is to a large extent routine clerical, rather than professional work. The widespread adoption of subject specialization in academic libraries is another trend in staffing structures which may lead to an increase in non-professional posts at the expense of professional posts, since surveys of graduate professionals employed in academic libraries (Roberts 1973;[10] Smith and Schofield 1973[11]) have shown that much of the job content in technical services was thought by the job-holders not to demand much training or intellectual effort.

A further factor which affects the growth or decline in the number of posts for professional librarians is the rate of expansion (if any) of their parent bodies. The massive expansion in higher education in the 1960s and early 1970s, which followed the *Robbins Report* (1963)[12] led to a rapidly growing market demand. In the late 1970s, however, cuts in teacher training led to the demise or mergers of most of the colleges of education, with the inevitable consequences for libraries of staff reductions through centralization, or staff redeployment. In some cases redeployment meant adding to the pool of librarians by appointing college of education lecturers to library posts. Cutbacks in teacher training came about partly because of the declining birthrate in Britain from the mid-1960s and partly, it must be supposed, from the failure of manpower planning to predict the effects of this decline, and attempt to control the expanding colleges in the 1960s.

This is an interesting example of the difficulties inherent in manpower planning. Even when trends in market demand have been at least roughly identified, it is a delicate and demanding matter to take action to curb supply. Davinson (1974) points out some of the pitfalls. It means 'denial of freedom of educational choice'. Students denied the opportunity to take a vocational degree course in which they are interested will presumably be channelled towards courses of a non-vocational nature which will leave them no better off in job-seeking at the end, since our society now seems to be developing an endemic graduate employment problem, whether the degree is vocational or 'pure'. Davinson adds:

> There is only one logical way to act out manpower planning to its ultimate conclusion. It is to create what the polite would call the planned economy, and the honest, totalitarian oppression. In this situation every qualified person is entitled to a ration of higher education in a discipline selected by the state. At the conclusion ... the grateful graduate goes where he is put, and the commissar in charge of leisure services, washhouses, libraries and dogcatching does with him what he can...[13]

It might be added that manpower planning techniques are not yet sufficiently refined for the calculations to be entirely acceptable. Furthermore it would seem that if manpower planning is to be applied by the state, it must be seen to be applied over a wide spectrum of occupations and professions, so that justice is seen to be impartially administered, if that is ever possible. If numbers of graduates in certain disciplines are to be controlled, then there must be effective control mechanisms in all sectors of higher education equally: in universities, as well as in polytechnics and institutes of higher education.

The question becomes if anything more rebarbative from 1983 onwards, when a marked fall in the numbers of eighteen-year-olds means that higher education institutions have fewer applicants from which to make their selection, and there is increased competition to attract the diminishing number of suitably qualified applicants. It remains to be seen whether employment prospects at the end of a course have a significant effect on student choice of course; to what extent government intervention to 'rationalize' the number of places in line with market demands will reshape the face of higher education; and to what extent the concept of academic freedom of choice in higher education is trimmed as the squeeze on resources tightens during the remaining decades of the twentieth century.

The role of the professional associations in manpower planning is an interesting one. The Law Society and the Royal Institute of British Architects appear, from their various public statements in the press, to take the view that entry to their professional education should not be restricted on the basis of the number of jobs available at the end of the course. They support freedom of choice in higher education (even for professional and vocational courses), and argue that what is called overproduction gives employers an excellent choice of applicants for jobs, thus raising standards in the profession. They further argue the inestimable value of professional courses in developing students personally in the practical skills which make them just as competitive (if not more so) as the traditional university graduate in the wider job market. The Library Association Commission, on the other hand, states:

> There might be an increasing number of entrants who regard a degree in librarianship or information science as non-vocational, and treat it as an alternative to a general degree with a possible view to obtaining a post outside the particular profession. While recognising this possibility the Commission feels that comparatively few people will embark on librarianship studies without a desire to obtain a post in librarianship. Indeed we note that it is common practice for schools of librarianship to place considerable emphasis upon a motivation towards librarianship when they are selecting students, and we know of no attempts to inform potential students that the courses offered are non-vocational.[14]

The nuances in this passage are an interesting contrast to the stance taken up by other professional bodies like the Law Society and RIBA. There is little recognition that a degree in librarianship or information science is an education, not just a training. Most young people 'desire to obtain a post in...' a particular occupation these days, but they know enough about the general employment situation to be realistic in accepting the possibility that they may have to find jobs outside their chosen sphere. Every survey of the unemployment situation which has been carried out emphasizes the point that qualifications do give people a head start in the difficult search for jobs. It is always better to be qualified than unqualified when looking for work.

Schools of librarianship do indeed emphasize motivation when recruiting their students, but they are increasingly also careful to point out the effects of recession on the job market and how this is particularly bad in those professions like librarianship, which rely traditionally on public service employers to place their graduates.

Qualitative aspects of manpower planning

In the mid-1970s the Sheffield Manpower Project was carried out in Britain, and its findings are a major source of information on the qualitative aspects of manpower planning in the library and information world.

The principal investigator Sergean comments:

> The matching of people to jobs depends upon continuous selection, assessment, training and allocation, and the matching of jobs to people upon a continuous process of work, job and systems design. However these activities can only be carried out on the basis of a prior knowledge of the nature of jobs and the personnel available.[15]

In order to establish the nature of jobs in library and information work, the research team took a 5 per cent sample of library and information units in Britain, and administered job description questionnaires to individual members of staff in these units. The questionnaires explored work demands (what intellectual, social and physical skills does a particular job require?) and the work environment. The degree to which existing staff were meeting the demands of their work was also considered, but the investigation was based solely on information provided by job-holders, and not upon, additionally, information provided by supervisors. The main findings[16] were published in 1976, and consequently two forums[17,18] were held to discuss the implications with educationalists and with practising librarians.

The problems of personnel management raised by the Sheffield project are of lasting relevance, although the information on age structure, job mobility and staff structures refers to the mid-1970s situation. The following paragraphs take up some of the main issues raised by the investigation, and consider them by type of library.

Academic libraries In the growth enjoyed by academic libraries in the 1960s and early 1970s staff development normally came about through promotion and job mobility. Since this pattern appears to have faded out, due to increasing periods of time likely to be spent by academic librarians in the same post, more reliance needs to be placed on staff development within the individual library. There may be some frustration among academic librarians because of diminished promotion prospects, even within their own libraries. The motivation of a fairly static work force requires new approaches to staff deployment and staff training. The Sheffield Project highlights in particular the problems of staff attitudes, cultivating a willingness to innovate, and communication with the unions. It is suggested that consultation, in the sense of communication *up* the staff hierarchy would be an important element in job satisfaction. The Report found that 53 per cent of academic librarians were dissatisfied with prevailing forms and levels of consultation. This compares with 64 per cent of public librarians and 51 per cent of special librarians. Communication between academic librarians and teaching staff was also thought to be insufficient, and capable of being improved, for mutual benefit.

The Project investigators found that the work done in academic libraries indicated a bias towards technical services, rather than user services. The survey findings showed that many of the tasks and activities carried out were not seen as intellectually demanding or professionally rewarding by the job-holders. It suggested that perhaps academic libraries had failed to set up staff structures that would make the most effective use of professional librarians' expertise. Certain lines of development are proposed to improve the situation. These include a different ratio of professional to non-professional staff (in the direction of fewer professionals and more senior non-professionals), a stronger emphasis on user services and less emphasis on conservation, and increased activity by academic librarians in the academic community, rather than on technical duties of a routine kind in the library itself.

The academic librarians who took part in the follow-up discussion on the findings of the Manpower Project considered that academic libraries could scarcely operate if there were rigid distinctions drawn between professional and non-professional duties. They saw some difficulty in meeting librarians' expectations of change and improvement, should these expectations be aroused by getting staff to write their own job descriptions. However they were 'generally agreed on the need to find ways of describing jobs and analysing the match of the job with the job-holder'. They further agreed that the emphasis on in-service training should be greater, and that an increased service or user orientation 'might have to be associated with forms of education calculated to alter prevailing attitudes', so this too would be a focus for staff training and development programmes.

Since then support has been given to the idea of restructuring academic library staff to take account of some of the questions raised by the Sheffield Project. Winkworth (1980) proposes that para-professional staff will take over jobs hitherto carried out by professionals in the traditional academic library. He cites as examples cataloguing, classification, straightforward enquiry work, and staff supervision. Professional work will therefore be upgraded to include a higher content of responsibility and initiative, but this will mean fewer jobs for professionals, unless services are expanded, and that depends on the state of the economy. Winkworth provides figures to show how in a large polytechnic library this proposed new structure might affect the allocation of work, levels of qualification, and ratio of professional to para-professional and non-professional staff (see Tables 3.10 and 3.11). Note that this takes into account the new structure of qualifications approved by the Library Association, and effective from 1981. The main differences between the old and the new qualificational structures are that the length of experience needed to be admitted to the Associateship of the Library Association (ALA) has been extended, and a new level of qualification has been introduced, the Licentiate (LLA). This requires more formal training for the new graduate or postgraduate librarian out of library school. The Library Association has also given support to the national development of courses for para-professionals, under the auspices of the Business Education Council (BEC), which may be recognized by employers as worthy of

Table 3.10. Qualifications, grades and duties[19]

Local Government Grade	Minimum Qualifications	Duties
SO+	Degree + ALA + more experience	Section Head
AP5)	Degree + ALA (which requires 2 + years' experience)	Information work, Sub-section Head
AP4) possibly linked	Degree + LLA (which requires 1 + years' experience)	Some subject work, difficult cataloguing and classification
AP3)	Degree + librarianship course (require 3-5 years' study)	1-year trainee
C3	BEC Higher + 8 years' experience	Supervising many staff
C2	BEC National + 5 years' experience	Inquiry work, supervising 1-4 staff
C1	4 "O" levels + 2 years' experience	Work requiring judgment, initiative
C1 to bar	4 "O" levels	Little initiative needed

Table 3.11. Staff structure of a polytechnic library

Number of Staff at Present	Local Government Grade and Maximum Salary (as at 1.1.80)		Possible Future Staff Structure	Change in Salary Bill
				£
13	SO and above		13	0
8	AP5	£5547	7	−5 547
1	AP4	£5067	3	+10 134
8	AP3	£4533	1	−31 731
30	TOTAL LIBRARIANS		24	
0	C3	£4302	3	+12 906
0	C2	£3894	5	+19 470
8	C1	£3585	10	+ 7 170
27½	C1 below bar £3165		23½	−12 660
35½	TOTAL ASSISTANTS		41½	
65½	TOTAL STAFF		65½	−£258 net

Note: Secretarial, administrative, design and other staff are excluded from the above totals.

financial upgrading, so that there might be some career progression for this category of library staff.

Public libraries. The Sheffield Manpower Project drew attention to a number of problems arising from the structure of public library staffs, and the patterns of work allocation. Questions were raised about the undue amount of routine work on which professionals spent a proportion of their time. The unsocial hours worked by public librarians had to be accepted as the inevitable result of a user-oriented service. Increased use of automated systems might lead to job impoverishment or even the disappearance of jobs.

The Report showed that 66 per cent of the graduates working in public libraries felt that they were over qualified for the work they were doing. This again raises the question of employing para-professionals (with training in technical skills), for more of the routine tasks. Further educational implications were raised as to the nature of the skills required by professionals. It seems that they needed more social skills than they had acquired during their educational courses.

Compared with academic and special librarians, public librarians 'have the lowest level of educational attainment', it appeared from the survey, and 'place a lower value on educational levels than their colleagues'. This has doubtless changed considerably over the intervening period, since public libraries have increasingly been recruiting graduates and postgraduates, and there has been a strong emphasis on staff training and development in many of the systems, so that existing staff have been engaging in more continuing education than at the time of the Sheffield Survey. The librarians who attended the follow-up seminar thought that public libraries needed staff just as well qualified as those who worked in academic or special libraries. It was considered that an improved system was needed for educating and training senior non-professionals, and that this should be complemented by improved job prospects for non-professionals, to increase their motivation. This echoes the views of academic librarians, and it now remains to be seen how the BEC courses will attract library workers, and whether employers will recognize them for financial upgrading.

Since the mid-1970s there have been widespread changes in staffing structures in public libraries, the major trend being the introduction of professional teams with geographical and specialist responsibilities. This has meant an increase in the professional content of jobs, where the structure is effective, and also more responsibility for senior non-professional staff, who run service points on a day-to-day basis, referring matters to the professional team as necessary.

The LAMSAC study of public library staffing. One of the problems of the Jessop Report was that not enough was known about what librarians actually did, and how they were deployed in libraries, and how their qualifications were used. So in the early 1970s the Department of Education and Science commissioned (on the recommendation of the Library Advisory Councils) an extensive study of public library staffing. This was undertaken by the Local Authorities Management Services and Computer Committee (LAMSAC), which presented its three-volume findings[20] in 1974.

The object of the LAMSAC study was to determine staffing standards for both professional and non-professional staff in public libraries. This was seen as an important step in assessing manpower requirements for each local authority, thus contributing to a general picture of national needs. The assumption made by the DES was that 'with the present constraints on public expenditure the recommendations should not be used to justify any increase in expenditure and that no additional financial or manpower resources can be made available for the implementation of the Report's recommendations'.[21] So library managers were being asked to make more effective use of their staff, by revising their staffing structures and/or job descriptions in the light of the LAMSAC formulae, which covered tasks and methods at local, area and headquarters levels, for general and specialist services, ranging from headquarters administration to mobile library staffing and outreach. In addition formulae were provided for the work of non-professionals at local/area level. The formulae were arrived at by investigating the staffing situation in 'an urban type county, a rural type county, a London borough, and the equivalent of a metropolitan district'. The measurement approach was 'that of interviewing library staff to obtain descriptions of duties in as much detail as possible, together with estimated time factors... in terms of decimal hours per week, e.g. if an activity occurred once every four weeks and the time estimated for its performance was two hours, then the time factor would be expressed as 0.5 hours per week'. In addition to interviewing 220 staff in depth, the researchers spent a great deal of time building up background information on how the present state of staffing had been reached, the range and scope of services provided, and the strengths and weaknesses of the system, in each of the five authorities who took part in the project.

Two examples will show the type of formulae which resulted from the study. Figure 3.1 considers one of the formulae for determining non-professional staffing (LAMSAC 1976, Section 6(i)[22]).

FIGURE 3.1. FORMULA FOR THE STAFFING OF FULL-TIME STATIC LIBRARIANS

A. Issuing, renewing, discharging and fines collection
  Photocharging: 4.96 weekly hours per 1000 weekly issues
  Browne: 9.16 weekly hours per 1000 weekly issues
  Browne/Token: 5.88 weekly hours per 1000 weekly issues
B. Shelf tidying
  0.50 weekly hours per 1000 'live' stock (i.e. lending stock other than that housed in closed access)
C. Stock ordering, processing, editing, repair, withdrawals and stocktaking
  0.52 weekly hours per 1000 total stock

These are just some of the range of non-professional staff duties, given to illustrate the kind of detail presented in the LAMSAC formulae. They draw attention to some of the problems in applying the formulae. Already these methods of issuing have been largely superseded by computerized issue systems, such as the Plessey light pen. The figures may therefore be taken as no longer relevant for most public libraries. On the other hand the actual measurement methods can still be used, and the list of tasks produced by the

LAMSAC analysis can be of help in drawing up job descriptions or modifying existing job descriptions in staff restructuring.

Figure 3.2 gives an example of a formula for professional work.

FIGURE 3.2. FORMULA FOR THE STAFFING OF REFERENCE AND INFORMATION WORK[23]

$$\frac{E}{3,000} \times F =$$ Number of full-time staff required, where the library has a separate reference section

E = Annual total of recorded enquiries

F = A factor based on average time taken to answer enquiries, since this varies between different subjects, and depends also on whether the query is a simple information one, or requires personal assistance from the librarian

3,000 represents the average number of enquiries per staff member per year

The Report is careful to point out in relation to this reference work formula, that further consideration must be given to local conditions. If, for example, a local government information service is offered, or the library has any special deposit collections (patents for example), or it carries out a strong publishing programme in, say, local history studies, then additional staff will be required. On the basis of its investigations, the Report recommends that of the total reference staff, 45 per cent to 55 per cent should be professionally qualified.

An important aspect of the LAMSAC recommendations was their support for training and professional development, though at the time of their fieldwork investigations, they found a wide disparity among experienced librarians as to how long was needed for this. Twenty-one librarians failed to arrive at any consensus as to how much time was needed to train a new member of the non-professional staff. Periods suggested varied from a few hours to several months. The Report drew up a checklist of training activities for non-professionals (Section 5), and assigned times to these, ending up with the formula of 51 hours needed by the staff giving instruction, and 64 hours needed by the person receiving instruction. Professional staff training was also considered, and many of the recommendations for professional and non-professional staff have since been taken up and expanded in the Library Association's 1977 working party report on training.[24] The growing concern for in-service training meant that most public library systems appointed training or personnel officers in the late 1970s to co-ordinate and plan their staff development programmes. Many systems have compiled training packages (some multi-media) and training checklists for non-professionals especially, no doubt partly influenced by the

LAMSAC findings and the LA's Report. Coventry public Libraries and Leicestershire County Libraries are examples of systems which have been active in building up training materials.

The intention of the LAMSAC Report was to provide information of a detailed kind on most of the tasks carried out in libraries. The help it can provide for staff managers is, at the most basic, a means of calculating staffing costs for existing and new services. It does this by providing a simple means of calculating the number of hours of non-professional and professional staff-time needed to carry out, for example, a children's service, or a service to the housebound, at an acceptable standard based on existing libraries' experience. The formulae could also be used for reallocating duties among existing staff, so that, for instance, non-professional work might be winnowed out from professional work to a greater extent. This would leave professionals with more time for expanding professional services, or introducing new services, at least in theory, though attitudes and resourcing problems may still inhibit such developments. In times of financial pressure, the LAMSAC formulae might provide a framework for assessing whether certain services are taking up too much of the staff effort, in proportion to other services. The Report suggests that 'few organizations have as yet the capacity for measurement to be able to know that they are staffing at the optimum, and the possibilities of over-provision or lack of balance between sections and services should be explored'.[25]

In some libraries, levels of staff prove to be higher than the standards recommended in the LAMSAC study. The answer may be that certain services are highly developed in some systems, because of their philosophy of public librarianship (for example outreach services in inner city areas, such as the London boroughs of Brent and Lambeth), which is based on responses to particularly extreme information deprivation. The development of community profiling alongside area-based teams has led to different emphases and priorities in systems, based on local needs, rather than national standards.

The application of the LAMSAC formulae is limited therefore by contextual factors such as local needs and specific philosophies of librarianship. The formulae also need to be updated as new methods (particularly computerized systems) are introduced. The danger inherent in uniform national standards is that they may be used without due regard to local variations, in terms of user groups, priorities in information needs as seen by the staff, and individual excellence in specific parts of the service. In the last case, for example, an above average service to business and industry, or to the institutionalized, might be cut, if national costing standards were to be applied and used in the allocation of funds. This seems to be an approach which government may favour as a means of achieving economies in public spending, since already purely quantitative measures based on cost per thousand population, and cost per issue have been discussed as a basis for decisions on how much should be spent by individual local authorities on their library services.[26]

Special libraries: job characteristics. In the area of special libraries the findings of the Sheffield Manpower Project highlighted a number of problems concerned with staffing. In general the smallness of the units creates difficulties in staff development and training. Junior staff in particular have difficulty in getting release to further their education. However, it appears from the investigation that many staff in special libraries have a low regard for, and feel little need for professional qualifications. Qualifications gained outside librarianship are more highly esteemed. Information scientists, however, did see themselves as appropriately qualified for their work, and attached less importance to working experience, or learning from the job.

The need for management expertise was stressed, and in particular it was thought important that special librarians should be able to produce and make use of aims and objectives for the information unit, that they should be capable of monitoring the work flow, and measuring output.

Another area of concern was the changing nature of the work, often in the form of additional duties and responsibilities taken on at the initiative of the librarian. It seems there is greater freedom and scope for development of individual talents in many special libraries, but grasping these opportunities requires a certain degree of nerve and self-confidence in addition to professional expertise. Since the mid-1970s on-line information services have perhaps constituted the greatest change in special library work, and have necessitated the development of whole new areas of expertise by the staff. Concern over diminishing resources was beginning to be expressed at the time of the Sheffield Manpower Project, and the follow-up seminar on special libraries commented:

> Linked with job characteristics and staffing needs of special libraries is the necessity for increased productivity, for practical methods of monitoring work flow and for means of establishing reliable output comparisons between libraries. Advice from the British Library Research and Development Department, based on specific research projects in these areas, could well assist special libraries in the full utilization of staff potential and in the maintenance of services despite reduced resources.[27]

Common problems in staffing academic, public and special libraries

Certain problem areas recur in all the reports on staff deployment and job characteristics, to which reference has been made in this chapter.

1. There is a great deal of stress caused for staff by changes in organizational structures, leading to larger more bureaucratized library systems. Stress is

likewise caused by changes in the nature of librarianship skills, and in particular the introduction of computerized systems in libraries has left some librarians alienated and ill-prepared. But other rapid changes during the 1970s in philosophies of librarianship have been upsetting for many librarians; trends towards user-orientation, towards outreach, away from the materials-based bibliophile approach, have been seen by many traditional librarians as travesties of the 'true' librarianship, where information is neutral and cool.

2. Methods of staff deployment have emphasized the work group, rather than the individual worker, and staff have found themselves designated team members, and expected to be articulate with colleagues on professional matters, after years perhaps of a quiet life 'in the sticks', where it was rather *infra dig.* to use professional terminology. The opposite dilemma also occurs, as the surveys of staff deployment in academic libraries reveal. The enthusiasm of the professionally qualified graduate can be quickly dampened, if they are given little responsibility, few opportunities to use their professional skills, and are kept out of contact with users.

3. The librarian receiving his or her professional education in the 1980s needs to develop newer skills, in particular communication skills, as well as technological skills. Library educators need also to make better provision for para-professionals.

So far in this chapter the emphasis has been on manpower requirements for librarianship on a national level. The Sheffield Manpower Project investigated personnel in the profession as a whole, by examining job characteristics and job satisfaction in public, academic and special libraries. The LAMSAC Report confined itself to public libraries, but within that sector it made general recommendations on staffing standards, relating to numbers of staff needed, and levels of staff needed. The Barnes Report 1977, and the Jessop Report 1968 attempted to forecast the numbers of librarians that would be needed in the years ahead, on the basis of supply and demand statistics. These studies form the background against which the individual library must carry out its own manpower planning.

Manpower planning for the individual library

The questions raised are parallel to those covered earlier in this chapter. The concern is to enable the library manager to assess accurately how many staff are needed now and over the next five years, and what range of skills they should have, if the library is to be effective in achieving its objectives. The methods the manager uses are once again the four basic steps in manpower planning, at whatever level it is attempted. These are analysis of the existing situation, calculation of likely wastage, working out likely demand for the period under review, and bringing together these supply and demand calculations, in order to produce the actual manpower plan. The assumption is that staff are an expensive resource, and should be utilized as effectively as possible, not only in pursuit of the service objectives of the library, but in order to make wise use of their qualifications and skills and bring about some degree of job satisfaction for them. These four steps are now discussed in greater detail.

1. *Analysis of existing staff.* All libraries have personnel records, though the nature and extent of their contents differs very much from one organization to another. Sometimes application forms, references and other material dating from the selection interview constitute the entire record on file. Increasingly, however, schemes of staff appraisal or 'performance review' are being introduced (see Chapter 6 for details). These are generally carried out on a regular basis, once a year normally, in order to assist the manager in matching up qualifications and skills with posts where they will be most relevant. The dual aim is to make services more cost-effective and increase job satisfaction. Staff appraisal programmes, when linked with job analysis and description (see Chapter 4) enable the manager to make a more regular and systematic link-up between staff skills and developing services and techniques. For example, awareness of subject expertise, professional specialisms such as children's work or media librarianship, language ability, or management skills, is a useful basis when redeploying public library staff into area teams. It should be noted that staff appraisal is used also to spot 'high fliers', perhaps those with management potential or computer expertise, so that they can be given the necessary encouragement and training to fill newly-developing posts or to take over when vacancies are created by resignation or retirement.

2. *Staff wastage.* The Barnes Report draws attention to the social trends in Britain, which affect the wastage rate in libraries as in other occupations, and these should be borne in mind when compiling a manpower plan for a particular library, though there will be local factors which may cause national trends to be modified. In some areas wastage through marriage and/or child-rearing may be lower than in others. Difficulty in finding employment in libraries may cause women to take advantage of the present more generous maternity leave, to keep their jobs open, rather than resign outright. Wastage through death accounts for 17 librarians per annum (1970s figures), and since librarianship is a 'young profession, with 40 per cent of librarians in the under-thirties band at the time of the Barnes Report, this kind of wastage will remain negligible. Early retirement and voluntary redundancy, however, are two significant factors in the 1980s. These are the approaches to public expenditure cuts that local authorities and educational institutions are most likely to favour. It remains to be seen to what extent librarians take up these offers, and if they do, whether the posts vacated will be frozen, and for how long.

In September 1979 the Library Association issued a statement deploring the effects on libraries of government plans to cut local government expenditure in 1980/81. They noted that public libraries had been spending just over 52 per cent of their budgets on staffing between 1975/76 and 1977/78. The number of non-manual staff had already fallen between these years from 24,133 to 23,627, a 2 per cent drop (Library Association, 1979).[28] In addition there had been a fall in the number of professional posts, from 7,902 to 7,780, a decrease of 1.5 per cent. This decrease can be accounted for in two ways: frozen posts, and staff restructuring. The introduction of area teams of professional librarians, backed up by senior non-professionals to do the day-to-day running of service points, was a noteworthy trend during the late 1970s. This approach to public library staffing can, especially in periods of financial stringency, lead to fewer professionals proportionately to non-professionals, since one of the objects is to reduce the amount of routine clerical work for higher-paid professional staff, and transfer it to non-professionals.

As the cuts gained momentum in the early 1980s, it became clear that many local authorities were planning to cut library services more savagely than others, on the grounds that libraries must take lower priority than education, housing and the social services. The most extreme case in 1980 was Kingston-upon-Thames, where a reduction of 17 per cent in the library's budget was planned.[29] In many other authorities librarians were asked to prepare reports on the effects of reductions of between $7\frac{1}{2}$ per cent and 10 per cent. All this came at the end of a decade during which public libraries' share of local government money had already declined, ending up at rather less than 1.5 per cent of local government expenditure. Librarians were warned by the Library Association in September 1979 that:

> The current proposals are clearly going to affect staff numbers substantially. Several authorities are already planning to make library staff redundant. A reorganization in another authority has made a cut of 20 professional posts. Almost every authority which has contacted the Association mentions an embargo on appointments and 'frozen' posts. It is difficult to overemphasize the harmful effects of reduced staffing levels on the services which are provided for the public, and the complete withdrawal of services to small communities cannot be ruled out.[30]

School libraries also were weakened by a two-pronged attack. Schools reduced their library budgets, hours were reduced, and staff posts frozen (Wiltshire and Cumbria, for example). Public libraries' services to schools were affected by cuts in book-funds and staff. An extreme case was in Solihull where in 1974 there were ten established school library posts. By 1980 there was none.

Academic libraries were not immune either. Cuts of the nature of one million pounds planned by Leeds City Council for the 1980/81 Polytechnic budget could not be implemented without swingeing library cuts, in book-funds and frozen posts. Although the Labour leader promised that, if the Tories were voted out at the imminent local government elections, Labour would 'take steps to rectify any unjust cut in their budget so that he could help this fine institution', he also noted that staff savings could be made, in consultation with the unions. 'There is room for a staff review but I want to say that if we gain control in Leeds in May we will have a policy of no redundancies', added the Labour leader. (*Yorkshire Evening Post*, 13 March 1980). This did not rule out, however, early retirement and voluntary redundancy schemes being offered to the Polytechnic teaching and library staff.

The academic library sector was affected in different degrees, depending on local politics and local interpretation of central government guidelines on such matters as withdrawal of approval for undersubscribed courses, reductions in research grants, and capital expenditure. There were certain inevitable consequences of frozen posts and the low wastage rates in all types of library. Bowey (1974)[31] identifies the normal 'push' and 'pull' factors which lead to wastage. A synopsis of them is shown in Figure 3.3.:

FIGURE 3.3

Push factors	Pull factors
'Induction crisis', or people leaving due to adjustment problems in a new situation	Moving for higher earnings
	Moving for promotion, to further one's career
Leaving because of inter-personal conflicts	Attraction of alternative job opportunities
Redundancy policies of employers	Attraction of alternative roles, e.g. motherhood, early retirement
Pressures from changed working requirements	

In the early 1980s, it was becoming clear that the relative importance of these push/pull factors was changing. The age structure of the profession was such that there were a great many younger people seeking promotion, or a change of job opportunities at least, but not enough people were of the age to retire, and so opportunities for career prospects were decreasing. In the 'push' column, employers' policies on early retirement and voluntary redundancy were gaining importance, whereas people might no longer be so much influenced by the 'induction crisis' or by interpersonal conflicts at work, since they would be aware of the problems of finding other posts in a declining market. One implication here is the need for more subtle forms of staff development and in-service training, to offset the interpersonal conflicts of a rather more stagnating staff situation. Also, where internal promotion is becoming the rule, rather than recruiting 'fresh' staff from outside the system, greater attention needs to be paid to stimulating staff ideas, by encouraging more participative management, *ad hoc* working parties, and discussion papers on future development of services.

There are a number of simple formulae for measuring wastage rates in an individual library, in order to establish trends, and assist manpower planning for the years ahead. The simplest sum of all is:

$$\frac{\text{Number of staff leaving in year}}{\text{Average number of employees}} \times 100 = \text{percentage wastage}$$

This may conceal, however a high turnover in one area of the library, or at one level of library staff, say, junior non-professionals on the counter. So it is useful to get a more accurate picture by working out:

$$\frac{\text{Number of staff with over one year's service}}{\text{Number of staff employed one year ago}} \times 100$$

This gives a 'labour stability index', which can be used to keep check on staffing trends in a particular library.

3. *Forecasting the demand for staff in an individual library.* A consideration of the factors looked at in the previous section on staff wastage will show how difficult it is to produce an accurate forecast. So much depends on social, economic and political features. There is, moreover, no very clear relationship between number of staff, and effectiveness of service (as far as this can be measured). For example, during the late 1970s, use of public libraries increased (as measured by issue statistics), but numbers of staff decreased. Either staff were getting through more work, or more effective ways of deploying them had been evolved by management, or less obviously measurable services than issues were suffering lower standards, to compensate for improved lending services. It may be deduced from this example that forecasting demand for staff is very much dependent on the library's aims and objectives. To which services does management give priority? On this will depend the allocation of staff resources to various sections.

Secondly, the staff structure in operation will affect the demand for staff of different levels. A restructuring which makes use of non-professional or para-professional staff to carry out routine work, may lead to fewer professional staff, or it may free professional staff for genuinely professional work, which they may have been prevented from doing because of their heavy burden of routine tasks. A clear distinction is not always possible or desirable, especially in smaller library units, between professional and non-professional. But it is useful to bear in mind the following dictum of Herbert Schur:

It is the professional's ability and willingness to question current practices which distinguishes him from the non-professional (who is not able to question), and from the minor bureaucrat (who is not willing, even if able, to question).[32]

The basic method for calculating the number and nature of staff needed over the period under review is as follows:

(a) Consider the numbers and the skills and attributes of the staff, who currently keep the services going at existing levels of effectiveness.

(b) Note any apparent undermanning or overmanning (often as a result of restructuring of staff, or of automation schemes).

(c) Note any apparent mismatching of people to jobs. (This may result from poor recruitment procedures, or from job changes since the person was recruited).

(d) Consider to what extent the present levels of effectiveness meet the aims and objectives of the library. Pin-point specific areas of service which do not seem satisfactory in terms of objectives (for example, the requests service, short loan service, promotion and publicity). Is the source of the problem a staffing one, in whole or in part?

(e) Consider the development of new services, which have been planned, or are being contemplated (for example, housebound services, user education programmes, on-line information services). Calculate the numbers and necessary or desirable qualities and qualifications of staff needed to develop these services.

4. *Bringing together the calculations to produce the manpower plan.* In times of enforced economies, this set of guidelines can also be of assistance in working out how and where cuts can be made with least damage to the achievement of high priority objectives. As above, the first step must be a detailed analysis of existing staff and existing levels of service. This can be followed by decisions about priorities (in detail), and two sets of plans drawn up: a short-term economy scheme, and a long-term development plan.

For public libraries, the LAMSAC standards provide detailed guidance on the staffing levels which the project showed were necessary to maintain the range of services normally operated by public libraries. Time allowances are built in for staff training, and for holiday allowances. The project is not complete, since there were areas which defeated their attempts to establish standards. Bibliographical services, for example, were investigated in six authorities, as part of the fieldwork for the project, but no formulae could be hammered out, since 'differences in policies and practices produced differences in staffing, and the variations were too great and the sample too small to enable the production of standards that could be offered with any degree of confidence'.[33] Some of the differences in practice were in the requests procedures. These were handled in some libraries by professional staff, and in others by non-professionals. Some bibliographical departments were very active in producing booklists and other guides, and so needed more staff. There were significant differences in ordering procedures and policies, which meant that the number of staff needed varied considerably between different library systems. An increasingly significant influence here is the extent to which ordering is computerized. The amount of stock editing, revision and balancing of stock among all the service points, also varied greatly. 'In one authority there were four stock editors undertaking stock revision, allocation of new stock, etc., together with a Catalogue Editor to co-ordinate and balance the collections between service points. In another authority where the figures for total stock and additions were greater the number of staff used was considerably less.'[34]

It is clearly a difficult business, then, to establish staffing standards with any certainty, since so much depends on what a specific library is aiming to achieve. There is nothing similar to the LAMSAC standards for other types of library, so librarians there need to evolve their own standards, starting with the aims and objectives of their parent body, which they can use to establish the library's objectives. Does the college, polytechnic or university give priority to the development of certain areas of the curriculum? What changes have occurred in the courses offered, as a result perhaps of diversification in colleges of education, for example? Is there an emphasis on part-time and sandwich courses? Have teaching methods evolved towards resource-based learning? These are some of the background considerations which will help library management to decide where priorities should lie.

Examples of decisions which need to be taken are:

1. Should emphasis be on a high-turnover, three-hour loan collection, to make intensive use of limited resources, especially in new or expanding subject areas?
2. Are part-time students better served by longer opening hours or by judicious duplication of texts to put in a special part-timers' loan collection?
3. Who are the potential users of on-line information services? What policies and procedures need to be outlined before on-line services can be introduced?

Everyday decisions of this kind determine the numbers and levels of staff needed in a library (and vice versa of course, too often). Training needs are often revealed by the introduction of new or extended services, or indeed by changing methods in traditional services such as information work and user education.

If, as seems likely during the next decade, manpower plans are needed not so much to shape and plan for developing services, but rather to cope with the maintenance of existing services run by a diminishing staff, then close attention must be paid to staffing structures and staff development.

Lack of job mobility and poorer promotion prospects for young professionals mean that staff must more than previously be provided with planned opportunities for professional growth, through variety and stimulus and recognition of their achievements. Rather than cutting training budgets it becomes ever more vital to maintain or expand them. But the heart of the matter is whether or not the library can cultivate as an organization the climate for growth, a more subtle and difficult objective than carrying out a structured analysis of how staff see their training needs, or how much money and time may be taken each year to go to conferences and workshops. These matters must underpin any manpower plan which an individual library draws up, and the plan must be continually questioned and monitored, if it is to have any significance.

At its simplest the manpower plan provides the basic outline of staff deployment over the next few years, and may also indicate what training developments are needed to support this outline of staff deployment. Manpower planning is a complex series of activities, rather than the production every few years of a single document called the manpower plan. Not only senior management but other levels of staff are involved. Job analysis, job description, personnel specification invariably require the co-operation and participation of the staff whose posts are under consideration in any phase of staff management, whether it be recruitment or appraisal or training.

These activities are carried out in the light of the library's objectives, and are intended to ensure that the library's most expensive resource, its staff, is deployed in the best possible way, by which is meant not only best in terms of effective services, but also best in terms of job satisfaction for the staff. There can, naturally, be a certain amount of conflict here, and a delicate pathway must be trodden between the work-place as a ruthless machine chewing up and spitting out its hapless victim workers, and the personal idyll immortalized by Jerome K. Jerome: 'I like work. It fascinates me. I can sit and look at it for hours. I love to keep it by me. The idea of getting rid of it nearly breaks my heart.'

In conclusion, Figure 3.4 summarizes much of what has been discussed on the various phases of manpower planning, and shows some of the connections with subsequent chapters. Moore in 1980 neatly summarized what it is all about:

> Manpower planning is concerned with making sure that the right number of workers are in the right place at the right time; it is also concerned with ensuring that the workers have the appropriate skills and expertise.[35]

FIGURE 3.4. STAGES IN DRAWING UP A MANPOWER PLAN FOR AN INDIVIDUAL LIBRARY SYSTEM

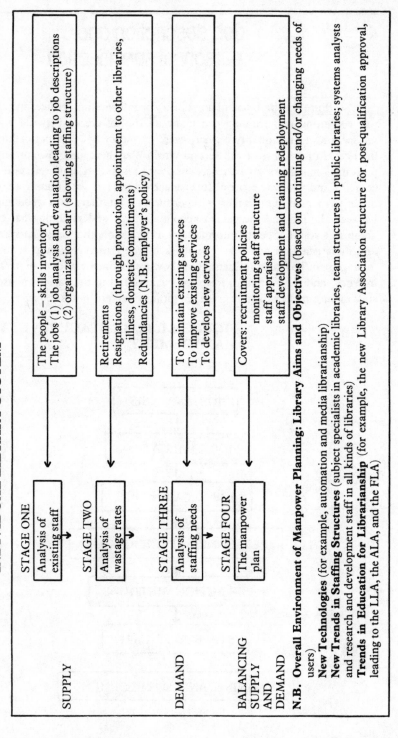

SUPPLY

STAGE ONE
Analysis of existing staff → The people – skills inventory
The jobs (1) job analysis and evaluation leading to job descriptions
(2) organization chart (showing staffing structure)

STAGE TWO
Analysis of wastage rates →
Retirements
Resignations (through promotion, appointment to other libraries, illness, domestic commitments)
Redundancies (N.B. employer's policy)

DEMAND

STAGE THREE
Analysis of staffing needs →
To maintain existing services
To improve existing services
To develop new services

STAGE FOUR
The manpower plan →
Covers: recruitment policies
monitoring staff structure
staff appraisal
staff development and training redeployment

BALANCING
SUPPLY
AND
DEMAND

N.B. Overall Environment of Manpower Planning: Library Aims and Objectives (based on continuing and/or changing needs of users)
New Technologies (for example, automation and media librarianship)
New Trends in Staffing Structures (subject specialists in academic libraries, team structures in public libraries; systems analysts and research and development staff in all kinds of libraries)
Trends in Education for Librarianship (for example, the new Library Association structure for post-qualification approval, leading to the LLA, the ALA, and the FLA)

97

4   Job description and personnel specification

Staff are the life-blood of any library or information service, and effective recruiting and training can make all the difference between a poor service and a high quality service, even, or especially, in times of limited finances. In Britain since the Second World War there has grown up among personnel managers an increased understanding that staff selection is a complex and two-way process. It is concerned not just with finding a highly qualified person, but rather with ensuring that there is a good match between the job and the person appointed. This understanding has come about as a result of better information on the factors that cause satisfaction and dissatisfaction at work. The work of the human relations school of management has been influential in showing the importance of motivation at work, and their findings form the background to the various phases in staff management which form the remaining chapters in this book.

FIGURE 4.1. MAIN STAGES IN STAFF MANAGEMENT

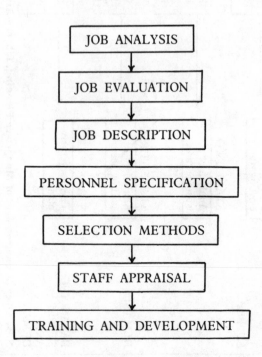

JOB ANALYSIS

JOB EVALUATION

JOB DESCRIPTION

PERSONNEL SPECIFICATION

SELECTION METHODS

STAFF APPRAISAL

TRAINING AND DEVELOPMENT

The work of the National Institute of Industrial Psychology has been significant in developing systematic techniques for recruiting staff. Although the original applications were in industry, these techniques are now widely used in the professions as well, and this includes library and information work. A notable example is the use of Professor Alec Rodger's Seven-Point Plan for drawing up a list of attributes desirable or essential in the person appointed to a particular post (see page 146 for an example of how this has been used in the library context). The diagram above shows the systematic approach to staff management which has evolved gradually in this country due to pressures which revealed the inadequacy of previous informal approaches.

These pressures may be summarized as: higher expectations of candidates whose educational levels have risen in the post-Robbins boom; rapid technological changes (automation has changed the content and context of many jobs); changes in aims and objectives of employing organizations (e.g. outreach in public libraries, and learning resource orientation in some academic libraries); and manpower planning, or at least attempts at manpower planning, which have led to much argument about the match or mismatch, in quantity and quality, between the products of library education and the jobs they get.

Job analysis and job description

As Plumbley[1] (1974) points out, the first step in recruitment is to 'measure the "hole" so that in turn we can measure possible "pegs", and if we can use identical measuring devices, so much the better'. This preliminary measuring up of the purpose and components of a job is called job analysis, and leads to the production of a job description. If the job is not clearly defined and justifiable in terms of the library's objectives, the member of staff appointed to fill it will suffer frustration and indeed often conflict with other members of staff. A job is defined as a collection of tasks making up the work of one member of staff, but in reality some jobs appear to exist only because there is a person holding them. Technology and changes in the environment may diminish job content, or cause jobs to disappear entirely, but this is not always reflected in unrevised staffing structures.

The two absolutely classic cases invariably quoted in the literature are the extra man in the artillery team, whose job was originally to hold the horses, and whose post continued when mechanization took place; and the civil service post (in its later stages an office job) still on the establishment in the 1950s, the purpose of which was to patrol the cliffs of Dover to give early warning of Napoleon. In the context of library and information work vigilance is equally necessary to ensure that posts are modified or created so as to make sense in terms of the organization's current commitments and priorities. This is made especially difficult, but even more necessary, when posts are frozen by the employing institution. Individuals and their unions are naturally suspicious when job analysis is carried out, especially where it is part of an Organization and Methods investigation by, say, a local authority, with a view to economies in staffing. Nonetheless there have been striking examples of changes in staff deployment and job content during the 1970s in all three main types of library, in response to two major trends in librarianship, automation and user-orientation.

In public libraries a major regrouping of staff into area teams has taken place, with the aims of both increasing job satisfaction for professionals by giving them greater variety and increased responsibilities, and of making the services more effective by increasing the range and providing more specialized expertise. This has changed the job design of professionals and non-professionals. Professionals, as members of the team, now have a geographical responsibility to a number of service points (where previously they may have been confined to one branch library). In addition they are given a specialist function, such as children's and schools' services, or information work. And in some systems they have a third responsibility, that of stock management within a particular subject for all the service points in their area. Non-professionals in many cases now carry out the day-to-day running of the branches, and so the role and content of their posts have changed fairly substantially to give them more responsibility and a greater range of duties. Where the team system is working well, the effects on job satisfaction are admirable. Jones (1977) reports on the basis of a survey of middle management librarians, that:

> authority is more dispersed and this is a positive source of job satisfaction. However the system fails to provide satisfaction when librarians feel that they have not enough delegated power, when they suffer a sense of being out of touch with the work of the service points, and only intermittently engage in staff supervision. Although some of the teams have open-ended duties and are free to develop projects there can be a sense of frustration arising from lack of support staff, technical aid and suitable accommodation. Communication up the management hierarchy has not been developed as effectively as the traditional downwards communication, and this lies behind the plea for more participation, or more genuine participation.[2]

In academic libraries the main trend in staff deployment during the 1970s has been subject specialization. The stimulus has come from research into user needs, and an increased awareness of how users, rather than librarians, think about and find their way around libraries. The result has been a gradual shift in emphasis from the functional basis (where staff were designated cataloguers or acquisitions or circulation staff) to a subject basis. It should be noted, however, that the two approaches or principles of staff deployment remain complementary, and even where subject specialization is consistently applied, it requires a majority of the library staff to remain engaged in functional tasks to provide the necessary support and backup in technical services. So while the subject specialists may form a team to cover readers' services (stock selection in liaison with academic staff, user education, information services, and consultancy on cataloguing and classification in their subjects), technical services continue to engage the larger proportion of staff. While subject specialists are conscious of the potential of their work as a means of giving better services and greater job satisfaction, academic librarians on the whole may not be satisfied with the proportion of time and effort which goes into technical services. Roberts reported in the follow-up of the Sheffield Manpower Project that:

> In terms of 'critical activities' the performance of technical services was thought ... to be the most time-consuming activity (46%) and the most important (42%) [in academic libraries]. For public libraries the proportions on this issue were 22% and 23%. For special units 28% and 29%.[3]

The Sheffield Report suggests that perhaps the current processing activities are unnecessarily complicated, and raises the ambition of 'a closer match between tasks, duties and responsibilities, and staff capabilities'. Indeed a more fundamental question is raised as to whether subject specialization and its attendant structure of technical support services is the best way of providing a user-oriented service.

Subject specialization presents many problems from the point of view of job content. Only a minority of graduate professional staff can make use of their subject degrees. The rest suffer from lack of contact with users and user services, which is an area of strong preference for entrants to the profession. The subject specialists suffer from lack of experience in staff supervision, since they are not line managers directly in control of support staff, but have usually only a consultative role in relation to acquisitions and cataloguing. This is a difficulty if they wish to move later to managerial posts.

It appears that subject specialization does provide more effective user-oriented services, so how far does it matter that a proportion of graduates in academic libraries find their work frustrating, and consider that their jobs could just as well be done by people with lower qualifications and less experience? How far is it possible in designing jobs to reconcile the needs of staff for job satisfaction with the needs of the users for effective services?

The situation perhaps suggests that some of the staff in technical services are indeed overqualified for the work they do. It is argued that paraprofessionals might be perfectly capable of coping, and that graduates are not always necessary. A proposed staffing structure for a large polytechnic library which follows these reforms is outlined by Winkworth[4] and is shown on page 83 in Chapter 3. It should be observed that transferring a proportion of the routine procedural work to senior non-professionals (as has happened in many public libraries with the introduction of professional teams) does lead inevitably to a reduction in the numbers of professional librarians needed to operate a library system, unless times are prosperous and the extra staff time released can be channelled to the development and extension of services. This is very much a manpower planning problem which the profession will have to face over the next decade.

In special libraries, according to the findings of the Sheffield Manpower Project,[5] the jobs are more heavily slanted towards the provision of user services, and a great deal of time is spent on preparing information bulletins, compiling critical bibliographies, translating and abstracting, and report writing. In many special libraries users are a demanding and specialized group or series of groups, more so than in academic libraries, it seems. Another striking aspect of special library work is the extent to which job-holders can enlarge or enrich their own jobs. This was discussed at a Leeds careers seminar held by the Institute of Information Scientists in 1980.[6] There are many examples of special librarians rewriting their job descriptions, reshaping their duties and responsibilities to fit better with how they see the role of the information unit in the firm or organization. Of course the corollary is that in times of economic recession the job description may again be rewritten to merge the work with another post, or to remove it entirely, or alter its level from professional to clerical.

Job analysis can be a normal and regular phase in staff management, or it can be an intermittent swoop (predatory or otherwise) by an employing organization such as a local authority or an industrial organization, intended to achieve staff economies or savings through automation or restructuring. As indicated in the chapter on manpower planning, those responsible for staffing can profitably carry out a regular analysis of staffing needs, in the light of the library's objectives and priorities. This entails looking at the job content and context of existing jobs, and considering how they may be affected by changing needs and developing services.

Objectives approach to job analysis

Jobs are ultimately only justifiable in terms of the library's objectives, so every job should be seen as in some way contributing to what the library is trying to achieve in the way of services to its user community. Job-holders need to be made aware of how their work fits in with the work of the rest of the library, and of the parent institution. For example in Brighton Polytechnic Library the library's aim is to provide very strong educational support for the teaching and learning programmes. The specific objectives by which this aim is pursued are set out in the job descriptions of the 'Course Resources Officers', a clumsy title perhaps, but one which implies the priority which is given to the library staff developing a close working relationship with the teaching staff. These officers are required to play an active part in curriculum development meetings with the faculty, to develop a variety of programmes and media for user education, and to gear their information services to proven need, which implies a close knowledge of content, teaching and assessment methods for the courses they cover. The extract from a Brighton job description indicates how the key tasks of an individual are related to the key tasks of their section, which are in turn related to the library's overall objectives (see page 104).

Liverpool Polytechnic Library has experimented with classic management by objectives (MbO) in drawing up its job descriptions. The extract below shows how the job-holder is expected to achieve (by the end of the academic year or term) a clear cut output of work, quantitatively expressed. He or she will have completed so many bibliographical guides, so many sessions of user education... While making the content of a job undeniably obvious, and showing how it relates to the work of the library as a whole, the MbO approach is very much open to criticism on the grounds that it specifies too rigidly and too minutely. It could become a strait-jacket around the post holder, inhibiting him or her from exercising imagination and initiative, or preventing attention to evolving needs which arise during a particular period, because of commitment to the detailed MbO job description. However, the success or failure of the approach would depend very much on how it was applied. The member of staff would have an annual opportunity to agree specific objectives for the next year, within the key task areas relevant to the job (information services, user education, and the others). So it has the advantage of involving members of staff in their own planning, of giving them the chance to take some responsibility and exercise initiative in their work. And these are important motivators for professional workers, according to the findings of surveys of job satisfaction among librarians.

A further criticism of the MbO approach is that the job descriptions express output in mainly quantitative rather than qualitative terms. A librarian might be expected to carry out so many periods of library instruction, but what is the measure of success in terms of improved reader facility in the literature of a subject? Further performance measures would have to be incorporated to evaluate that the objectives had been achieved for the user as well as for the librarian. In the case of user education, for example, has there been, in the opinion of teaching staff, any marked improvement in the range of sources used in projects, and in the quality of the bibliographical citations?

Practical advantages of job analysis and description

Perhaps the most common way in which librarians make use of job analysis and description is in the recruitment of staff. A necessary preliminary to appointing new staff is to have a clear idea as to what kind of person is needed for a post. With existing jobs, it may be found that ideally the new member of staff should carry out a mixture of new and existing

FIGURE 4.2. BRIGHTON POLYTECHNIC JOB DESCRIPTION FOR COURSE RESOURCES OFFICERS

1. To know the detailed structure and educational goals of the course, including the way it is administered, the methods of teaching and learning employed in it, and the relevant characteristics and problems of its students. To know the course's entry requirements, validation process and assessment methods.

2. To obtain after appointment such subject knowledge of the topics covered by the course as to make possible an understanding of the syllabus's content, range and emphasis.

3. To obtain after appointment some understanding of current developments in educational thought and practice.

4. To possess a high degree of competence in professional librarianship.

5. To have some familiarity with non-print material and with media equipment, and to gain after appointment some experience of media production.

6. To serve on the relevant course boards, committees and working parties in order to:

 (a) understand the course's resource needs, and to evaluate these in qualitative, quantitative and financial terms;

 (b) draw attention to the range of resources and facilities provided by Learning Resources;

 (c) support and encourage within the course the development of new approaches to teaching and learning;

 (d) convey information about course developments and needs to both academic staff and the appropriate Learning Resources staff.

7. To be aware of all significant works and sources of information for the course, so as to be able to select stock, and to develop the collection to its maximum level of effectiveness; and to ensure that the collection contains all relevant formats of material, print and non-print.

8. To apply the techniques of a professional librarian to ensure that resources are fully exploited, such exploitation to include:

 (a) the selective dissemination of information;

 (b) the analytical analysis of library materials for information retrieval purposes;

 (c) the introduction of staff and students to the range and depth of resources available both within the Polytechnic and elsewhere; formal and informal instruction in the use of library resources.

9. To consult with other members of Learning Resources so that the general developments and particular needs of the courses may be known and financial provision made for further growth; such consultation to be with other Course Resources Officers, and the Site Resources Officer, the relevant Educational Development Unit staff, the Media Librarian, the Technical Facilities Manager and the Technical Services Librarian.

FIGURE 4.3. EXTRACT FROM LIVERPOOL POLYTECHNIC JOB DESCRIPTION (MbO)

The subject specialist will:—

1. In order to identify the teaching/learning needs which may be met by multi-media sources and services:

	Activity	Objective	Hours	Total Hours
(a)	Sit on relevant faculty or departmental boards in order to keep in touch with current planning and course development	Attend all meetings held during the year	6.25 × no. of meetings (c. 15)	94
(b)	Advise on the impact on the library of academic developments and changes in student numbers	Report changes in departments' teaching methods, courses and enrolments at senior staff meetings	3 × 20 meetings	60
(c)	Take part as a member of the senior management team in library planning	Attend all senior library management team meetings	AS ABOVE	
(d)	Advise on policy decisions on reader services, class and cat., and user instruction programmes	AS ABOVE	AS ABOVE	

tasks, omitting some of the present job-holder's tasks and taking on one or two others. These changes need to be considered because few jobs remain or should remain completely static. Changes in the library's range of services, changes in emphasis perhaps as a result of a new Chief Librarian, changes in technology, may all affect the nature of certain jobs, either to diminish them or to enlarge or enrich their content. So, as the first stage in the recruitment process, job analysis and description assist in clarifying the content and context of the post that is to be filled, and in modifying the job where changing conditions indicate.

Analysis helps also in the problem of designing new posts. Examples of new posts which have been created in recent years in public libraries are those concerned with developing and running 'outreach' services to minority groups in urban areas. For instance in 1979 the London Borough of Hounslow advertised a new post for a 'forward-looking and energetic librarian, who has real ability to develop and maintain services to the borough's sizeable ethnic minority community, the majority of whom are from the Indian sub-continent'. Another reason for new posts is when new library service points are opened. Also in 1979, for example, Devon County Library advertised for someone to run their new library about to be opened at Dawlish. They were seeking someone with the 'necessary blend of drive, initiative and post qualification experience to take control of this service and develop its full potential'.

In the special library field posts are created as existing services expand, or because new subdivisions are established in the existing parent body. For example the Building Services Research and Information Association opened an International Air Infiltration Centre in 1979, and advertised for a librarian to set up the necessary technical information service. The job analysis done prior to advertising had shown that what was needed was someone with 'competence in the use of automated data retrieval systems... and fluency in a second European language'.

Automation has brought into existence a number of new posts concerned with systems analysis, as well as reducing posts in library housekeeping areas, such as circulation work. Teesside Polytechnic advertised for a Programmer/Analyst (Library Systems) to assist Polytechnic library staff to develop automated cataloguing and issue systems. The appropriate person would need 'COBOL programming ability and experience of systems analysis or library systems'. Other ways in which new jobs evolve are through significant trends in the parent body of, say, academic libraries. In a number of schools, colleges of education and polytechnics the development of resource-based learning by the teaching staff has been the stimulus for a more positive, educationally-based mode of librarianship. For example Gayton High School for Boys in Harrow advertised a post in their newly equipped library, where, 'in addition to normal duties, the Librarian will be expected to develop the library as a resource centre which can be used across the school curriculum ... applicants should be Chartered Librarians with good educational library experience and a desire to apply his/her own ideas in the development of the Service'.

How do you design a new job? The manager needs to have some knowledge and understanding of what makes a satisfying job, rather than simply listing tasks which need to be carried out if a new service is to get under way. This brings us back to the relevance of motivation theories to deploying staff in library and information work. The manager should bear in mind the positive motivators, such as responsibility, sense of achievement and opportunity to use professional expertise, as well as the 'hygiene factors' of pay, working conditions and status.

In academic librarianship in particular, it has been noted that a source of dissatisfaction and frustration is the sharp division often encountered between technical services and readers' services, with the majority of professional staff engaged solely in technical services. Can anything be done to alleviate this problem when new jobs are to be created? The importance of the work group has been convincingly established by motivation theorists from Mayo onwards, so attention should be paid to the place of the new member of staff *vis-à-vis* existing staff, to establish him or her with some sense of belonging to a particular team or group with common objectives. It is also useful to bear in mind security needs as well as esteem or self-actualising needs, when designing a job. People may appreciate the challenge of a roving commission (as for instance in setting up outreach services in public libraries), but they also need a stable base, giving them a geographical centre and colleagues to support them. Thus in the team structure in public libraries, it is important to maintain for team librarians a fairly high number of hours of attendance every week at service points.

In addition to designing new posts, library managers have in recent years been heavily engaged in redesigning jobs, or staff restructuring as it is often called. The most obvious examples are related to the introduction of the team structure in public libraries. People previously employed as branch librarians (in many cases with a rather high proportion of routine non-professional work in proportion to professional tasks) have been redeployed as members of a professional team, each with functional and sometimes also subject responsibilities as well as a geographical responsibility for a number of service points in the area (Hinks).[78] This is an example of what job designers call 'job enrichment', that is, adding to a job tasks of a higher level. This should be distinguished from 'job enlargement', which means adding further tasks of the same level, in order to provide more variety within a job, and alleviate boredom. Team restructuring has also meant job enrichment for non-professional staff in public libraries, since very often senior clerical staff have been given a supervisory role in the day-to-day running of a branch (previously done by a professional Branch Librarian).

Another example of job redesign intended to lead to job enrichment is the grouping of cataloguers so that each one takes responsibility for a particular group of subjects, in which they do all the cataloguing and classifying. Job enlargement is sometimes used to give cataloguers contact with users, and add variety, to their work. This usually consists in academic libraries of assigning them to evening counter duties. At the level of routine counter work job enlargement is used to prevent tedium. The normal procedure is to give people limited shifts, of say two hours at a time, on issuing, or

FIGURE 4.4. EXTRACT FROM THE NATIONAL JOINT COUNCIL JOB EVALUATION SCHEME

JOB EVALUATION

GUIDANCE FOR EVALUATION PANELS

DECISIONS MADE

This factor deals with the responsibility of the postholder for taking decisions during the course of his duties. Decisions to recommend courses of action are included. The extent of the effect of a decision becomes progressively relevant in making assessments beyond level 4.

Level 1   Course of action limited to choices of a routine nature.

Level 2   Course of action limited to choices of a less routine nature.

Level 3   Decisions in accordance with established policy where judgements between limited alternatives are necessary.

Level 4   Decisions within established policy where many factors must be weighed.

Level 5   Occasional decisions leading to minor changes of procedures affecting others.

Level 6   Difficult or important decisions within established policy where many factors must be weighed. Decisions leading to changes in procedures affecting others.

Level 7   Decisions to recommend changes of major procedures affecting others or contributing significantly to policy changes.

Level 8   Decisions leading to a change in major procedures or to recommend changes in policy affecting others.

Level 9   Reviewing major policy and deciding to recommend changes in, or the initiation of new, policy.

overdues, or shelf tidying. The problem is how to reconcile this with the need to give people some area of their own to look after, so that they have some sense of achievement. This is done in some academic libraries by, for example, making each member of the counter staff responsible for a particular section of the stacks. The trouble with job enlargement is that it often means redesigning routine jobs so that a person has several boring tasks, rather than one or two. But they can be varied in such a way that, for example, social needs are taken into account. Thus periods of backroom work may be alternated with periods of contact with the public, and periods of working on one's own can be alternated with periods of working with others.

Job analysis and description are also seen as important means of diagnosing training needs. The personnel or training officer has a basis for drawing up relevant programmes for staff development, if he or she has

JOB EVALUATION

PANEL: . . . .   POST No. . . . .

. . . .   POST . . . .

. . . .   SECTION . . . .

. . . .   DEPARTMENT . . . .

PLEASE READ THE NOTES 'GUIDANCE FOR JOB EVALUATION PANELS' AND PLACE TICK IN APPROPRIATE COLUMN

	1	2	3	4	5	6	7	8	9
	1	2	3	4	5	6	7	8	9
Supervisory and Managerial Responsibility									
Decisions Made	1	2	3	4	5	6	7	8	9
Supervision Received	1	2	3	4	5	6	7		
Work Complexity	1	2	3	4	5	6	7		
Special Conditions	1								
Contacts	1	2	3	4	5	6	7	8	
Creative Work	1	2	3	4	5	6	7	8	
Education	1	2	3	4	5	6	7	8	9
Experience	1	2	3	4	5	6	7	8	9

Chairman's signature . . . .   Date . . . .

organized the production of a set of job descriptions. These can be used as the basis for assessing staff abilities and competences in a particular job, and where necessary arranging for training appropriate to a job-holder who has difficulties in certain aspects of the job, (interpersonal skills in dealing with the public, perhaps, or computer appreciation, or updating in AACR 2).

In special libraries in particular, more often than in public or academic libraries, job analysis may be used as a preliminary to job evaluation. Job evaluation means (Dutton 1976) 'the process of analysis and assessment of the relative content of jobs, to place them in an acceptable rank order, which can be used as the basis for a pay structure'.[9] Job description is more simply a broad statement of the purpose, scope, duties and responsibilities of a job, and is the product of job analysis (identifying the component parts of a job and the context in which it is carried out). It should be added that an important stimulus to the compilation of job descriptions for library posts has come from the employing bodies, and has in particular affected public libraries and special libraries. Since local government reorganization in 1974, public libraries have been heavily affected by new management approaches in local government generally, and may be asked to conform in their personnel practices with the local authority's policies. Special libraries likewise may find, especially in industry, that they are required to do as the other sections do, in matters of staffing, and draw up descriptions and evaluations of the tasks performed.

Methods of analysis and evaluation

Dutton identifies the 'qualitative' and the 'quantitative' approaches to these matters. The quantitative method is to assign values in numerical terms to the various job components identified in the analysis. That is, some tasks are rated as more professional than others. A weighting or score is given to them higher than that given to less professionally demanding tasks. When the scores are added up for all the components in a specific job, the total indicates roughly the extent to which a job might be appropriate for various levels of professional or non-professional staff.

The qualitative approach is more usual in library and information work, and implies that certain factors are borne in mind that indicate professional levels of work, without actually assigning scores. A guide to what tasks are considered professional or non-professional can be found in the Library Association's *Professional and non-professional duties in libraries,* 2nd edn., 1974.[10] In local government the National Joint Council job evaluation system takes into account factors such as supervisory responsibility, decision-making, work complexity, creative elements in the work, and also factors related to the person who could do the job (education and experience necessary). A matrix scoring system is shown in Figure 4.4.[11] This shows that within each factor, the score assigned to a specific job may be

FIGURE 4.5. COVENTRY PUBLIC LIBRARY – EXTRACT FROM JOB DESCRIPTION

ANALYSIS OF PERFORMANCE REQUIREMENTS AND CONDITIONS FOR POST OF HOSPITAL LIBRARIAN

A. *Education*
Chartered Librarian.

B. *Experience*
(Implied in 'A').

C. *Supervisory Responsibilities*
Directly supervise the work of the Assistant Area Librarian(s) (Hospitals) and any voluntary staff seconded or assigned to the library service.

D. *Decisions Made*
Within the framework of Departmental and Area policy (City Libraries) and the guidelines as set down by the Hospital authorities, responsible for all day-to-day decision making for the unit.
Responsible to the Community Area Librarian for the spending of *assigned* portions of the Area funds of the City Libraries.
Responsible to the Hospital Secretary for all spending from Hospital funds.

E. *Supervision Received*
Works under the general supervision of the Community Area Librarian and the Hospital Secretary (at professional/operational levels, respectively).

F. *Work Complexity*
A complex situation, owing to the range and diversity of activities undertaken within the Hospital/community, and the dual nature of the post, with responsibilities to both the Hospital and the City Libraries.

G. *Responsibility for Assets*
None.

H. *Contacts*
Regular contacts with the professional staff of the Community Area.
Contacts other Departmental personnel as the need occurs.

I. *Creative Work and Reports*
a) Monthly statistical and narrative report on the work of the unit (To the Community Area Librarian).
b) Annual statistical and narrative report (as above).
c) Such other reports as may be necessary to the forwarding of the Area's activities (either solicited or at the postholder's initiative).

J. *Other Factors*
Ability to drive a car is desirable.

K. *Age*
Not relevant.

111

along a continuum of nine levels. For example, if decision-making in a post is restricted to very routine matters, the lowest score (level 1) would be assigned. If however the kind of decisions made would lead to changes in procedures affecting others, the score would be level 6 in the matrix, and where decisions would lead to changes in policies affecting others, level 8 score would be assigned.

The way in which this approach has affected job descriptions in public libraries is shown in the example from Coventry (Figure 4.5). At the bottom of the actual description of duties and responsibilities attached to the post of Principal Librarian (Hospitals), there is an 'Analysis of performance requirements and conditions'; in effect an evaluation of the level of the job. Education, experience, supervisory responsibilities, decision-making, work complexity, responsibility for assets, creative work, and contacts are the headings used. These are in fact the headings shown in the National Joint Council extract, as can be seen if a comparison is made between the extracts which are provided as examples.

An American version of job evaluation, using a scoring system, is that of Rothenberg,[12] compiled for evaluating jobs in a survey by mailed questionnaire which she sent to a sample of school librarians in the US. She assigned tasks to four groups: high professional job tasks, low professional job tasks, high non-professional job tasks and low non-professional job tasks. This was done on the basis of skills and knowledge required to perform the various tasks. Then an individual librarian's 'job-task index score' was compiled by assigning an appropriate score for each task included in their work. This would be from 4 for primary involvement in a high professional task like budget preparation or formal library instruction, down to minus 4 for primary involvement in a low non-professional task like photocopying or shelving. The final score was computed by adding up scores for each task checked off as part of an individual librarian's work, and dividing by the number of tasks. In the questionnaire sent to librarians the tasks were not of course grouped into professional and non-professional, but were arranged in a single alphabetical sequence. Rothenberg's scoring sheet is shown in Figure 4.6.

Classification of job-task index items. The 'job index score' is compiled by asking employees to tick off all their duties on a form which lists the following tasks, indicating whether they have a primary or secondary involvement in each task ticked. Their returned forms are then scored as shown, and this provides the personnel manager with a quantitative evaluation of the posts covered, for use in recruitment, for example.

Common factors in job evaluation schemes. In most schemes of job evaluation a list of 'job factors' is drawn up as a preliminary step. These factors commonly include accuracy, accountability, complexity, creativity, decision-making, dexterity, effect of errors, educational requirements, mental and/or physical effort, problem-solving, resource-controlling,

FIGURE 4.6. ROTHENBERG'S SCORING SHEET

Group 1. High professional job tasks
Score – primary involvement 4, secondary involvement 3

Bibliography	Formal library instruction
Budget preparation	Personnel coordination
Choosing publications	Policy determination
Choosing subjects	Program planning

Group 2. Low professional job tasks
Score – primary involvement 2, secondary involvement 1
Assisting readers
Descriptive cataloguing
Informal library instruction
Responding to information requests
Verifying requests

Group 3. High non-professional job tasks
Score – primary involvement minus 2, secondary involvement minus 1

Bindery preparation	Inter-library loan
Bookkeeping	Periodical checking
Data processing	Searching catalogs

Group 4. Low non-professional job tasks
Score – primary involvement minus 4, secondary involvement minus 3

Bookmarking	Repairing and mending
Filing cards	Shelving
Filing and maintaining	Typing cards
circulation records	Typing correspondence
Photocopying	

responsibility for money, materials, data and equipment, social skills, supervisory load and work pressure.

Each of these factors is then weighted, and a score assigned by a panel of evaluators. Standard forms are then drawn up, like the National Joint Council form shown earlier, for use by the evaluators. Job-holders are then given an explanation of evaluation, and very often trade unions take an active part in discussing with the employers the context of evaluation and the reasons why it is being carried out. Their object is obviously to try to prevent the disappearance or downgrading of existing posts. Job-holders then fill in questionnaires, and sometimes in addition take part in interviews covering the content and context of their work. On the basis of these returns, job analysts compile job descriptions for each post and apply the points rating system to it. On the basis of the results jobs are graded and paid accordingly, for example the system of A.P. grades in British local government library jobs. The National Joint Council has agreed that there will be no personal reduction in grading for any staff as a result of job evaluation, but transfers are always possible.

In the sphere of special libraries, Don Mason comments on the importance of job evaluation as a means of ensuring that salary grades and working status are fair both to the occupant of the job and to the employer. He discusses the use of factor analysis in evaluating jobs in information work, and identifies as significant factors:

1. Amount of specialized knowledge which the job demands.
2. Level and extent of staff management involved.
3. Range of relationships within and without the company which the job-holder needs to maintain or build.
4. Value of the decisions which have to be made.[13]

Examples of different levels of decision-making, which lead to a job being rated high or low on this last factor might be:
Highest level; Decisions on the information unit's budget, staff deployment, planning and evaluation of services, research into user needs.
Level 2: Decisions on search strategies for published and unpublished information, selection and subject analysis of materials.
Judgement in evaluating materials/information retrieved.
Level 3: Decisions on search strategies for published materials. Advisory decisions on selecting material, and subject analysis of material.[14]
Similar levels can be established for other aspects of information work, such as enquiry work, which can range from the lowest level of quick reference and textbook enquiries for simple data, to the highest level, which calls for critical evaluation of materials, and selective and analytical assessment of the enquiry, and contacts with outside organizations.

Methods of collecting data for job descriptions. Methods used by employing bodies to evaluate jobs for salary grading purposes involve detailed analysis of job content. Job analysis also takes place within a particular library system very often with the object of producing job descriptions to use in the selection, appraisal and training of staff. The range of methods used includes the following:

1. Jobholders write out a description of their own job.
2. The immediate supervisor writes the description, with or without the participation of the job-holder.
3. The supervisor or a job analyst from outside the library carries out a detailed 'observation' of the work being done.

4. Jobholders are asked to keep work diaries over a period. Often a combination of these methods is used.

Updating job descriptions is important, since they often become quite misleading after two or three years as jobs evolve or regress due to technological or other environmental changes. The problem is that job descriptions are often only used in libraries when jobs are vacant and new staff are to be appointed. Many years may elapse therefore while they gather dust in the personnel files. Job descriptions however have considerable potential in other areas of staff management besides recruitment. In particular they provide a useful basis for staff appraisal schemes, since they provide a yardstick for identifying strengths and weaknesses which staff are experiencing in carrying out their work from year to year. In turn this kind of appraisal can help in planning training and staff development opportunities.

Content of job descriptions
1. *Statement of purpose, objectives of the job.*

The examples of job descriptions from Brighton Polytechnic and Liverpool Polytechnic (on pages 104 and 105) show clearly how a particular post is related to the library's objectives, and outline fairly specific objectives for the specific post. A further illustration from a public library job description is given in Figure 4.7, where the Bradford Public Libraries Staffing and Development Officer has for objectives:

to provide, develop, co-ordinate and advise on all matters relating to staffing and training in the Division.

to provide, co-ordinate and advise on research and on service development projects.

to participate in the corporate management of the Division.

Another example from Coventry Public Library's post of Hospitals' Librarian, cites as the objective or 'job purpose':

to ensure the provision and ready availability of those resources essential to the educational, recreational and cultural development of the Hospitals and local community, in liaison with the Hospital Secretary, and under the general supervision of the Community Area Librarian.

It might be argued that these statements of objectives verge on the obvious, but they set the scene for more detailed description of what the job is about, and the best ones make strong links between the job and the library's work and overall aims, so that the jobholder has a strong sense of playing a purposeful part in the organization's activities and services to its public.

2. *Main tasks and duties.*

This is often a straightforward list of the activities which the job-holder will be expected to perform. So that, in the Bradford example, quite detailed

FIGURE 4.7. OUTLINE JOB DESCRIPTION – BRADFORD PUBLIC LIBRARY

POST TITLE	STAFFING & DEVELOPMENT OFFICER	POST GRADE		POST REFERENCE	E	4	S	0	0	2

The following information is furnished to assist staff joining the Metropolitan District Council to understand and appreciate the work content of their post and the role they are to play in the organisation. However the following points should be noted:

1. Whilst every endeavour has been made to outline all the duties and responsibilities of the post, a document such as this does not permit every item to be specified in detail. Broad headings therefore may have been used below, in which case all the usual associated routines are naturally included in the job description.

2. Officers should not refuse to undertake work which is not specified on this form but they should record any additional duties they are required to perform and these will be taken into account when salaries are reviewed.

PRIME OBJECTIVES OF THE POST:
To assist the Chief Librarian in the overall objectives of the Libraries Division, particularly to provide, develop, co-ordinate and advise on all matters relating to staffing and training in the Division. To provide, co-ordinate and advise on research and on service development projects throughout the Division. To participate in the Corporate Management of the Division.

SUPERVISORY/MANAGERIAL RESPONSIBILITIES:
Direct supervision of (1) clerical assistant and up to (8) professional trainees.

SUPERVISION AND GUIDANCE:
Directly responsible to Chief Librarian, arranging own work programme, receiving guidance on overall policies and objectives, and on complex problems, with specialist advice available from Principal Librarians.

RANGE OF DECISION TAKING:
Responsible to the Chief Librarian for decisions on all personnel matters throughout the Division; manpower audit and planning; recruitment selection; placement training and staff development; direct supervision of trainees, communication, appraisal and reporting, welfare and working conditions, advising and assisting all staff; co-ordination and advice on research and for co-ordination of work of project teams engaged on development projects; recommending changes in policy where appropriate; decisions have to be taken which do not fall within established Policy guidelines. Next in seniority to Chief Librarian with membership of Divisional Management Team which includes consideration of all policies, and responsibility for special projects outside the prime objectives of the postholder.

RESPONSIBILITY FOR ASSETS, MATERIALS ETC.:
Responsible for the safe custody of the assets of the unit, particularly confidential staff files and papers. Also for advising on safety and security of staff and their property.

116

RANGE OF DUTIES:

STAFFING

Manpower Audit and Planning – prepare short and long term manpower forecasts. In conjunction with senior staff prepare and revise job descriptions: participate in reviews of staffing and gradings; advise on staffing levels, for new and existing services, in conjunction with Divisional Admin. Officer, monitor and report on staffing budget.

Recruitment and Selection – Publicise work in libraries, to schools and universities career meetings and conventions, with colleagues where appropriate, to promote awareness of Service opportunities. Participate in interview and appointment of professional staff; interview and appoint non-professional and manual staff, prepare and, in conjunction with Personnel Office, place advertisements; prepare and distribute information for staff as appropriate; liaise with schools of librarianship on placing of Bradford staff and receive students on attachments and other appropriate matters (research projects).

Communication – Recommend to senior management, and monitor, an effective two-way communication network.

Welfare and working conditions – Ensure that all relevant Conditions of Service are applied throughout the Division, and that, as far as possible, they equal the best current public library practice; be available to any member of staff requiring guidance or help with any problem and be an appeal officer in grievances not satisfied locally.

RESEARCH
Co-ordinate and participate in a programme of research; produce reports as appropriate.

DEVELOPMENT
Co-ordinate the work of the project team leaders engaged in development projects throughout the Division, e.g. new or enhanced services, new buildings; liaise with the Building Section of the Directorate and any other appropriate agencies, and with Directorate of Development Services (Planning and Architects Divisions).

CORPORATE MANAGEMENT
Participate in the corporate management of the library service by attendance at meetings, discussions with colleagues, writing reports, policy statements and similar documents, etc., for Chief Librarian, use at Panel and Committee meetings, etc., attend Panel and Committee meetings as required. Other projects as allocated from time to time beyond the scope of the postholder's prime objectives.

CONTACTS
Chief Librarian, Principal Librarians and all other staff of the Division (250 office, 60 manual) senior staff of other Directorates of Divisions (particularly Educational Services, Admin. Division, Personnel Office, Management Services Division, Planning; and Architects Division); members of the Council; staff and students of Schools of Librarianship; staff of other libraries at Chief and Senior Officer level; careers teachers and officers; British Council; professional bodies; Dept. of Employment; Dept. of Education and Science; management service organisations, within and without local government; school pupils and other members of the public.

lists of the range of duties are set out under the headings 'Staffing', 'Research', 'Development' and 'Corporate management'. Often a distinction is made between 'key task areas', and the range of duties or activities which make up the job. For example in the post of Hospitals' Librarian at Coventry, one 'key task area' is to 'establish links with the community served'. The activities by which this is to be achieved then follow: the post holder will provide display and publicity materials for hospital events, will maintain up to date directory information on local societies and organizations, for example. Setting out key task areas is often a helpful way of building a bridge between the objectives of the job and the concrete duties to be carried out.

3. *Place of the post in the library's staffing structure.*

This section of the job description should indicate clearly to whom the member of staff is responsible, and whom they are required to supervise in turn. This is sometimes conveniently set out in the form of an organization chart, or it may simply be given as in the Bradford example:

> Direct supervision of 1 clerical assistant and up to 8 professional trainees.
>
> Directly responsible to Chief Librarian, arranging own work programme... with specialist advice available from Principal Librarians.

It is important to make clear the range and level of decision-making involved in the job, in addition to a bald statement about position in the staff hierarchy. This involves some indication of the amount of guidance which will be given by the post-holder's superiors, the existence or lack of existence of clearly outlined policies and procedures and precedents, the gravity of the problems likely to arise, degree of innovation likely to be required in the work, and the effect on other staff (how widespread and significant) of decisions taken by the holder of this job. Note the paragraph in the Bradford example, headed 'Range of decision taking'.

4. *Contacts outside the library.*

These give a useful indication of the range and level of people in the community with whom the post holder will be required to develop and maintain contacts. In the Bradford post, for example, the Staffing Officer is expected to build contacts with schools, careers officers, schools of librarianship, the Department of Employment, and the British Council, among others. In the Brighton and Liverpool Polytechnic examples, the subject specialists are required to build up close contacts with teaching staff, by sitting on Boards of Studies, and other formal bodies, as well as by continuing informal contacts, throughout the academic year.

5. *Salary scales and working conditions.*

These are part of the contextual information (as opposed to content of job) which is essential on job descriptions, particularly when used in the recruitment process. Working conditions include details of working hours, holidays, opportunities for staff development (such as time and expenses for attending professional workshops and conferences), and prospects for promotion. These days it is often the case that information about trade union membership is given as well. If there is a union membership agreement with the employer, the post holder may be required to join the appropriate union as a condition of taking up the post.

6. *Organizational factors.*

In some job descriptions the library takes a lot of trouble to convey the philosophy and structure of the service as they operate it, in order to attract the right kind of staff for them. This is the case in the Brighton Polytechnic job description for subject specialists, which makes it very clear that Brighton places a high priority on educationally literate librarians, who can communicate knowledgeably with teaching staff and educational technologists, and who regard learning resources as an integral part of their work, and not something to be left to others.

Problems associated with job descriptions.

1. They need to be continuously updated; otherwise they become irrelevant and ignored.
2. They need to leave some scope for initiative and innovation on the part of the job holder. If they are too specific and detailed, this can encourage the job holder to continue merely to do the things the predecessor did, without bothering to create and improve.
3. They are generally careful to state that the post holder may be required to undertake 'such other duties as from time to time the chief librarian may decide'. Otherwise they could become a force for reaction. There may however be difficulties in this area, when unions consider that duties from frozen posts are being reallocated to increase the work-load of other staff. They may instruct their members to refuse to take on extra duties when they are of this nature.
4. If the post holder has not been consulted or personally involved in compiling a job description, it is likely that he or she will not be anxious to carry out its injunctions, and will ignore it as far as possible.
5. The value of job descriptions depends very much on how they are used in a library. Their value extends beyond the recruiting phase, but often this is the only area in which they appear to be used. They need to be referred to, when staff appraisal and staff development are taking place, and when policy decisions are being taken on manpower planning.

Personnel specification

The job description describes the *job*; the personnel specification describes the *person* capable of doing the job. The job description should be sufficiently informative to enable a realistic picture to be outlined of the

FIGURE 4.8. JOB SPECIFICATION

Dept.   County Library   Post Ref. No. N11

Section   Bury St. Edmunds, Ipswich, Lowestoft   Responsibility level PO2/1

Designation of Post   Area Librarian, Bury St. Edmunds, Ipswich, Lowestoft

JOB DESCRIPTION	FACTOR	REQUIREMENTS
Direction and control of all lending, reference, information and mobile library services, and services to schools within the Area.	Education	Chartered librarian. Post-qualification training relevant to a post at this level of library management.
Maintenance of special services – old people's homes, hospitals, prisons, etc. Supervision of book selection and supply. Contact with District Council Consultative Committee, and with community and user interests, activities and needs in order to monitor library performance and progress.	Experience	Minium age 30. Non-graduates and CNAA graduates to have ten years' practical experience (five after passing appropriate examination). Graduates to have eight years after passing post-graduate professional examination.
	Supervision	Responsible for direct control of approximately 38 professional, 65 non-professional and 7 manual staff.
Routing of mobile libraries within Area, co-ordination of routes between Areas. Arrangement of cultural activities, exhibitions, concerts, film shows, meetings, etc. in libraries in the area and the letting of accommodation for use by local societies. Supervision of public catering facilities provided in libraries.	Decisions made	Considerable autonomy of action within agreed county policy, referring only most complex problems to County Librarian. Constant review of policy and major procedures, submitting recommendations for changes of policy to the County Librarian and of procedures to the operational group of librarians.
Safe custody and maintenance of buildings and vehicles within the Area.	Supervision received	Responsible to County Librarian for the efficient administration of the Area library service within a policy of accountable management.
To play a full and active part in the corporate management of the library authority. To take executive action as required in the absence of the County Librarian, including the ability to deputise if required to do so.	Complexity	Wide range of executive duties.

FACTOR	REQUIREMENTS
Contacts	Library representatives and adviser on District Consultative Committees. Collaboration with library headquarters and Areas, with senior officers of other departments on siting and planning of libraries after consultation with County Librarian. Direct contact with appropriate officers on building and vehicle maintenance.
Reports and Records	Maintenance of catalogues, submission of statistical reports, supervision of maintenance of vehicle records. Prepare reports on the library service within the Area.
Staff	Responsible, subject to county council policy, for appointment of staff to Area services with the advice, where necessary, of the appropriate specialist officers.
Staff Position	One of a group of five officers sharing operational responsibility for the library service and able to deputise for the County Librarian if required to do so.

attributes required in a successful applicant. What are the qualifications, experience and personal qualities, the skills, abilities and specialist interests required to carry out a particular job?

Very often the job description and the personnel specification are combined in one document for recruitment purposes. Job applicants who send off for further details receive information on the duties and responsibilities of the job, and also on the qualifications, experience and qualities required in the person who will be appointed. An example of a detailed 'job specification' combining job description and personnel specification from Suffolk County Library is shown in Figure 4.8.

FIGURE 4.9

JOB SPECIFICATION	PERSONNEL SPECIFICATION	HOW TO DISCOVER APPLICANTS FOR JOB
1. Specialized technical/ professional activities?	What knowledge? What skills are required to what level? (other than those below)	Qualifications, contribution to the literature, prof. activity; well read in the current lit. and abreast of current developments; references; selection tests.
2. Social requirements: how extended is the role set and how heterogeneous? Extent and kind of relations with users and other out-of-library people?	Ability to communicate clearly? Ability to handle conflict? To lead?	Difficult to assess! Past experience – type of job? References? Social interests? Handling of interview situation? Group selection methods? Personality tests?
3. Does the job require to be *developed*, qualitatively and/or quantitatively?	Enthusiasm, drive, initiative, ambition?	As for 2. What does the candidate expect and want from this job? Can you find out by oblique means?
4. Is this a relatively unprogrammed job, with many open and 'one-off' situations?	Autonomy, originality, imagination, creativity, critical capacity but not scatty?	Again, much as for 2. Situational case studies of value. Better: 'Well, you have seen the job; what would you do if you were landed with it?'
5. Alternatively, is this a relatively programmed job, needing continuous accurate and systematic work?	A steady, reliable, orderly-minded applicant, with plenty of staying power – but not too inflexible!	Interview impressions, and aptitude tests.

6. What kinds and degrees of stress characterize this job? Speed, deadlines, responsibility, people stress?	Stable, self-reliant, relaxed, sense of humour?	Past experience, personality tests, interview – but easy to be misled here.
7. Personal circumstances: how much travelling, shift work, possibility of transfer? Must we really have someone who is going to be heavily committed to this job?	Domestic commitments, other commitments? Where would the *job* fit into the candidate's *life*? What's she looking for? Where is she going?	Interview (Careful, not only out of respect for privacy, but because it is particularly easy to make wrong inferences.) Honesty needed on each side, in the best long-term interests of each side.

Strictly speaking the term 'job specification' in personnel management means the intermediate stage between job description and personnel specification, in which the characteristics of a job are listed, in terms of complexity, responsibility and supervisory load. These characteristics of the job are then used to determine the characteristics of the person needed to do the job. In library practice the job specification is usually merged with the job description. Figure 4.9 shows the connections.

The employing organization may not have complete control over the requirements they ask for in job applicants, since both professional bodies and trade unions may lay down certain guidelines as to hours of work, what jobs may or may not be carried out by the post holder, what qualifications are appropriate, and what salary grades should apply to a particular post. In public libraries Nalgo (National Association of Local Government Officers) is the relevant union for professional librarians; in college and polytechnic libraries it is Natfhe (National Association of Teachers in Further and Higher Education) or APT (Association of Polytechnic Teachers) or Nalgo; and in university libraries it is AUT (Association of University Teachers). In special libraries there is a wider range of unions because of the diversity of the parent institutions, but some of the commonly found unions are ASTMS (Association of Scientific Technical and Managerial Staff), NUPE (National Union of Public Employees) and also Nalgo.

The Library Association from time to time draws attention to jobs which it has decided to black, because of what is considered to be inadequate salary grading or conditions of service. It is not necessarily successful, however, in dissuading librarians from applying for, or accepting such jobs, since the sanctions it can impose seem to depend on members' solidarity and this is not always evident, probably because of the wide range of levels and types of library. In periods of economic recession, moreover, librarians may have to be less choosy about getting a toe-hold in the profession, or a step up the ladder.

The Library Association, it should be emphasized, is not a trade union for professionals, and activity over salaries and gradings and conditions of service is very much more in the hands of the white-collar unions, to which an increasing proportion of librarians belong. However the Library Association has of recent years appointed a member of its Headquarters staff to be responsible for industrial relations, in the sense of advising members, and developing contacts with the main unions, so as to have an indirect say in safeguarding the rights of members.

How to compile a personnel specification

Provided that the job description gives a clear and accurate account of the content and context of a post, and the levels of performance required in terms of decision-making, policy and planning, and such matters, it is comparatively straightforward to decide on the kind of person needed to do the job. But there are pitfalls. Rodger, the formulator of the widely used Seven-Point Plan for selectors, says: If matching is to be done satisfactorily, the requirements of an occupation (or job) must be described in the same terms as the attributes of the people who are being considered for it.'[5] The Suffolk County specification for an Area Librarian shows how the matching can be closely done.

Plumbley adds a further point, that 'it is not helpful to ask for attributes that cannot be assessed by the selector or the selection process'.[16] It might be added that the most common selection process in libraries is the interview, and this is often very inadequate for the purposes it is used for, since it cannot, for example, test people's executive capacity or problem-solving skills, though these are very often needed in library services.

To help managers draw up a personnel specification, there are two widely-used classifications of attributes:

Rodger's Seven-Point Plan[17]	*Fraser's Five-Point Plan*[18]
Physical make-up	Impact on other people
Attainments	Qualifications
General intelligence	Innate abilities
Specialized aptitudes	Motivation
Interests	Adjustment
Disposition	
Circumstances	

Each of these categories (the two classifications overlap almost completely, so are not to be seen as alternative guidelines in drawing up a personnel specification, but rather as suggesting common categories to be considered) is likely to be considered when staff are appointed to library jobs. Although Rodger and Fraser were concerned with recruitment in general and not with any particular occupation, there is much coincidence between their categories and those derived from librarians' own accounts of their jobs and the skills they require (Sheffield Manpower Project findings):

1. Special knowledge: bibliographic; subject knowledge; particular type of work or procedure; foreign languages; users and users' needs; locality.
2. Special abilities and skills: mental or intellectual; organizing or administrative; staff management; social skills; clerical skills.
3. Other qualities: those relating to temperament, disposition, personality, interest, motivation.
4. Formal qualifications and experience: education, previous work experience.[19]

The Sheffield Manpower Project also elicited from librarians the factors in their work that put pressure on staff. The replies mentioned pressures arising from the pace of work, from the variety of tasks in many jobs, physical demands (sheer stamina), contact with people, and changing environment and techniques.

It should be noted that in drawing up a specification a distinction can be drawn between 'essential attributes', 'desirable attributes' and 'contra-indicators'. This may help the selectors in refining the process of sifting candidates. Another helpful source of information may be provided by the exit interview. The departing job-holders may give some useful clues about the kind of person who could best succeed them. Was the departing member of staff able to use his qualifications to a satisfying extent? Did the individual's disposition prove mainly suitable or unsuitable for the range of personal contacts involved in the job? Were there specialist abilities needed which they felt they did not have, or had been inadequately trained to develop?

The points focused by Fraser and Rodger may be used either as actual headings in drawing up a personnel specification, and under each heading the selectors can jot down notes relevant to the job in question, or the points can be used as general guidelines which should be taken into account when sifting applications for the shortlist, and in interviewing applicants. Some librarians prefer to avoid too much specificity in a personnel specification, on the grounds that it may lead to good applicants being ruled out, if their education and/or experience has been unconventional. Another criticism of using the points to check off an applicant's characteristics is that the whole individual is often greater (sometimes less) than the sum of his or her parts.

The selection process must remain open to overall impressions, and beware of fragmentation into stylized categories.

Physical make-up and impact on others. In Fraser's and Rodger's plans, this means appearance, bearing and speech, and the reaction which these elicit in other people, both colleagues and users. In addition are covered aspects of health and physique necessary for library work. Very closely related to this is Rodger's 'disposition', since this is the set of attitudes and personality traits, which to a large extent determine the impact made on the public and on other staff in the work group.

Very often in recruiting library staff it is the subjective impressions of the interviewing panel that count in determining applicants' general disposition and impact, but there is now an increasing tendency to emphasize the informal parts of selection. Other members of staff, and particularly the colleagues who will be working with the new member of staff, are given an opportunity to show the applicants around, and lunch with them, and sometimes even take part in the interview. They can then give their views on how well they think candidates may fit in (or as necessary not fit in but act as a lively stimulus).

Ability to express oneself reasonably fluently may well be more effectively assessed informally, rather than in the awesome atmosphere of the interviewing room. The qualities thought desirable appear to be articulacy on matters where knowledge might be expected (previous work experience, professional issues, higher education courses, studies); an ability to be clear in communicating; and a degree of amiability in responding to other people.

In terms of physical stamina, some library jobs (counter work, for example) make quite high demands, perhaps surprisingly so in the light of the public image of librarians. There are plenty of jobs, however which are mainly sedentary, and selectors should take account of the policies of their employing organizations on providing jobs for the physically handicapped. Some local authorities, for instance, stipulate that approximately 1.5 per cent of their posts should be held by the handicapped.

Qualifications and attainments. Fraser makes the distinction between general education, specialist training and work experience. Rodger likewise includes under 'Attainments' all those educational and professional experiences which the applicant has had from school through higher education to the previous job.

The requirements differ from one type of library to another. Academic and special libraries, for example, may be more concerned with the subject and level of the first degree, than with the applicant's professional education in librarianship or information science. In the more traditional university libraries more weight is likely to be given to research degrees in, say, history or theology or literature, than to professional research in librarianship. The argument seems to be that assistant librarians must be able to communicate with academics in their own terms, and display some personal experience of the research process which is the *raison d'être* of the academic way of life. Another argument concerns the problem of status, which it is felt might be lowered if it is based on professional rather than academic attainments. This seems a curious argument when most professions have now built up an educational framework which reflects the academic framework at every level, from first degrees, to taught master's degrees, to research degrees at M.Phil. and Ph.D. level. It is unusual in these circumstances for a professional group to argue, as some academic librarians continue to do, that to improve one's prospects in the profession, it is important to work for a qualification in a different discipline, such as English literature or history.

The complexity of higher education in Britain, divided as it is into a public sector (polytechnics, institutes of higher education, and colleges) and a private sector (the universities), with the Open University as a third channel by which mature students can study for degrees, makes for a confused situation on the comparative worth of different kinds of degrees. CNAA degrees and Open University degrees had to fight hard for recognition during their early years, until it became known that their standards of validation, and their teaching and assessment methods were actually setting an example, in many respects, to the more traditional universities.

In professional education for librarians and information scientists the situation is perhaps just as confusing for many employers, who are confronted with a bewildering range of qualifications. There are first degrees in librarianship and information science, postgraduate diplomas or masters' degrees (which are only postgraduate in the chronological sense, since they are not a follow-up of the subject of the first degree). There are masters' degrees which are a follow-up of previous professional education, and so are more genuinely 'masters'' level, some people would argue. There are research degrees at M.Phil. and Ph.D. level awarded for theses based on research in librarianship. Some of the first degrees in librarianship have a much lower librarianship content than others, since they are joint honours degrees, where the students may spend half their time on another subject such as economics or languages. Some of the polytechnic degrees in librarianship have a higher content of 'fringe' subjects than others, so that they may spend considerable time and effort on sociology or languages, although being awarded a degree in librarianship. In other schools the 'fringe' subjects have been gradually integrated more closely with librarianship, so it has become possible to look on them as support subjects relevant to user studies, for example, rather than some kind of intellectual ballast needed to turn librarianship into a worthy degree subject.

For selectors to assess whether an applicant is suitably qualified for a job, then, means that they need a considerable knowledge of what has been happening in education for librarianship over the past decade. Although the various courses are all approved by the Library Association as a means whereby successful graduates are accepted onto the Register of Chartered Librarians (on completion of the appropriate period of supervised post-school practice), there is considerable diversification and emphases among the different library schools. Some examples of curriculum development where the pace of change has varied between schools are: teaching the management and technology of library automation; teaching communications skills; the integration of media skills into the course; and teaching library management at a level appropriate to the needs of the young professional.

Again, in teaching and assessment methods there is much diversity between schools, and selectors should be aware of the connections between the skills they are seeking and the educational experiences in these skills which their applicants have had, or not had.

For more senior appointments the whole area of continuing education is relevant, and there are many opportunities open to practising librarians, by which they may develop professionally and achieve formal qualifications or pursue interests informally. These were investigated by Jones[20] in 1976 and librarians' preferences listed. The most significant activities in the view of practising librarians for keeping up to date professionally were discussion with colleagues, being active at staff meetings, visiting other libraries, receiving in-service training, reading librarianship literature, attending conferences and workshops, taking part in working parties, and studying for further qualifications. Low down in librarians' preferences were giving papers at conferences, writing articles for publication, holding professional office, and secondment to other libraries.

In the appointment of young professionals to their first post, the selectors need also to be aware of the problems for young entrants to the profession in gaining work experience. Few libraries retain the pre-library school trainee schemes which were once so common, so it may be that the only work experience the applicant will have had will be a few weeks of field work during the librarianship course. Recognition of this problem has been one of the factors in the Library Association's decision to restructure the requirements for acceptance on the Register of Chartered Librarians from 1981. The library school leaver is required to complete one year of supervised professional work (monitored by qualified staff) before becoming a Licentiate (LLA). Another two years of approved service is required before the Associateship is awarded, so the ALA now demands three years of practice plus a written report.

This moves a great deal of the responsibility for work experience back into the practitioners' world away from the library schools, and increases the onus on personnel managers to provide the appropriate level of experience for young professionals.

General intelligence/innate abilities. Fraser and Rodger here diverge a little in what they argue selectors should consider in applicants. Rodger emphasizes rather more the ability to apply intelligence. How much intelligence is displayed by the applicant in his or her usual mode of working? To test this some library employers have devised practical problems or decision-making simulations for the applicants to tackle, in addition to having the traditional selection interview.

Fraser's interpretation of 'innate abilities' seems to be those rather indefinable qualities which stem from a person's education and experience, but go beyond these, to give 'a general quickness in the uptake' and 'special aptitudes'. It is generally agreed that western education systems reward academic achievement at the expense of other important skills, so it is useful for selectors to investigate the presence or absence of such other skills as communication skills, or aesthetic skills (for promotion and display, for example).

Rodger's category of 'special aptitudes' includes mechanical aptitude, manual dexterity, facility in written or verbal expression, facility with figures and creative talent in, say, designing or graphics.

Motivation. Fraser defines this as the way in which the individual applies his or her abilities in practical situations, and to what extent he or she achieves effective results. This is a complex area, and it is important to refer back to Chapter 2 on the relevance of motivation theories to library staffing. The importance of assessing applicants' motivation is inestimable, since staff frustration and ineffective results are likely when there is a mismatch between the post and the person. For instance, the kind of person who would be effective answering routine queries, or doing issue-desk work in contact with users, might well be someone whose motivation to work stems mainly from social needs, rather than what Maslow calls identity needs or self-actualisation needs. If the person appointed to this job was motivated rather by self-actualisation needs (who wanted to be stretched to the limit of their potential, and be faced with challenge, and responsibility) the results would almost certainly be disappointing.

Another example might be the person who is motivated mainly by security needs. The problems generally arise in this case when innovations take place, say in staffing structures, and the individual becomes a member of an area team, say, rather than working as a fairly isolated professional in a branch library where there was a secure niche and familiar routines. For the person motivated by identity needs and social needs the change would be a source of positive satisfaction, but for the staff member mainly concerned with security at work the change may lead to unease and withdrawal symptoms.

Adjustment. Fraser describes this as emotional stability, and is concerned with the amount of stress a person at work is capable of standing, particularly in interacting with other people (public or colleagues). As with motivation the important thing is to achieve some sort of match between the individual's needs and the specific job requirements. It is probably true to say that there are fewer places for people to 'hide' in libraries than there were in the more tranquil years up to the late 1960s. Libraries are larger, more bureaucratic because of their increasing complexity, and there have been determined efforts to manage them better, through the application of management ideas and techniques. Very often these include an objectives approach to running the library, which usually leads to changes in staff deployment, since the library plans to move to a more user-oriented stance, and traditionally staff were deployed in functional technical duties, rather than in service-oriented jobs. When staff are restructured, for example, into professional teams, there can be serious problems of adjustment for some staff. Those whose temperament finds it difficult to accept the new ways will devise evasive measures. Subject specialists have been known to seclude themselves in backroom offices, and to resent live readers 'intruding' upon their work with queries and an exchange of views. Team members in public libraries have similarly been observed to have problems in communicating professional ideas to their fellow members, and to revert to non-professional routine work when visiting service points, because of not knowing how to cope with their new role of planning projects and letting the non-professionals look after the routine.

If aware of these problems of adjustment, selectors can do their informed best at the recruitment stage to avert future difficulties by choosing the right people. For staff already on the establishment the problem becomes an appraisal and training question.

Interests. Rodger argues that the questions of interest to the manager compiling a personnel specification are: 'To what extent are a person's interests intellectual? or practical-constructional? physically active? social? artistic?'[21]

Application forms and curricula vitae invariably include a section on 'Interests'. This can cover both professional interests and leisure interests, which need not necessarily be entirely separate, though very often they are, for few categories of workers manage to achieve the consonance of interest between their work and their leisure that traditionally belongs to writers, musicians, professional sportsmen and academics. Rodger's view is that selectors should try to match up the demands of the job with the characteristics shown by the category of interests listed by the applicant, artistic, intellectual or other.

Circumstances. The personnel specification provides an opportunity to mention job requirements which may well be affected by a person's domestic circumstances. Is mobility an essential part of the job? Are the hours irregular, with evening and weekend duties? Are training opportunities going to occur that would mean the job-holder being free to get away at weekends or for two- or three-day courses midweek? Is the applicant prepared to move to be within reasonable travelling time of the library?

This is, since the *Sex Discrimination Act* of 1975, a rather tricky area for selectors to deal with, when interviews take place. It is important therefore that the personnel specification is carefully and clearly expressed, and that women applicants are treated with scrupulous fairness, which is generally interpreted as meaning they should not be excluded because of domestic circumstances, unless it can be shown that men too have been excluded for similar reasons.

Work assignments

1. Read through several times the following account of the work done by a subject specialist in engineering in a university library. Draw up a job description for the post, in as detailed a manner as possible, using the headings provided in this chapter.

2. Draw up a personnel specification for the same job, using your job description as the basis. Check that you have covered all or most of the points in Rodger's and Fraser's plans.

LIBRARY SUBJECT SPECIALISATION AT WORK
Charles Crossley, Engineering Librarian

The Subject Specialist Librarians at Bradford are a team concerned to ensure that the users of the Library, from Fresher to Professor, obtain access to information. The objectives of the service and the means of attaining them may be explicitly stated, but may also be perceived by observing the team in action during a fairly typical day.

9.00 a.m.

In the J. B. Priestley Library the Engineering Librarian is opening his mail. Among a mixed pile are requests from a lecturer to purchase a couple of new books and a batch of British Standards for Mechanical Engineering. He passes over to the Assistant Engineering Librarian three books obtained on approval, which have been returned from examination by Electrical Engineering lecturers. They want two and reject the third. The Assistant Engineering Librarian puts them to one side for the moment; she'll deal with them later. Right now she's pretty busy proof-reading the typescript pages of the current awareness periodical she edits – *ACE: Articles in Civil Engineering*. There are 950 items to check this month.

Next door, the Life Sciences Librarian has an early visit from a lecturer who is anxious about the effects of the periodicals cancellation exercise the Library has to conduct this month. This is going to take some time...

If anyone is looking for the Physical Sciences Librarians now is the time to catch them. One of them is just on his way to the Computing Laboratory – which is mercifully in the same building – to collect the output of the Nottingham-based computerized search system in chemistry and allied subject fields. The Computing Laboratory runs the tape which is supplied to us weekly, and the Assistant Physical Sciences Librarian will have to sub-divide the printout for distribution to various lecturers. The Physical Sciences Librarian is departing in the direction of the bookshelves upstairs, bearing a sheet of blue paper. This is a worksheet he will give to first-year Chemistry students, which will guide them around the Library on their first visit, and he will set them tasks requiring them to consult various reference works as they go. In a new library this is obviously going to need wholesale revision.

Meanwhile, over in Wardley House, the Social Sciences Librarian is working at his book selection. He has the whole of this week's British National Bibliography to wade through (700 items, any one of which may be a relevant book to add to stock). He must then turn his attention to the foreign language needs of the Library and scan *Novye Knigi* for new Russian works; this must be done without delay each week, because these books go out of print so quickly and are lost for ever. The Assistant Social Sciences Librarian comes in to ask about the format of a new self-help guide for students he is preparing, designed to assist readers to find their way through the literature of Applied Social Studies.

10.00 a.m.

If we hurry back to the J. B. Priestley Library again we shall be just in time to see the Engineering Librarian disappearing upstairs to a Seminar Room, where a group of third-year Mechanical Engineers are assembling for the last part of a six-hour course of information retrieval and handling. This morning they are to have a brief discussion on the problems of literature searching, followed by an explanation of the conventions of bibliographical citations. They will be given a post-instruction criterion test and – oh dear! – some practical work to be done in the Library and handed in next week.

The Life Sciences Librarian has turned his attention from periodicals, because another lecturer colleague has rung up with a request for statistics on the prevalence of helminth infections in the UK. The search is only just beginning, and we can leave him for a time with his lists of government publications and his search through *Index Medicus* and the rest. Hindsight will tell us that this is not going to be an easy one, and a few 'phone calls to outside sources are going to be necessary in the next day or so.

The Physical Sciences Librarian has returned from the Reading Room, has refreshed himself, and is now engaged in tearing up a Journal! This is an extra copy of the Physical Sciences edition of *Current Contents,* obtained specifically for the purpose of providing an alerting service on new periodical articles in their field to a number of staff in the Mathematics and Chemistry Schools. As he scans, he is bearing in mind the need to watch out for items which would usefully serve as topics for the individual course-work assignments he sets for postgraduate students in Archaeological Sciences. Ah! Here's one: the implications of the Mossbauer Effect for archaeological investigations – this will do admirably. The students will have to identify and find relevant papers and evaluate them.

The Social Sciences Librarian has hurried upstairs in Wardley House to attend a discussion with Modern Languages staff about an afternoon seminar for their second-year students, designed to offer guidance on dissertation topics: how to select them, how to research them, how to exploit library resources, how to compile a bibliography, and how to present the dissertation. It is sheer coincidence that the Engineering Librarian, who has

133

been asked to contribute to the teaching, is at that very moment engaged in teaching the subject elsewhere.

11.00 a.m.

At the end of his hour with the engineering students, one of them takes up his offer to seek help at any time and buttonholes him. How can he trace details of a company report on automobile gears? A few minutes' talk elicits the information that this is almost certainly a confidential report, prepared for internal use only and therefore not listed in, and not traceable through, the published guides. A quick check in the relevant sources demonstrates the truth of this, and the student realizes that he will have to make his own private approach to friends outside the University if he is to get anywhere on this one.

The Physical Sciences Librarian is returning to his office. He had just assisted a student with the microfiche reading equipment, and was about to turn his mind to book selection and scan a dealer's catalogue. On his way however, he had been waylaid by another reader who wanted guidance on the complexities of the catalogue. And now for that book list... But no! 'Where do I get change for the photocopier? 'Where are the books on physical chemistry?' Oh well, the Physical Sciences Librarian *is* expected to know these things. From little acorns... Back to the office. That book list has come from a well-known second-hand dealer. It's the very thing for helping to build up the stock in archaeology. We have a long way to go yet in this subject.

One of the cataloguers has just caught the Life Sciences Librarian as he scans the abstracts journals for those helminth infection statistics. Whereabouts should this new book on the toxicology of insecticides be classified? If that one was straightforward how about this one on prostaglandins?

12 noon

The Engineering Librarian has been over to the Chemical Engineering Building to discuss the timing and content of the four-hour Sources of Information course given to first-year students. Last year their course work showed insufficient use of up-to-date statistical sources for production and consumption data for various chemicals. This needs attention. He makes a mental note to call on the specialized know-how of the Management Librarian up at Emm Lane. As he returns to his office he finds one of the Electrical Engineering students who graduated last Summer waiting to see him. He has come across to Bradford to pass on his comments about the tape/slide guide to literature searching in electrical engineering which the Engineering Librarian had sent him for examination. Contacts with past students and help of this kind are especially gratifying.

The Assistant Engineering Librarian has completed her proof-reading, and is now assembling entries for a typed list of newly acquired books in Civil

134

Engineering subjects. This will be typed and duplicated and distributed within a few days – always provided the typist is not already doing a similar list for the Life Sciences Librarian.

He, at this moment, is talking to a lecturer from Pharmacy who wants a Medlars literature search done – another computer-based information search – this time in the medical field. Guidance is needed about the formulation of the search profile, by which the stored literature is accessed.

How was the Catholic vote split-up in the Netherlands in the 1960s? The lecturer who is seeking the answer in the Social Sciences Library at this moment is hurrying off to Leeds in a few minutes to fulfil a radio interview engagement. The Social Sciences Librarian must get his skates on! When that's done he can get lunch. There's not much time left, because he has a School Meeting to attend at 2.15 p.m.

2.00 p.m.
The Life Sciences Librarian spends a fair portion of the afternoon preparing the contents page bulletins for Pharmacy and Biological Sciences staffs. There are ten subject areas to provide for and the service is much appreciated. But when you have only one pair of hands...! The Engineering Librarian makes time to go upstairs to continue listing the subjects which will be printed on shelf guides to make the book stock in his area easier to use. It's no use having a large collection of books unless the readers can find their way through it.

In Wardley House, the Assistant Social Sciences Librarian is examining the shelves for material to include in a new holdings list of works on Ethnic and Linguistic Geography. Lists such as these are valued because they are linked to a course syllabus, and bring together for the student the books and pamphlets which the classified scheme in the Library unavoidably scatters.

The afternoon mail brings the Engineering Librarian a copy of a book, written by colleagues elsewhere in the University, to which he has contributed a chapter. After publishing delays this is a welcome sight.

The Social Sciences Librarian has returned from his School Meeting to find a colleague from Yugoslav Studies in the Library, and they talk of the exchange agreement whereby we obtain much-needed books and other publications from that country. The mutual benefits from such a scheme provides the only means whereby many publications are easily obtainable in both countries. Added to material in other languages on Yugoslavia they constitute rich resources. The Social Sciences Librarian will use these more and more in the preparation of his book on the bibliographical resources of that country.

The Physical Sciences Librarian found a note on his desk from a lecturer in Textiles. Could he arrange to introduce a research student to the Library and have a chat with him about his research topic and show him how to do a literature search – he knows nothing about abstracts and bibliographies? Several unsuccessful attempts to make telephone contact later, the arrangements are made.

The end of a day for Subject Specialist Librarians. Been a messy day, thinks one, on his way out. Must tackle that periodicals cancellation problem tomorrow, promises another. Why can't it always be as quiet as this? I could settle down to some uninterrupted work now, muses a third, while another packs a few professional journals into his case – perhaps I'll find time to read them tonight, he thinks.

Recruitment and selection of staff

Assuming the personnel specification effectively lists the attributes required of a person for a particular post then the task of any selector is to discover to what extent these attributes are present.

Sources of information

It is useful to have a total view of the information sources available because there is a tendency to think so much of one source, such as the formal interview, as to make insufficient use of others. Figure 5.1 indicates the main sources used in selection.

FIGURE 5.1. THE MAIN INFORMATION SOURCES USED IN SELECTION

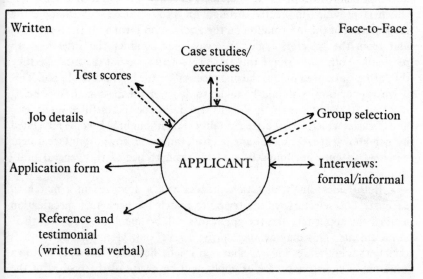

The diagram helps to illustrate a number of ideas that are central to a discussion of selection. As important as any is the idea that information is being obtained throughout the process by both selectors and applicants. Too often selectors will perceive the exercise as one-way only and forget that the

137

applicant is all the time finding out about the post and the library. This is very important not only because the applicant may pick up quite erroneous ideas about the job but also significant information is likely to be missed due to the haphazard nature of the exercise. Effective management demands systematic planning and so one should be thinking from the very beginning about the information to give the applicant throughout the selection process as well as how to obtain information about the applicant.

The diagram also suggests that information is communicated in two main forms: written and face-to-face. The written information can be read and re-read at leisure and compared. On the one hand the applicant can compare job details for several libraries while the selectors can compare the written applications, references, test scores, etc. of all those applying for the post. Case studies and exercises may be completed in written form or can be carried out orally. Group selection methods and the interview are oral exercises and, although written summaries and assessments might be made, the applicants and selectors acquire their information by listening and observing.

In selection two sorts of information are obtained. The most obvious is that which is obtained directly from the applicant, for example the actual information which is given by an applicant in response to a question in an interview or on an application form; and from the selectors' side, the information provided in the job details. The other sort of information is that which is provided indirectly through the process itself, for example the presentation of the information on the application form or at the interview; and from the selectors' side, the way they conduct the interview. In particular both 'sides' have to be aware whether or not the message they think they have presented is the one received by the intended audience. This is why opportunities should be taken to discover the message that is being received. At the very least, applicants who fail to be successful at interviews and libraries which do not attract quality recruits ought to become interested in such knowledge. It can be quite painful, but so can any hospital treatment designed to cure an illness beyond the competence of the general practitioner.

Both 'sides' in the selection process will be involved in a matching exercise. The selectors will be trying to match the personnel specification against the applicants and the applicants will be matching the job to their requirements. This may or may not be carried out systematically but it is certain that both sides will have built up a rich, 'holistic' picture of their own situation. The selectors, for example, will be aware of the history of the library's achievements, the management style of the library, and the various individuals with whom the successful applicant will be working. The applicants will be aware of their own domestic situations and their likes and dislikes concerning jobs and people. The richer pictures may contain elements which neither side particularly wants to present to the other.

The selectors and applicants also have to beware of treating the present situation as an unchanging one. Both need to look to the future especially when the economic circumstances are such that mobility of staff is restricted and a mistake made is hard to rectify. The library must think very carefully about predictable future developments and the likely changes in the jobs of successful applicants. That is why selection needs to be seen as something more than describing existing posts and filling them.

Stages in the selection of staff

1. *Advertising*

There are a number of standard advertising outlets used by librarians for the recruitment of staff. Certain constraints may be laid down by the parent body such as the advertising of a post internally as a first step or the use of particular publications such as local newspapers. It is unlikely that a search for new outlets will be worth the effort since librarians seeking posts will regularly peruse familar sources. In Britain such sources include:

The Times Literary Supplement
The Times Higher Education Supplement
The Library Association Record Vacancies Supplement
The Guardian
The Daily Telegraph

Local newspapers are frequently used for non-professional posts and special librarians may use Aslib's staff appointments register.

The first 'message' about the library is passed to the potential applicants by the advertisement and therefore it deserves a great deal more thought than it is often given. The typical page advertising library posts displays a poverty of imagination that some would think characteristic of the profession as a whole. The objective of the advertisement is to attract those potential applicants whom the library would wish to attract and to discourage those who would be unlikely to make a success of the job. The advertisement needs to be drafted with that objective in mind and to help to achieve it the librarian needs to be aware of the sort of information the potential applicant would like to have. In our experience library advertisements make very little use of the information in the personnel specification. Perhaps the librarian does not want to give too much away but we feel that it should contain something about the qualities required to perform the job successfully and fit in with the preferred style of management. There are constraints of space and money but existing space could be better utilized. Consider the two advertisements in Figure 5.2 bearing in mind the points which have been made.

FIGURE 5.2. TWO TYPICAL ADVERTISEMENTS

County Library

Local Government Library and Information Service

Assistant Librarian

This challenging post offers a first rate opportunity for an enthusiastic, chartered Librarian to organize and run the Local Government Information Service in the County.

Reporting directly to the Assistant County Librarian (Reference & Information) the successful candidate will be expected to build on and develop the current service and to meet demands for extending it where possible. The holder of this post will work with the minimum of supervision in a job that calls for a high degree of personal initiative and the ability to communicate at all levels.

The successful candidate is likely to be a chartered librarian who is, in addition, a graduate with four to five years' post-charter experience, probably in reference, technical or college librarianship.

The post is within the Librarian's Career Grade AP3-5 (£5652-£7878). Suitably qualified candidates would be appointed within grade AP5.

Further details and application forms from County Library, County Hall
Closing Date: **29th February 1982**

ASSISTANT LENDING LIBRARIAN

Post N157

Librarians Scale £5064 to £6333

(minimum £5652 for Chartered Librarians)

Applications are invited from qualified librarians for this post at Central Library.

Application forms and further details available from the Assistant County Librarian, Central Library, to whom completed forms must be returned by 11 March 1982.

It is necessary to appreciate that, unlike other stages of the selection process, advertising is carried out in public and therefore has an important public relations dimension as it gives the library an opportunity of presenting its image to the profession and beyond. Many librarians make a habit of reading through advertisements whether they are looking for a post or not and their attention can be held by the information and design of a carefully thought-out advertisement.

Library posts can be publicized in other ways particularly through the use of agencies set up to provide employment opportunities. When unemployment is high local and central government tend to encourage and support such agencies. In Britain the Manpower Services Commission operates programmes to help young people looking for jobs and there is a specialized service for professional people called Professional and Executive Recruitment.

When a library wants to fill a vacancy quickly library schools can be contacted directly to find suitable candidates who merit support by their schools. In some cases the library may have employed a person as a trainee or as a fieldwork student and systematic appraisal records can be used to suggest persons who would be fairly certain to prove a success in the appointment.

The selection process presents an opportunity to involve staff as a staff development activity, as a means of maintaining morale, and in order to ensure a good choice is made by those who know most about the job and with whom the person appointed will be working closely. Guidelines from the City of London Polytechnic illustrate these objectives (see Figure 5.3).

2. Short-listing

When a number of people apply for a post it is normal to draw up a list of those whom the selectors consider strong contenders. As travel and subsistence costs increase it is likely that shortlists will become smaller and, with prospects for promotion generally diminishing, libraries are likely to look more favourably upon internal candidates. It is difficult sometimes to decide which internal candidates to short-list because a failure to make the list can easily be interpreted as a lack of belief in their abilities and future prospects.

The personnel specification should act as the basis for the short-list with the application forms, references and testimonials being measured against it for clues which either qualify or disqualify the applicants for further consideration. Application forms should therefore be designed to facilitate this analysis although as members of larger organizations libraries are frequently obliged to use less helpful forms. A useful discussion is provided

FIGURE 5.3. AN EXAMPLE OF SELECTION PROCESS GUIDELINES

CITY OF LONDON POLYTECHNIC LIBRARY AND LEARNING RESOURCES SERVICE
INTERVIEWS: Proposed guidelines for the involvement of library staff with prospective candidates.

POST	SUGGESTED PANEL	STAFF TO MEET IN ADDITION:		
		1. Essential	2. Desirable	3. Achieved by pre or post interview visit to:
Chief Librarian	Directorate including Co-ordinator of LLRS	Deputy, All Grade 1s, Staff Development Librarian	As many other staff as possible e.g. Site Librarians, Library Assistant representatives	All sites and Technical Services
Deputy Chief Librarian	Directorate, Chief Librarian	All Grade 1s, Staff Development Librarian		
Technical Services Librarian	Chief, Deputy, Readers' Services Librarian, Staff Development Librarian	Other Grade 1s, Chief Cataloguer, Acquisitions Librarian, Serials Librarian	Assistant Librarians (Cataloguing) TS Library Assistants, Site Librarian, Moorgate	Technical Services, CA Site, BS Site
Readers' Services Librarian	Chief, Deputy, Technical Services Librarian, Staff Development Librarian	Other Grade 1s, Site Librarians	Subject Librarians, Library Assistants (Services)	CA and BS Sites + one smaller site, Technical Services
Archives and Special Collections Librarian	Chief, Deputy, Readers' Services Librarian/Technical Services, Staff Development Librarian	Other Grade 1s, Fawcett Library Staff	Site Librarian, Calcutta House	Fawcett Library, CA Site

by Edwards[1] which includes a summary of an Industrial Society survey of fifty application forms. However, some of the questions which are frequently asked, according to the survey, would not pass muster with bodies aiming to eliminate discrimination from employment. In Britain the Equal Opportunities Commission has produced guidelines which include the elimination of detailed questions on marital status, children or other dependants since they could be construed as indicating a bias against married women.[2]

A certain amount of doubt exists concerning the value of written references. In a small profession like librarianship deliberately dishonest references are unlikely although it is common for reference writers to highlight strengths rather than weaknesses and this tendency could increase as staff are allowed access to their own personal files, though the evidence from staff appraisal is that this is not true in the long term.[3] Naturally the personnel management in the library needs to be such that an accurate reference is possible. An effective staff appraisal system will yield helpful information and a participative style ought to ensure that those who know most about the person have a hand in writing the reference. A writer of references needs to be asked about the knowledge, abilities, skills and personal qualities that are considered important for the particular job. This is precisely what the personnel specification aims to do and if one is not compiled it makes the job of the reference writer more difficult. Even those who compile personnel specifications do not always use them when obtaining references.

It is common practice to ask for two references and to insist that one is from the applicant's current employer if there is one. In many cases the current employer will be a librarian and it is reasonable to assume that opinion on performance in a job, which has similarities with the one for which the person is applying, is more helpful than a reference from a personal acquaintance. Some potential applicants will be unhappy about revealing their interests in another job to their current employer, but on the other hand it is not unknown for employers to look more favourably on those seeking employment elsewhere if they are valuable members of staff.

Since doubt does exist about the value of written references, selectors may choose to obtain verbal references in addition or instead. A telephone conversation with a professional colleague can be quite revealing especially as no permanent record is kept. In fact, it is our experience that selectors ask the very questions and provide the very information which they fail to provide when seeking written references.

Testimonials are written without a particular job in mind for use by the person about whom it is written whenever an appropriate occasion arises. They are only of minor value and are rarely asked for by selectors though they may be provided by applicants as additional evidence.

When vacancies become scarcer and the number of applicants is very large selectors tend to search more assiduously for disqualifying data and sometimes this will represent a further refinement of the original specification. For example a narrower age range may be decided upon and any uncertainties about domestic problems or illnesses will be more likely to cause an applicant to be rejected.

3. *Informal interviews*

Surveys of English public and academic library selection practices other than the traditional interview were carried out in 1978[4] and 1979 and showed that the most popular method was the informal interview. There is plenty of evidence that where this is practised the informal interview can be as important as the formal one. In a few cases the informal one is used for short-listing professional posts. At Birmingham Polytechnic, for instance, at Principal Lecturer level 'a shortlist is drawn up and each candidate invited separately to the Polytechnic. They meet the Polytechnic Librarian and other senior colleagues, see appropriate parts of the library operation and visit as many Polytechnic sites as possible. After this a shortlist for formal interviews is drawn up.' In most cases informal tours and discussions will take place on the same day as the formal interviews and may well include lunch. A number of libraries have found it appropriate for a member of staff on the same grade as the vacancy to accompany the applicants on the tour and in one case the outgoing member is specifically mentioned. One respondent to the public library survey neatly summarized the advantages of the informal interview as he saw them: '(a) The candidates get the "low down" on the post. (b) The present postholder gives his/her opinion on the candidate's suitability. (c) An opportunity to test the "chemistry" between the candidates and some of the people with whom they will work.' These advantages can be seen as counteracting two major criticisms of the traditional formal interview: it fails sufficiently to simulate the situations in which successful applicants would find themselves after appointment, and it does not provide the applicant with enough information about the job.

For some people informal discussions are a welcome and relaxing contrast to the formal interview while for others, as one respondent remarked, 'a too detailed preamble to the interview can cause confusion or make candidates ill-at-ease in interview'. There is no indication that any systematic method of assessment is used for informal interviews although one may be adopted for the formal interview. If the informal sessions are to be used in making the final decisions then there has to be some form of feedback to decision makers by those involved. In most public services the decision will be given on the same day as the final assessment is made so communication has to take place fairly quickly. In the private sector it is common for a longer period of time to elapse between the interview and the final decision.

4. *Formal interviews*

The favourite, and in many cases the only, face-to-face method used in selection is the formal interview. In librarianship the number of interviewers can range from one to quite a large number. The largest numbers will often be members of a committee responsible for the library.

Once again the starting point should be the personnel specification because this spells out what the interviewers should be searching for. The use of an interview form which is directly related to to the specification helps to ensure that the interview keeps on relevant lines. A form which has been used by Liverpool Polytechnic is a good example (see Figure 5.4).

As far as possible interviewers should want accurate information to be communicated to both 'sides' directly through the information given and indirectly through the process itself and factors that inhibit should be minimized in favour of those that facilitate the flow of relevant information. A helpful framework is provided by R. L. Gorden.[5]

Attention needs to be paid to:

(a) *The environment of the interview.* The place in which it is held will communicate a whole range of information. Interruptions and outside noise should be avoided, comfortable seats should be provided at the same level for interviewers and interviewee and there should be no physical barriers such as desks and tables between them. The interviewee should be considered the most important person in the library on that day.

(b) *The pattern of the interview.* Interviews often follow established lines and, if these norms are adhered to, interviewees are likely to be more relaxed especially when they become used to the experience. In fact 'it can be very useful for the interviewer to go and introduce himself to the candidate in the waiting-room, so that contact is made quickly, unexpectedly, and on neutral territory and the rapport stage of the interview when it begins later is made easier'.[6] With similar intention, it is usual to begin the interview gently and lead up to more difficult questions and allow candidates to ask questions of their own at the end. A minority believe in making the interview a much more stressful experience in order, perhaps, to simulate the stresses in the job. We are inclined to agree with Higham[7] that stress interviews are 'anathema to those who take interviews seriously. It is sometimes assumed that by subjecting a candidate to stress – such as rudeness and hostility – in an interview you can somehow get an indication of how he will stand up to stress in the job. There is, of course, no evidence to support this view: the two situations are entirely different, and the causes of stress on the job include many other frustrations besides those in a superior position being deliberately discourteous.'

Interviewers should get together well before the interviews and plan the progress they want to make. This should not mean that the interview will not

FIGURE 5.4. AN EXAMPLE OF AN INTERVIEW FORM

LIVERPOOL POLYTECHNIC LIBRARY SERVICE
(Based on 7-point plan of National Institute of Industrial Psychology)

Interview report on _____ DoB _____ Age _____

1. **PHYSICAL MAKE-UP**
   defects of health or physique   A B C D E
   hearing   A B C D E
   speech   A B C D E

2. **ATTAINMENTS** (and previous experience)
   type of education (school and later):
   educational level reached   A B C D E

3. **GENERAL INTELLIGENCE**
   new situations capacity to learn   A B C D E
   level ordinarily displayed   A B C D E

4. **SPECIAL APTITUDES**
   mechanical aptitude   A B C D E
   manual dexterity   A B C D E
   facility in use of words   A B C D E
   facility in use of figures   A B C D E
   talent for drawing   A B C D E
   talent for music   A B C D E

5. **INTERESTS**
   intellectual   A B C D E
   practical-constructional   A B C D E
   physically-active   A B C D E
   social   A B C D E
   artistic   A B C D E

6. **DISPOSITION**
   how acceptable (will he/she
   adjust to the job?)   A B C D E
   how influential (will he/she
   change the job?)   A B C D E
   how steady and dependable   A B C D E
   how self-reliant (self-starter?)   A B C D E

7. **CIRCUMSTANCES**
   domestic circumstances (e.g.
   distance to travel, commitment)
   family occupations:

   ADDITIONAL REMARKS:

FIGURE 5.5. EXAMPLES OF
INTERVIEW QUESTIONS

Some of the following questions have been framed in order to test attitude or disposition, that is *favourable, hostile, indifferent*; this can indicate such qualities as *leadership, acceptability, diplomacy, stability* and *self reliance*. Most questions have however been devised to test *technical library knowledge*, with the expectation that a systematic reply or otherwise will give an indication of an *ordered or logical intelligence*.

QUESTIONS FOR INTERVIEWING QUALIFIED LIBRARY STAFF

2. Q. *How do you think media selection should be conducted?*

    A. (a) By *consultation* at Boards, Committees (early warning of new courses), Teaching Staff, Students, Library, Admin. and Research staff.

        (b) By *collection and study of Bibliography of literature in all subjects* covered by the Polytechnic and important fringe areas.

        (c) By collection and study of *Bibliography of Literature of Education Careers particularly HE. and ET.*

        (d) By collection and study of *Bibliography of literature of information and Library Science.*

        (e) Examination of all records particularly inter-library loans and circulation, to test coverage and effectiveness.

        (f) Use of *subject experts on library staff* if available.

3. Q. *What is your attitude to non-print media?*

    A. (a) As another important *channel of communication* it must be *acquired and documented* as required by the College teaching programme.

        (b) The theoretical method which the use of educational technology implies, namely data collection, *analysis, design and feedback* of programmes, can also *usefully be applied to library instruction* programmes.

        (c) In view of the central position and large commitment to software and hardware, an academic library would seem to be a useful centre to observe and *evaluate teaching programmes.*

move spontaneously but it should ensure that it progresses in a logical manner and covers all key points.

(c) *Questioning*. Obviously the questions should not be unnecessarily complicated or vague. Interviewers may want to use this form of questioning in a deliberate way to test candidates but must always remember they are communicating their own vagueness to candidates. As far as possible the wording of the questions should be decided in advance to ensure that the question is an effective vehicle for discovering whether items in the personnel specification are present or not. An interesting list of interview questions for different grades of staff has been compiled by the library of the Polytechnic of the South Bank, London and an extract is shown in Figure 5.5. 'Closed' questions, which require no more than yes or no answers, should be avoided because, from the selectors' point of view, the object is to hear what the candidate has to say and therefore to ask questions which invite the candidate to do this.

Richard Frear,[7] who has written a comprehensive work on interviewing, says that when interviewers are thoroughly trained in his methods they do only fifteen to twenty per cent of the talking. He suggests a number of ways of asking open or exploratory questions including the use of 'laundry-lists' – listing a number of possible responses and giving a choice to the interviewee. This method can help particularly where an interviewee is having difficulty with a question which requires considerable analysis or in following up a 'clue' provided in previous questioning. For example the interviewer may want to discover a person's strengths and weaknesses by saying, 'Some librarians like working with readers best, others like working with books and others like classifying and cataloguing. What gives you most satisfaction?' Another way is to to offer two responses that are more or less opposites and to ask which view is held by the interviewee. For example, 'In your last post did you publicize the library as much as you would have liked or, on hindsight, would it have been better to have spent more time on it?'

The opportunity should often be taken to probe by following up general questions with a request for more detail by the use of such probes as, 'Tell me more about . . .' and 'Why does that appeal to you?' However, interviewers have to be beware of 'grilling' the applicants, which could cause them not to respond freely.

(d) *Listening and responding*. Selection interviews are rarely tape-recorded so the only chance to hear what is said is at the interview itself. Careful listening is very important because it also indicates the interviewers' interest in the candidate. Salient points should be noted as soon as possible although it is difficult to make notes without appearing not to be listening. In addition interviewees can be disturbed if notes appear to be taken when information of a highly personal or derogatory nature is imparted. Frear[9] sensibly recommends that interviewers wait until favourable information is given before writing unfavourable information previously given. What candidates fail to say is as important as what they do say. Interviewers should be careful to listen to, and if necessary wait for, all answers and not give a 'halo' to those candidates who start well or have certain outstanding qualities. Nor should one or two early mistakes disqualify a candidate for the rest of the interview. It is well known that interviewers often make decisions after only a short time in the interview.

The response that is made to answers is known to influence interviewees. The interviewer can control the pace of the interview and, through indicating approval or disapproval or responses, affect the course of the interview. At worst this can cause interviewees to withhold information and try to please the interviewers by telling them what they believe the interviewers would like to hear.

Although the primary interest will be on what is said, non-verbal cues will be playing a significant part and the good interviewer will be aware of them. In particular facial expression and body movement are important especially where they conflict with what is being said. There are some difficulties in applying kinesic analysis to selection interviewing because interviewees are often nervous and betray the nervousness under stress. On their part interviewers can ease the stress on the interviewee by responding facially to information given. It is well known that the raising of eyebrows and smiling helps to indicate interest and friendliness.

In spite of its popularity the traditional interview has often been criticized because of its artificial nature and its bias in favour of those who 'interview well' but may not be good at the job. Selectors have, therefore, to beware of ignoring the written evidence when coming to their conclusion. A number of librarians have been sufficiently dissatisfied as to devise additional methods which simulate more closely the actual work which the successful applicant will have to perform.

5. Group selection

This method is most applicable when testing what Fraser refers to as 'impact on others'[10] – the ability to get on with others, influence them, and display leadership qualities. The simplest form is to give the group of candidates a topic to discuss and then to observe them. This is practised by Coventry Public Libraries: 'topics given are usually items of current interest in the profession, preferably with a contentious element e.g. charging for loans, the relevance of library pressure groups etc. The topic is introduced and the discussion is then largely unstructured, the "chairman" deliberately taking a very passive role to allow the group to act, interact in an unstructured way.'

A second form is that of the case study or command exercise in which candidates take the chair in turn and outline their solutions to a problem, which will have been given to them some time before, and defend it before the other candidates. Readers will be aware that the War Office Selection Boards take this a stage further and require candidates to lead others through a practical difficulty such as crossing a stream.

Each of these group exercises can be done in written form by individual candidates, can be carried out with the selection panel or with the other candidates or, most realistically of all, they can be performed with the staff with whom the successful candidate will be working and the case studies can simulate actual problems encountered in the post for which they have applied. Here are a few examples of short exercises used by public libraries which could be either presented in written form or discussed with various groups.

For a medical librarian:
1. Prepare a written report – length at your discretion – justifying starting a current awareness service in a medical library context.
2. Prepare, in note form, a briefing to a senior member of the library staff on the current controversy over the place of the librarian in the medical team – the 'clinical librarian'.
3. Prepare a verbal presentation, as to a medical library management committee, on the value of MEDLARS to a postgraduate medical library with comments on on-line access.

For a team librarian:
You have been appointed Librarian within a Team in the County of Exshire consisting of four Librarians and a Leader. Prepare a schedule for a programme of induction and training for yourself to cover the first month of your taking up the appointment. Set out the programme in order of priority giving reasons for your choice of order.

A variation on the case study, reported by one public library in the survey, is the in-tray exercise:
Candidates are given an envelope containing 12–15 'situations' and are asked, immediately prior to the interview, to spend about 15–20 minutes putting these into priority order, making notes on any special points to watch etc. They then bring their answers into the formal interview with them, and are asked to go through their order of priority and to justify their placings, making any special observations etc. (the interviewers adopt a passive role in this).

Assessment of work in groups presents problems but one possibility is to draw on Rackham and Morgan's work in behaviour analysis.[11] A brief description of this and other methods is given by Jordan.[12]

6. *Tests*

One approach to staff selection puts the emphasis, as we have, on careful description of jobs and personnel specifications, another approach puts its faith in the development of more sophisticated and dependable tests:

> There are those who hold the view that subjective methods of assessing human beings will never prove to be adequately reliable and valid and who therefore turn to objective methods such as personality tests and questionnaires, objectively marked biographical questionnaires, interest questionnaires or other devices, in the hope of improving validities.[13]

If tests are to work really well, we should be able to measure how far candidates possess the various attributes required by the personnel specification and, like other methods, they should be good predictors of performance in jobs. This predictive validity is especially important of tests because there is so much opposition to them. While it is normally not difficult with most methods for candidates to appreciate what the selectors are trying to do (its 'face validity'), some tests appear at first acquaintance not to be related to the job for which the candidate is being tested. For example a numerical test may be used to measure intelligence but if the job involves very little number work there will be some suspicion about the validity of the test.

The user of tests needs to have confidence in the reliability of the test; that is that testees will perform in much the same way whenever they are tested. Sneath[14] says that reliability coefficients of .85 to .95 would be expected of well-constructed aptitude tests.

It is often recommended that training in the administration of tests is given before making use of them and several organizations have run courses planned according to a series of guidelines drawn up by the British Psychological Society and listed in Appendix 1 of Miller.[15] Many tests are not generally available but their use is controlled by such bodies as the Independent Assessment and Research Centre Ltd and the National Foundation for Educational Research. The main organizations are listed by Sneath,[16] and Buros[17] should be consulted for tests which are available and expert critiques of them.

The surveys of English academic and public libraries[17] showed that tests were rarely used. Two public libraries and three polytechnic libraries used tests for screening non-professionals. One library used tests to choose assistants who would produce computer input for the library catalogue. They were selected in co-operation with the Careers Advisory Service by a test of spatial ability and intelligence. Similarly, Birmingham Polytechnic used an aptitude test in selecting a team to undertake recataloguing: 'The heavy reliance on ISBN's for retrieving diagnostics suggested that any uneasiness with numerical sequences would be a disadvantage. Accordingly a small test was devised based on arranging ISBN-type numbers in correct sequence. Specimens of handwriting were also requested because of the importance of legibility on data sheets.

All the other examples are of short tests of abilities required in the assistants' work such as putting books in order, putting a list of names on cards in order, sorting catalogue cards into classification order, writing tickets and doing mental arithmetic with fines and giving change. Professional cataloguers at Liverpool Polytechnic are asked to classify a number of book titles using the Dewey Decimal Classification.

The effective performance of many jobs is certainly dependent on the employees' possessing a number of aptitudes but it is difficult to be precise about them because they can develop with training, experience and achievement.

Kingston[19] shows only 8 per cent of companies using intelligence tests regularly, and 33 per cent using them regularly or sometimes. Twenty-three per cent of companies make use of some intelligence tests, the most popular being NIIP's Group Test 70 and Group Test 90A, and NFER's AH4, Raven's progressive matrices and the Watson-Glaser Critical Thinking appraisal. NFER's AH5 and AH6 were most used in the Sneath survey. Intelligence is a difficult concept and tests are frequently criticized for their lack of face validity and for their cultural bias. The manager is also unsure whether test results will enable performance on the job to be predicted although they may indicate potential. All these criticisms can also be levelled at tests of creativity. Many personnel specifications for posts in libraries will contain items associated with the concept of creativity. J. P. Guildford[20] refers to five different factors associated with creativity: sensitivity to problems; fluency of ideas; flexibility; originality; and redefinition of situations. The tests which have been devised read like party games or brainstorming sessions. For example, in the AC Test of Creative Ability, questions pose a problem or an assumption to be made and the individual is asked to create solutions and possibilities. For example, assuming the statement to be true, give as many reasons or explanations as you can to explain the truth of the statement, 'April is the month of the most accidents of all kinds in the US.' This is scored for quantity (counting), uniqueness (statistical frequency) and quality or applicability (determined by experts).

If intelligence, creativity and aptitude tests seek to answer the question, 'Can he do it?', tests of interests and motivation try to discover whether he will do it. These tests seek to discover a person's interests and the amount of energy that person is prepared to devote to them. The Allport-Vernon-Lindzey Study of Values, for example, is designed to show the relative importance of six interests or motives: the theoretical , economic, aesthetic, social, political and religious.

Personality tests were originally designed as diagnostic aids in clinical and psychiatric medicine and are probably the most controversial of all. The majority are self-report, asking questions for the candidates to describe themselves in some way and this is related to scores for some known group. The best-known personality test is Cattell's 16 PF. The scores in this test are computed from the analysis of answers to around two hundred questions and personality is measured on a ten-point scale for each of the sixteen personality factors. Here are some of them:

Low score description	High score description
Reserved	Outgoing
Less intelligent	More intelligent
Humble	Assertive
Shy	Venturesome
Tough-minded	Tender-minded
Trusting	Suspicious
Self-assured	Apprehensive
Group-dependent	Self-sufficient
Relaxed	Tense

We do often refer to 'personality' in everyday speech but it is difficult to pin down its meaning in any precise way. Perhaps Kluckhohn's description[21] is the most apt – in some ways human beings are like all others, in some ways like some others and in some respects like no others. In the past personality was viewed as a characteristic mode which a person consistently chose to deal with the world – 'same old Bill' – but more recently it has been recognized that responses can change with experience and the way people behave will vary with the different situations in which they find themselves. The selector has to try to predict how a person will behave in the future and it has to be said that personality tests are of dubious value, especially those which are not satisfied with analysing external behaviour but wish to explore the values and psychological states which lie beneath through projective tests. Most of these are visual and subjects are asked to explain pictures which are usually ambiguous. Probably the best-known of these is the Rorschach Ink-blot Test. Kline,[22] a strong critic of the use of personality tests in employment selection, asserts that responses to projective tests 'are believed to show the deepest levels of personality. However, there is, in fact little firm objective evidence that projective tests can reveal anything of the sort. Indeed, there is often little agreement between examiners or the same examiner on different occasions.'

Another type of personality test is the objective personality test which can take any task which discriminates between one person and another and draw inferences from the scores e.g. handwriting, fidgeting, humour by asking subjects to rate jokes. At the moment we are inclined to support Kline in his objections:

> They are of unproven validity and to use them for selection purposes is unlikely to be useful. Secondly, and more important, I object to their covert and deceitful nature. Different personal qualities are obviously valuable in different occupations. With the old projective and psychometric tests, however, it was obvious, usually, what the test was about. Thus, if an applicant did not choose to reveal himself, he need not. With the objective test there is no such freedom.[23]

Work assignments

1. Using the personnel specification you drew up for a subject specialist in engineering (see Chapter 4), or any other suitable specification, take each item and describe how you would discover whether or not it was possessed by a candidate.

Note. It is best to use the list of methods provided in this chapter as a checklist and if the formal interview is to be used write out the actual wording of the question.

2. Role-play an interview and analyse it using the questions below. If a group is being trained questions can be divided up amongst it. It is more flexible to use a video-tape which can be re-run to emphasize points. An excellent one has been produced by the Polytechnic of North London.

(a) Observe the *non-verbal behaviours* especially whether they tell us anything about the suitability of the candidate and the performance of the interviewers. Are there any non-verbals which seem to contradict what was said? How facilitative are the *surroundings*?

(b) Score each question on a five-point scale for *relevance* to the particular job. (Score high for high relevance and add up the score at the end.)

(c) Collect evidence on:

Inhibitors. How far the interviewee appears to tell the interviewers what it is thought will please them and how far the interviewers control the pace and 'lead on' the interviewee.

Facilitators. How easily is the interview handled? Is the pattern appropriate? Do the interviewers listen well and ask non-rhetorical questions?

5. How effective is the interview in meeting its objective (discovering the presence or absence of items in the personnel specification)? Are other selection methods needed?

6   Staff appraisal

In Chapter 1 the idea of the management cycle was introduced and, if library staff are to be effectively managed, we have to pay more than lip-service to the last stage of the cycle by ensuring that we evaluate the performance of staff. Management is very much a matter of formalizing and systematizing activities, many of which already take place but in a haphazard manner. Staff appraisal provides a good illustration of this since staff are continually assessing each others' performances but the assessments may be unfair and inadequate and the information may not be used to improve the library's effectiveness.

The starting point for an appraisal system should be the desire to improve the performance of individual staff and to do this there has to be some monitoring of performance by appraisers. Naturally staff have to be informed about their existing performances in order to be stimulated to improve upon them and in some ways the most important objective of an appraisal system turns out to be the communication of such information to staff. It is surprising how so few staff have any accurate knowledge about senior management's views on their performance. Indeed, if they had known, their careers may have developed quite differently. It is interesting to note, and indicative of much management thinking, that few writings on appraisal refer to the possibility of formal appraisal of seniors by subordinates or by those on the same level, although we are aware that senior management's performance is a constant topic in staffroom conversation.

If staff are to improve they will frequently require help to do so. There may be a need for job descriptions to be changed by enlargement or enrichment. As outlined in Chapter 4, these descriptions will probably be changing anyway as a result, for example, of changes in the environment and in technology. Enrichment, however, may not be possible to any great extent without restructuring and we have already referred in Chapter 4 to the ways academic and public libraries have been restructured in recent years.

Appraisal should be viewed in association with the training and development of staff because it helps to identify training needs which have to be met if staff are to improve their performances. If appraisal is to be successful a library must be able to offer training opportunities to staff who are formally appraised. If it cannot do this then appraisal can cause frustration and resentment.

Randell[1] believes it is important to distinguish between three types of appraisal: reward reviews, potential reviews and performance reviews. So far we have discussed only the last which is concerned with the improvement of performance. Reward reviews are concerned with rewarding performance by pay and promotion. In public sector libraries pay is, of course, related to promotion but it is not usual for it to be directly dependent on performance. Librarians working in the private sector, however, are much more likely to have their pay reviewed annually and for it to be dependent on performance though Forbes and Anaya found only half their respondents using appraisals for salary reviews in their survey of United Kingdom manufacturing companies.[2] It would seem logical to make use of appraisal records for deciding on promotion and indicating potential but the evidence on practice is unclear. Ninety per cent of the organizations replying to Forbes and Anaya claimed to use results in considering employee promotions and eighty per cent to evaluate the potential of the appraisee but Walker's researches[3] showed that little or no use of appraisal reports was made in determining the field for selection and the final selection for promotion by one-third of the twenty-four respondents. Evidence comes from the 'Camden Newsletter' that some librarians favour systematic appraisal as providing a more accurate estimate of their worth for promotion:

> Many of us have been with the Department a long time; many of us have similar experience – so when we apply for jobs, the interview must be the only deciding factor. Is this enough? Regular Heads of Department reports would provide a constant record of our progress, staff not directly in the Management 'eye' would benefit, and interviewers would have more information about each applicant to help them in their decision-making. Reports would also help the Staff Officer to write constructive references when a person leaves the Department for a new job.[4]

It will be apparent that appraisal, like other management techniques, inevitably affects not only performance but motivation and job satisfaction. The theories discussed in Chapters 1 and 2 are therefore especially relevant. One of the objectives frequently claimed for appraisal is that it improves relationships and communications between managers and subordinates. Later in this chapter we will be looking at the most useful methods of appraisal for librarians and it is just as important as it is in staff selection to realize that all communications, whichever way they travel in the appraisal process, are significant and managers should plan the process carefully from the beginning if the end result is not to be a worsening of relationships. Messenger, in his description of the Shropshire system, echoes the Camden sentiments in criticizing the state of things before appraisal: 'Real knowledge of an individual's worth and attainments were frequently lacking. Opinions and impressions were too often substituted for facts.'[5]

As a result of appraisal there should accrue a better knowledge of the capabilities of the staff as a whole. Weaknesses should become more apparent and, in particular, skills and knowledge, which may previously have been overlooked, should come to light as individuals' hopes and aspirations are discussed. The good manager will be aware of the skills and knowledge required by the library and be able to match appraisal findings with them.

When a staff member is appointed the selectors usually believe their methods have enabled them to select a person who will fulfil their hopes. Appraisal should be seen as the check on whether those hopes have been justified. In this way appraisal is evaluation of the selection procedures. If, for example, there is a considerable shortfall between hopes and achievement by individual staff members it could be that the selection procedure is at fault.

Staff appraisal and styles of management

We have so far discussed the objectives of staff appraisal in a fairly general way but the reasons which appeal most will be those which support the style of management that is practised in the library. If we consider the two contrasting forms of management described in Chapter 2, mechanistic and organismic, it should become clearer how techniques like appraisal take their colour from the style prevalent in the organization and of course this may vary in different parts of it.

In a library managed on mechanistic lines a formal appraisal scheme is most likely to be instituted as a useful device for checking that staff are doing what they have been told to do. It may be rejected, however, where controls are already tight enough, or where management fear that their own competence may be called into question.

In an organismic system a scheme might be welcomed if it could be shown to improve staff performance but reservations would be likely concerning the constricting nature of a formal scheme because, in a truly organismic structure, appraisal of each other's performance would be taking place all the time. A formal scheme could easily stifle spontaneous action designed to meet problems as they arise. The mechanistic organization would be more likely than an organismic one to accept a method employing simple trait or numerical ratings as job performance would be viewed by the latter as a complex matter not amenable to simple ratings. By definition, in a mechanistic system the senior management would design the scheme and require staff to submit to it and the assessments would be limited to those of subordinates by superiors.

Joint discussion and agreement would characterize the organismic style with assessments being made by peers and subordinates as well as staff assessing themselves. Although most appraisal is, in essence, an assessment of individuals, it will be apparent that this could be unsatisfactory and unacceptable to those in truly organismic teams since it would be far more logical to assess the teams rather than the individuals alone; in such groups the individuals will be openly assessing each other and their contributions to the team objectives. For this reason the common practice of holding annual formal interviews when the manager 'plays God' would seem to be unnecessary in organismic systems. A survey carried out among appraisees in a government department suggests, however, that the effectiveness of the interviews is most likely to be affected by the frequency with which a manager discusses his subordinate's job outside the appraisal interview itself:

> The more often he talks over the interviewee's work with him, the more likely the interviewer will conduct an appraisal that is perceived as having positive effects on job performance and job satisfaction. This seemingly runs contrary to the conventional wisdom frequently voiced by students (and sometimes by trainers as well) on appraisal training courses, to the effect that 'if only we had good communications the rest of the time, we would not need appraisal interviews'. It also raises the question of whether the appraisal interview can contribute a great deal where, by accident or design, the manager seldom discusses matters with his staff – is it, in other words, an effective technique for increasing manager/subordinate communications? The findings presented here suggest that relatively little is achieved by the appraisal where existing communications are poor, though – paradoxically – this is where the need is greatest and the potential gains highest.[6]

Appraisal in a mechanistic organization would value such qualities as loyalty and obedience, 'not upsetting the apple-cart' and fitting in well whereas an organismic organization would value creativity, the use of knowledge and initiative in different situations, ability to adapt to change and supportive behaviour in groups.

Who does the appraising?

Most personnel management textbooks and, more recently, library management textbooks list and discuss available methods of appraisal. Robert Hilton has produced a helpful review of the literature[7] and there are now a few written accounts of methods used by particular libraries. We have also been able to obtain materials from a number of libraries and the emphasis in this chapter will be upon methods known to be used by libraries.

In most schemes it is the senior librarians who formally appraise the librarians who work directly for them. In some cases the next person above in the hierarchy ('the grandfather') plays some part, often by interviewing those whose appraisal reports are unsatisfactory. This happens in the British Civil Service. We have already referred to peer and subordinate appraisal and, although not usual, it is practised in a few American libraries. Anne Turner's reply to a request for information in *American Libraries* aroused so much interest that she wrote an article describing the system used in the Jones Library in Amhurst:

> The principal tool for the evaluation was a General Evaluation Form, which asked library workers to assess their own and others' performances using a numerical rating system. The basic form was in three parts 'Technical Performance (eleven criteria), Relation to the Public (eight criteria), and Relation to Staff (nine criteria). Additionally, each section had open-ended questions which invited comments, and the whole GEF ended with a final question, 'If I were in charge of this place I'd do something about————'. Workers who were supervisors were also evaluated for, and did evaluations of, Supervisory Skills.
>
> Except for the self-evaluation form all GEFs were filled out anonymously. Supervisors of the worker being evaluated received these forms and made a Composite GEF, which consolidated the ratings and comments of the subjects's co-workers. Thus a desk attendant filled GEF's on the other desk attendants and gave them to the circulation manager. The desk attendant also did a GEF on the circulation manager, and gave this to the circulation manager's supervisor (the director). Lastly she filled out a self-evaluation GEF, which she kept to use in her worker/supervisor conference.[8]

At the University of Texas at Austin reports are prepared by subordinates for the supervisor's private use[9] and anonymous peer and subordinate evaluations are made at the Southern Illinois University Carbondale library.[10] A letter written by David Weber, Director of Stanford University Libraries explains why we should be careful not to overvalue subordinate assessments:

> As in student evaluation of faculty, the views of subordinates may be based on narrower concerns than those of the organization. Subordinates are likely to give greater weight to practical matters, assistance with procedures, and departmental personnel issues. They may not see the vital contributions of the supervisor's fundamental planning or goal-setting roles, leadership of task forces and committees, and effectiveness in relations with faculty members and administrators.[11]

Weber's concern is with the interpretation of data collected and not with the method itself but many British librarians would consider the appraisal schemes described in this section too complex, time-consuming and unnecessary. One does have some sympathy with the British librarians whom David Peele met while researching appraisal in Britain and America who believed their appraisal role was fulfilled if their doors 'were always open' for staff who wished to see them.[12]

The impression is often given that appraisal is concerned only with evaluations of a person by others, usually superiors, and the contents are not revealed to the appraisee. Increasingly now the contents of the evaluations will be known, and possibly read by the person. A natural reaction to open appraisal might seem to be that appraisers will tend to be less candid where criticisms need to be made. However, the findings of Walker[13] suggest that there will at first be a deterioration and then an improvement.

Like the Jones Library in Amhurst, whose appraisal system is described above, Sheffield Public Libraries invite staff to appraise themselves using the form shown in Figure 6.1.

Some libraries adopting objectives-based appraisal systems require staff to review progress during the previous year 'towards the goals and objectives which were jointly established during the previous evaluation conference'.[14]

Forms of appraisal

The earliest form used by libraries appears to have been trait rating. In the United States the American Library Association published a standard rating form in its 'Personnel organization and procedure' manual[15] in which raters were required to score staff on thirty-three traits using a five-point scale, each point being denoted by a phrase or adverb, e.g.

THOROUGHNESS

Meticulous in checking. Always sees things through.	Usually thorough. Sometimes skips details under pressure.	Moderately careful. Inclined to take too many short cuts.

Superficial. Does not follow through if difficulties arise.	Does not complete assignments satisfactorily.

There are many variations on this system both in layout and scoring. Shropshire[16] and Gwyned, for example, have used a five-point scale with boxes to be ticked, sometimes referred to as a graphic rating scale (see Figure 6.2).

The British Civil Service has used a six-point scale with polar positions indicated by words, e.g.

RELATIONS WITH OTHERS

Sensitive to other people's feelings: tactful understanding of personnel problems, earns great respect	A B C D E F	Ignores or belittles other people's feelings; brusque; intolerant and doesn't earn respect

160

FIGURE 6.1. AN EXAMPLE OF A 'SELF' APPRAISAL FORM

Section 1   CONFIDENTIAL STAFF REPORT

Name . . . .
Age . . . .
Division . . . .
Section/Branch . . . .
Designation . . . .
Grade and present salary . . . .
Qualifications . . . .
. . . .
. . . .
Courses attended during previous 12 months . . . .
. . . .
. . . .
Qualifications obtained during previous 12 months . . . .
. . . .
. . . .

SECTION 2   PART A
             To be completed by individual being reviewed

1.   Summarise under 4 or 5 headings the key activities of your work
     during the previous 12 months

2.   State your ideas about your future career indicating particularly any
     further education, training courses, further experience etc. that you
     feel would be appropriate

SECTION 2   PART B

Performance Review

3. *The Immediate Superior/Head of Section* should assess employee's report, particularly commenting on results and performance in the light of prevailing circumstances, highlighting strengths and shortcomings

4. *The Immediate Superior's Proposals* to improve performance on the job (e.g. practical experience, private study, training course, further education etc.)

5. *Employee's Comments* – written after review interview with immediate Superior

Signed . . . .

Review completed by immediate Superior

GUIDELINES FOR COMPLETING THE REPORT

Section 1
Please check that these details are correct, and amend if not.

Section 2 – Part A
To be completed by individual being reviewed.

(Part A) Paragraph 1
Summarise the main areas of your work and indicate those which have given you greatest satisfaction, or have proved particularly difficult.

Paragraph 2
State your own ideas about your future career or development with particular reference to further training or experience. Mention any special job interests you may have or any other Divisions you would like to work in.

Section 2 – Part B
To be completed by immediate Superior.

(Part B) Paragraph 3
Comment on performance particularly relating to tasks given and how effectively they have been performed. Highlight good points and advise on shortcomings. Comment on statements made in Paragraph 1. Mention any aspects of personality which may have a detrimental effect on public service or staff relations.

Paragraph 4
Comment on any statements made in Paragraph 2 and recommend any action to be taken e.g. transfer, training, further experience. Discuss with member of staff points made above.

Paragraph 5
Pass back to individual being reviewed for completion and signing then forward completed report to Divisional Officer, Personnel and Training Office or Director of Libraries as provided in the staff instruction 'STAFF DEVELOPMENT SCHEME'

Endorsement of report by Area librarian/Divisional Head.

Signed . . . .

FIGURE 6.2. AN EXAMPLE OF A GRAPHIC RATING SCALE

Gwasanaeth Llyfrgell GWYNEDD Library Service

NAME   BRANCH or DEPARTMENT

CHARACTER AND   (tick appropriate   COMMENTS
PERSONALITY   boxes)

Responsibility.

Seeks and accepts responsibility at all times....1☐
Very willing to accept responsibility...............2...☐
Accepts responsibility as it comes....................3......☐
Inclined to refer up matters he could
himself decide..4.........☐
Avoids taking responsibility...........................5............☐

Relations with colleagues.

Wins and retains the highest regard of all.......1☐
Is generally liked and respected......................2...☐
Gets on well with everyone............................ 3......☐
Not very easy in his relationships...................4.........☐
A difficult colleague...................................... 5............☐

Contacts with public.

Outstandingly effective in dealing with them 1☐
Considerate and firm as required.................. 2...☐
Handles them quite well............................... 3......☐
Manner tends to be unfortunate................... 4.........☐
Poor at dealing with them............................. 5............☐

CAPACITY

Penetration.

Gets at once to the root of any problem.........1☐
Shows a ready appreciation of any problem...2...☐
Usually grasps a point correctly....................3......☐
Not very quick on the uptake........................4.........☐
Often misses the point.................................. 5............☐

Comments and Suggestions.

Always produces constructive comments
or suggestions on work routines.................... 1☐
Generally makes valuable suggestions.......... 2...☐
Comments and suggestions generally
well thought-out.. 3......☐
Seldom comments or makes suggestions........ 4.........☐
Never sees any reason for change................. 5............☐

Judgement.

Judgements consistently sound and
well thought-out.. 1☐
View of a matter is nearly always a
sensible one.. 2...☐
Takes a reasonable view on most matters...... 3......☐
Judgement tends to be erratic...................... 4.........☐
Judgement cannot be relied on.................... 5............☐

PERFORMANCE OF DUTIES

Output.

Outstanding in the amount of work he does...1☐
Gets through a great deal of work................2...☐
Work satisfactory...................................... 3......☐
Does rather less than expected..................... 4.........☐
Work regularly insufficient......................... 5............☐

Quality.

Distinguished for accurate and
thorough work.. 1☐
Maintains a high standard........................... 2...☐
Work is generally of good quality................3......☐
Performance is uneven................................ 4.........☐
Inaccurate and slovenly in his work............. 5............☐

Reporting Librarian's general remarks.

Date .... Signature .... Post Held ....

FIGRE 6.3. AN EXAMPLE OF A 'CONTROLLED WRITTEN' REPORT

BEDFORDSHIRE COUNTY LIBRARY
PROFESSIONAL STAFF ASSESSMENT

Name . . . .   Age..........
Professional & Academic Qualifications . . . .
Position . . . .   Post No...............
Date of Appointment to Present Post . . . .
Branch/Section . . . .
Period of Assessment: From....................   To....................

ASSESSMENT

1. PROFESSIONAL JUDGEMENT
    Ability to make sound proposals and decisions.

2. ABILITY TO PRODUCE CONSTRUCTIVE IDEAS
    The ability to innovate and provide fresh insight and broader perspectives.

3. COMMUNICATION ABILITY
    The ability to communicate clearly and concisely, both orally and in writing.

4. NUMERICAL ABILITY
    Handling and interpretation of figures and statistics (accuracy and under-
    standing).

5. ACCEPTANCE OF RESPONSIBILITY
    The degree to which responsibility is sought and accepted.

6. RELIABILITY
    Degree of reliability and competence, particularly when under pressure.

7. DRIVE AND DETERMINATION
    Application to tasks and degree of determination to carry a task through to
    conclusion.

8. MANAGEMENT OF STAFF AND RELATIONSHIPS WITH COLLEAGUES
   The ability to organise and inspire staff and/or colleagues to give of their best; ability to understand other people's problems, earn respect of others.

9. RELATIONSHIPS WITH THE PUBLIC
   Ability to deal with the public competently.

10. PROFESSIONAL KNOWLEDGE
    Degree to which equipped with an appropriate breadth of up-to-date knowledge.

11. APPLICATION OF PROFESSIONAL KNOWLEDGE AND SKILLS
    Degree of proficiency in the practical application of professional knowledge and skills.

12. GENERAL REMARKS
    Any additional relevant information, including any particular strengths or weaknesses.

TRAINING NEEDS

If, as a result of the assessments made, you consider that performance or potential could be improved by training, please specify these needs.

LONG TERM POTENTIAL

An assessment of the long term potential of the individual, as it would appear at the time of this interview (taking into account the views expressed by the individual).

COMMENTS OF ASSESSEE (if any).

Report discussed on . . . .

Signed by Assessee . . . .

(Signature does not necessarily imply agreement with the assessment).

Signed by Assessor . . . .

Date . . . .

This form of appraisal has a number of advantages. It is relatively easy for the appraisers to fill in the form. A cynic might say that they don't have to think up their own pet phrases because they are already prepared by somebody else. Trait scoring does give the impression, because values are being assigned, that the process is scientific and in some libraries the scores for each trait are aggregated and a total score given for the appraisee. This may leave the appraiser with a comfortable feeling of a job neatly completed but critics would argue that evaluating staff is a more complicated matter and a person does not consist simply of the sum of the traits chosen for an appraisal scheme.

In a few cases a weighted trait system is used in order to give greater weight to those traits which are considered important and it is concern for performance on the job which distinguishes what we believe to be the better trait systems from others which concern themselves too much with personality traits. The reader is invited to assess any trait-rating they experience on the basis of relevance to the job being rated.

Any scoring system faces the problem of standards. As Peele points out: 'The real problem... comes when we try to answer the question, "What is the standard?"... the unanswered question – perhaps the unanswerable one– is, "performance compared to what?"' [17] Peele then goes on to illustrate the problem by asking how we know what standard to use when rating 'Judgement' on a five-point scale and how we are to take into account the constraints under which each individual works when rating that person's performance.

Perhaps the simplest form of all would be a free-written report in which appraisers could write what they wished. In practice this would most likely prove to be disappointing as a management tool since essential aspects could be omitted and it would be very difficult to analyse and compare evaluations. Consequently a more popular form is the 'controlled written report' in which appraisers fill in a form under a number of chosen headings. An example is the one used by Bedfordshire County Library and the headings are reproduced in Figure 6.3. It should be noted that the headings relate directly to job requirements and not to personality.

Appraisal has frequently been criticized because of the very low motivation on the part of managers to appraise, to discuss appraisals with subordinates, and to initiate any follow-up action on the appraisals. [18] It is the last deficiency which has been chiefly responsible for the adoption of objectives-based systems of appraisal in which the manager and subordinate agree on targets for the future. Targets can cover a range of areas and should concentrate on those which the library has deemed important. This will be made easier if, as is likely, a management by objectives system is in operation. A model recently devised by two American librarians for academic reference librarians incorporates target areas, degrees of emphasis, criteria for measuring achievement, degree of accomplishment and final evaluation for each target area. The reference librarian's target areas include library instruction, publishing, reference questions answered (measured by unobtrusive tests, opinions of users and opinions of peers), teaching, liaison with academic staff, membership of committees, involvement with professional associations and continuing education.[19] Objectives-based methods can certainly bring about an improvement in staff performance and systematize its evaluation but, more than any of the appraisal methods di cussed, are dependent on management style for their impact on individuals. Many librarians would be appalled by the introduction of an objectives-based system like the one described by Ellison and Lazeration and one can sympathize with them but at the same time most managers would not feel the organization was progressing in the way it should if each person were allowed to work without any guidelines and evaluation of performance.

Appraisal interviewing

In most organizations where systematic appraisal is practised each appraisee discusses the results with his or her appraiser. This meeting is crucial for the achievement of a number of the objectives of appraisal already noted in this chapter. Although open appraisals, in which appraisees read their own appraisals and are often required to sign that they have done so, are becoming more common, a discussion of points made can help to interpret and explain them.

A form like the Bedfordshire one provides a useful guide to topics for discussion. It will not be difficult to discuss the appraisee's strengths but weaknesses have to be carefully handled. In Western Europe open confrontation or 'levelling', is not so popular or effective as it is in the United States so more subtle methods are required. It will also be recalled that one of the objectives of appraisal was to improve communication among staff of various grades in the library and communication in the interview must be successful to achieve this objective. The questions listed in Figure 6.4 are designed to indicate features of a successful appraisal interview and have been used by the authors as an analytical tool for training purposes. The questions follow closely those used for analysing the effectiveness of groups[20] by Jordan and lists produced by M. R. Williams[21], Anstey, Fletcher and Walker[22] together with Honey's 'hallmarks of an interactively skilled person'.[23] Transactional analysis also offers valuable help by stressing the importance of positive adult attitudes by both persons. Readers who are interested could study Barker[24] with considerable profit.

It will be plain that the interview requires careful preparation by both participants. The appraisee should see the appraisal form well in advance of the interview and be asked to prepare any topics for discussion which the appraiser thinks necessary. The appraiser has to be especially certain about strengths and weaknesses with evidence systematically collected to support the assessments being made and should welcome and encourage suggestions of topics for discussion put forward by the appraisee.

FIGURE 6.4. TYPICAL QUESTIONS USED TO EVALUATE AN APPRAISAL INTERVIEW

Objectives
1. Is the purpose of the appraisal made clear by the appraiser and does it appear to be understood and accepted by the appraisee?

Procedure
2. Does the appraiser make clear what pattern it is hoped the interview will take?
3. Do the participants appear to understand the points made by each of them? Is clarification sought where necessary?
4. Does the appraiser summarize what progress has been made in the interview from time to time and receive confirmation that the summaries are accurate?
5. How far is the discussion a two-way one and how far is it dominated by one of the participants? Are they both good listeners?
6. Is sufficient time given for each person to explain his/her position to his/her own satisfaction?

Relevance
7. Does the interview keep in step with the purpose of the appraisal or does it wander off into irrelevant side-tracks?

Conflict
8. Is disagreement used constructively or does it lead mainly to dissatisfaction?
9. When one criticizes the other is it made in a constructive way producing suggestions along with every criticism?
10. Do participants admit it when they are in the wrong or inadequate in some way rather than pretend to be right or adequate all the time?

Non-verbals
11. Are there any contradictions between the verbal and non-verbal behaviour? Do the non-verbal behaviours of the two persons help to create an atmosphere of trust and openness?

Action
12. Are the participants clear about action that is required before the next appraisal interview and is there a firm commitment to carry it out?

Work assignment

Read the following case study and role-play a staff appraisal interview between Bill and David. Participants might also be asked to compile a staff appraisal form based upon the job description and the Bedfordshire form and to use the information given to complete the form with reference to Bill Johnson. The opportunity can then be taken to evaluate the appraisal form as an effective one. The interview can be observed and analysed using the questions posed above and also the transactional analysis questions below. Reference should be made to Barker (1980) by those unfamiliar with transactional analysis.

Ego states

1. Identify the states (parent/child/adult) as they develop through the interview.
2. Analyse any key transactions in the interview especially where the transaction is 'crossed'.

Strokes

3. Note any significant use of strokes or lack of them. Are they negative or positive?

Games

4. Is there any evidence of games being played e.g. 'harried', 'wooden leg', 'poor me'.

Life positions

5. Is there evidence of the life position of each of the participants, i.e.

I'm not OK You're OK	I'm OK You're OK
I'm not OK You're not OK	I'm OK You're not OK

Case study: *Bill and David*

Leyton Polytechnic was formed on 1 April 1970 from the four former colleges of Art and Design, Building, Commerce, and Technology. The main buildings of the former colleges are on sites within a half to one mile of each other. A faculty structure has been set up and the faculty is seen as the basic unit of the Polytechnic. The faculties are Art and Design, Construction, Business and Management Studies, Humanities and Social Studies, Engineering, and Science.

Bill Johnson, A.L.A. (42 years old) was appointed Faculty Librarian for Business and Management Studies in 1970 after ten years as librarian of the College of Commerce. He carried on as if the Polytechnic had not really happened, running a traditional library service concentrating on keeping a tidy, well-catalogued library of books and periodicals, most of which were

171

bought as a result of suggestions by faculty staff. Bill is not against new ideas in librarianship but feels that most of them are old wine in new bottles. He read a book on how computers work a few years ago when it looked as though he might have to bring technology to the Commerce library and got quite interested and he looked at it again before his interview for Faculty Librarian.

He feels that library management is largely common sense although academic staff in the faculty and their students have caused him some uncertainty about this. It does seem to him that no sooner has he begun to hear about a management technique than it is said to be out of date.

The first Polytechnic Librarian allowed things to continue much as they were and let Bill get on with his work. Six months ago *David Drive*, B.A., A.L.A. was appointed Polytechnic Librarian. David cut his professional teeth in a College of Education library where he tried out a number of his ideas with a small enthusiastic staff and was raring to go when he came to the Polytechnic. He is 35 years old.

Within two months of his appointment he had written a 12-page report on library development in which computerization and increases in the number of audio-visual aids in all faculty libraries were central points and to aid this development a Management by Objectives system was recommended together with a staff appraisal scheme. David has had a few minor brushes with Bill already but he did not prolong these as he felt things could be sorted out properly once the staff appraisal scheme got under way. David's ideas on what a faculty librarian's duties ought to be were contained in a 'discussion paper' on 'Subject Specialists in the Polytechnic Libraries':

Faculty Librarians should regard themselves as Subject Specialists responsible to the Polytechnic Librarian for the management and development of services in their subject areas. Their roles are both those of a librarian and an educator.

Main activities.
1. Member of relevant faculty board which helps to keep the librarian in touch with current planning and course development.
2. Advise on the impact on the library of academic developments.
3. Take part as a member of the senior library management team in library planning.
4. Advise on policy decisions concerning reader services, classification and cataloguing and reader instruction programmes.
5. Develop the collections of book and non-book materials in relevant subjects.
Allocation of time
Faculty Librarians are expected to divide their time more or less equally among:
1. Readers' advisory services

2. Materials' selection and stock editing
3. Work outside the library – liaison, faculty and other meetings, publicity and promotion of the library, etc.

   Bill felt he did most of the duties listed but knew in his heart that David Drive would not agree and anyway he felt it would be impossible with the present staffing levels. He thought David was inexperienced, too attracted by new theories and gadgets but would mellow with time.

7   Staff training and development

Identifying training needs

We have already seen how staff appraisal can be a valuable aid in identifying individual training needs and, as the last chapter showed, the good manager does not view appraisal simply in terms of an annual event but is constantly observing and noting deficiences. These can be categorized as weaknesses in knowledge, skills and attitudes.

A start can also be made by analysing job descriptions and specifications for the knowledge, skills and attitudes required and the deficiences which exist. In some cases it may be necessary to start at an earlier point and draw up accurate descriptions and specifications where none exist. 'Exit interviews' with staff who resign can also reveal deficiences which training could go some way to repairing. If there is a high turnover of staff it will be especially important to discover the reason.

In some libraries, where an effort is being made to take training more seriously, surveys have been made of the whole staff to discover the training needs which staff feel they have. The example shown in Figure 7.1 is taken from a recent survey of Leeds Public Library carried out by one of the staff.

Training needs, however, are not simply a matter of individual benefits, not even the sum total of them. At the general level there are organizational training needs which relate to the general weaknesses in the library which can be remedied, or partly so, by training. As Boydell observes, the weaknesses can only be properly assessed if they are related to the present and future objectives of the organization.[1]

For training to be effective it must be viewed as an essential element in the management cycle and thus the starting point really lies in the changing needs of the communities which libraries serve and the different responses the library is able to make to fulfil those needs by utilizing new skills and technologies. For example, the development of degree courses in polytechnics has brought with it the need for wider reading by students and more systematic literature-searching to support project work. The library has needed to respond by improving and enlarging its teaching role:

> Many of the new CNAA degree courses at Sunderland now include units of up to 15 hours on information retrieval and techniques of library use. As these units are undertaken by the library, the staff concerned require expertise in teaching and the presentation of information. The ability to communicate effectively and with confidence is essential if library teaching is to have any impact, hence the urgent need for in-service training in this area.[2]

Frequently libraries have employed audio-visual materials such as tape-slide programmes in this teaching role and in the future are likely to make more use of computers for self-teaching purposes and this will constitute a training need for staff involved.

In public libraries staffing structures have been changing partly to enable the library to respond more quickly to community needs (see Chapter 4) and where this has happened the better-managed libraries have recognized that staff cannot be expected to perform differently simply because the structure has been changed and therefore training has been provided. A good example is the training package produced by Leicestershire on 'The effective use of team time'.[3]

Training needs may also be identified through a scrutiny of jobs being poorly performed in the library. If there are written quantitative standards in use for routine jobs it will be known whether these are being met and observation can reveal where qualitative standards are not being reached. In addition there may be complaints from the community served that can be analysed, possibly revealing training needs.

Checklist of training activities

Although we would hold firmly to the view that the starting point lies in the changing needs of communities, it is nevertheless helpful to use a checklist of training activities like the one used by Suffolk County Libraries (see Figure 7.2).

Group needs

The evidence obtained from the analysis of both individual and organizational needs will show that particular groups have their own training needs. This is so likely, and makes training so much easier, that analysis by group should be an essential part of needs' identification. Where group members are working closely together it is particularly desirable for them to put forward what they believe to be their training needs as a group. In this way training can much more easily be perceived as being intimately connected with the work rather than an extra that can be indulged in when there is an excess of funds, which is almost never.

A useful group checklist is produced by the Library Association:[4]

1. Library assistants
2. Senior library assistants
3. Pre-library school trainees
4. Unqualified subject specialists
5. Staff in first professional posts
6. Intermediate professionals
7. Specialists
8. Senior management
9. Clerical staff
10. Manual staff
11. Specialist technical staff
12. Other professions working in libraries

FIGURE 7.1. A RECENT SURVEY TO ASSESS STAFF TRAINING NEEDS

STAFF TRAINING AND DEVELOPMENT

1. Please indicate which general educational qualifications you hold at present (tick as appropriate and indicate the number of passes).

G.C.E. O level	( )	Degree (other than in Librarianship)	( )
G.C.E. A/S level	( )	Open University Degree	( )
C.S.E.	( )	City and Guilds Library	
R.S.A.	( )	Assistants Certificate	( )
School Certificate	( )	Other (please specify)	( )

2. Please indicate any professional library qualifications held (tick as appropriate)

Degree in Librarianship	( )
F.L.A.	( )
A.L.A.	( )
Member of Aslib	( )
Member of I.I.S.	( )

3. Do the qualifications held in 1 above have any special value in relation to your everyday work?

4. What aspects of library training have been covered by Leeds City Libraries in your own case? (tick where appropriate)

General induction (aims of the Library Service, conditions of employment, etc.)	( )
Library routine operations	( )
Visits to Headquarters	( )
Visits to other branch libraries	( )
Visits to the Central Library	( )
Visits to libraries other than those belonging to Leeds City Libraries	( )
Customer Relations	( )
Management/Supervisory Skills	( )

5. Has the training you have received under the headings in question 4 been valuable to you in your everyday work?   YES/NO
(Please comment on specific areas if necessary)

6. Have you attended any courses/seminars, etc. organised by outside bodies (e.g. Library Association , Aslib, School of Librarianship).

YES/NO

If yes, please specify subjects/topics covered.

7. Do you have any responsibility in your present post for training staff? YES/NO

If yes, how many staff do you have to train and what broad areas of training do you cover?

8. Are there any areas of your everyday work in which you feel that you are inadequately trained? Please specify.

9. Do you experience any difficulty in dealing with library users? If so please specify.

10. How confident do you feel about your knowledge of all the services offered by the Central Library and Branches when you have to answer enquiries at the counter? (Tick as appropriate.)

a. not at all confident   (   )
b. not very confident   (   )
c. quite confident   (   )
d. completely confident   (   )

11. Do you feel well-informed about new services and developments throughout the library system. YES/NO

12. Have you made a point of reading any book or periodical article on library services this year? YES/NO

13. Are you aware of the training policy, and any courses offered by:-

Leeds Department of Personnel   YES/NO
Leeds Department of Leisure Services   YES/NO
Leeds City Libraries   YES/NO

14. Does a supervisor discuss your training needs and career development with you on a regular basis? YES/NO

15. Please add any comments you might have regarding the present training policies and programmes.

FIGURE 7.2. A CHECKLIST OF TRAINING ACTIVITIES

TRAINING TOPICS

1. *Stock: selection and management*
   a. selection of books
   b. selection of recorded sound media
   c. selection of other materials (including ephemera, pamphlets, etc.)
   d. stock editing/withdrawal/ disposal
   e. stock circulation and exchanges
   f. cataloguing and classification (including computerized systems)
   g. information retrieval systems (including indexing & scanning)

2. *Services*
   a. enquiry handling techniques
   b. use of reference materials
   c. use of outside resources
   d. use of *internal* resources!
   e. identification of users' needs
   f. services to the disadvantaged and minority groups
   g. services to children and young people
   h. community information services
   i. local studies

3. *Management*
   a. objective setting
   b. allocation of resources
   c. financial planning and control
   d. policy analysis
   e. decision making
   f. committee procedures
   g. designing library buildings and plant
   h. mobile library routing
   i. computer appreciation and use

4. *Staff management*
   a. selection and interviewing techniques
   b. training
   c. delegation
   d. supervision
   e. trade union relations
   f. personnel management
   g. staff development

5. *Administration*
   a. systems design
   b. work study
   c. organisation and method study
   d. clerical procedures
   e. design of internal records
   f. statistics

6. *Communications/promotion*
   a. public speaking
   b. written communications: letters, memos, reports
   c. liaison with outside bodies
   d. internal communications
   e. community profiling
   f. user studies
   g. promotion of services generally
   h. promotion of stock (booklists, displays etc.)

The responsibility for training

In the classic model, identification of training needs is followed by the production of a written training policy, priorities are determined and the programme gets under way. While it is valuable for managers to have such an ideal in front of them, reality is sure to be more messy.

For training to be successful there must, first of all, be senior management support. Undoubtedly the chief librarian will be the most crucial figure but training, like any other organizational activity, will flounder if line managers do not believe in it but have to subscribe to it sufficiently to put up with the inconvenience of being without staff when off-the-job training is taking place. Because training is one of those management activities which is not automatically in the forefront of the manager's mind (it is not usually an issue which lies on the managers' desk awaiting decisions every day), there is a requirement for a person to be given overall responsibility for the management of training. This means that this person's job is to ensure that the stages of the classic model are adhered to and that training which does take place is continually evaluated. Ronald Edwards' survey results and guidelines[5] together with the Local Government Training Board's recommendations[6] provide valuable help in producing the training officer's job description. It is especially important for the training officer to be a member of the Senior Management Team and be acknowledged as the link with training personnel of the parent body.

As indicated at the beginning of this chapter, the link with personnel work is very strong and the Library Education Group directory[7] provides plenty of evidence that the opportunity has been taken to combine the functions. Where this is not the case there should be close links between the functions.

Whenever a specialist post is created there is a natural tendency for other staff to leave that specialism to the specialist and neglect it themselves. It cannot be emphasized too strongly that it is not the training officer's job to carry out all the training. The job of the training officer is to operate as a 'fulcrum of training activity' and the 'catalyst for training change and development'[8] and in this role has to create a training atmosphere in the library and an acceptance by line managers of their training responsibilities. One way of doing this, used by some libraries, is to form a training group led by the training officer. This has been successful, for example, in Glasgow, and in North Tyneside Libraries and in Kent each division provides a 'Training Co-ordinator' as a result of a recommendation by the Working Party on Training.

Resources for training

One of the group's main tasks will be to discover training resources in the organization itself. In particular a position statement should be drawn up concerning accommodation, equipment, expertise, and, of course, available funds.

1. *Accommodation:* Rooms for large and small groups which allow flexibility of use are desirable. The following measures, adapted from those used to evaluate accommodation by Peter Smith, provide a helpful checklist:[9]

Thermal – air temperature, air movement, ventilation.
Visual – natural and artificial lighting.
Acoustic – reverberation, background noise, sound levels.
Teaching aids – sockets, controls available.
Room form – size and shape, ease of vision, nature of exit and entry.
Toilet and washing facilities.
Eating and drinking facilities.
Furniture – tables, chairs, writing facilities.

2. *Equipment:* Screens, overhead projectors, slide projectors, tape-slide equipment, audio tape-recorders, video tape-recorders and monitors, film projectors.

3. *Expertise:* Two main types of expertise are required. The first is knowledge of areas in which training is required. Here the checklist of training activities (p. 178) can be used and names attached where expertise is available. The other type of expertise relates to the skills required to teach and train and this may be more difficult to discover. Staff may have had teaching experience or they may be known as good instructors but, on the other hand, expertise may be lacking and in that case an important early consideration will be how to train the trainers, since it could be harmful to launch a programme only to have it poorly taught.

4. *Funds:* Money available for training in the library budget, or from other funds such as those of specialist training and management departments in the organization.

The mechanistic/organismic paradigm on p. 23 shows how staff training and development claims a larger share of resources in a library managed in an organismic style. A library, therefore, which acts positively in the areas so far discussed in this chapter almost by definition will have organismic characteristics. Staff training and development are intimately affected by management style in the same way that staff appraisal is affected. Not only will training flourish under certain management styles but training will itself affect that organization and its style of management in the way it is meant to in an organismic library.

Stages of training

As we investigate the various groups and their training needs we can distinguish:

1. Maintenance training, which enables the library to maintain its existing procedures and includes induction training for new entrants to the library system or to particular posts.

2. Basic up-dating and improvement training in areas identified as requiring improvement. An example of such training for improving trade union relationships is introduced later in this chapter.

3. Staff development which is discussed on pp. 188-190.

Even libraries which do little other training involve themselves in induction training. In a sense they have to, otherwise new staff would be unable to perform existing tasks adequately but many induction programmes are more systematic and recognize that all new staff need a general introduction to the service. It has to be recognized that induction introduces staff to the social and cultural aspects of the organization as much as to the jobs themselves. 'Systematic induction provides the basis for integrating the newcomer into the library as quickly and effectively as possible, and building a foundation for later job training and development. Additionally the positive interest by management in the newcomer can be an important motivator and help to reinforce the enthusiasm with which most newcomers tackle their job.'[10]

Trafford Library Service has been especially systematic:

1. *Pre-employment information:* to confirm the appointment, give information about the place of work, ensure the employee knows where to report and what to bring with him/her.

2. *First day orientation:* to welcome the new employee to HQ, provide brief information and complete necessary documentation, introduce members of the Library Management Team, take to library at which to be based, introduce to District Librarian and Librarian in charge of service point.

3. *Introduction to the job:* to ensure that all new employees understand their duties. Basic training programme to be completed within three months.

4. *Induction interview:* interview with District Librarian at which certain basic information is imparted and progress to date monitored. Interview to take place after approximately one month.

5. *Formal induction course:* to broaden the scene and help the employee see his/her job in relation to Trafford Library Service as a whole. A one-day course to take place within six months.

To ensure that all staff are systematically inducted a checklist is frequently employed and there is a timescale for its completion. An example from North Tyneside is shown in Figure 7.3 and other examples can be seen in P. Robertson's contribution to the Library Association's 'Guidelines for training in libraries'.[11]

FIGURE 7.3. NORTH TYNESIDE INDUCTION CHECKLIST

NAME:–

DATE OF APPOINTMENT:–

Item No.	Item	Responsibility	Completed
1	Layout of library, including staff facilities	AL	
2	Emergency and accident procedures (fire exits and equipment; first-aid box)	AL	
3	Hours of duty; time-sheet; meal-breaks; tea-breaks; procedure in case of absence from work	AL	
4	Staff hierarchy within the Area	AL	
5	Use of the telephones, both internal and external – telephone manners and correct answering, and telex	AL	
6	Dealing with the public in person on enquiry desks	AL	
7	Staff hierarchy within the Department	(PL(S)	
8	The catalogue – arrangement and use; type of alphabetization	AL	
9	Request system (books) including the correct completion of forms; Inter-Library loans	PL(BS)	
10	Requests systems (recordings and pictures)	(PL(A)	
11	Schools Service	PL(SIS)	
12	Local Studies Centre	PL(LS)	
13	Housebound Service – Homes	AL	
14	Book selection; General principles; Buying for Area and Branches	AL	
15	Book selection in the specialism	Relevant PL	
16	Book issue methods; scope of work of reception/Senior Assistants	AL/SA i/c	
17	Drafting and signing of letters	AL	

The great danger with induction is information overload caused by too much information being handed out, usually with the best of intentions, in too short a time. Here, as in many management activities, it is desirable to enter into the perceptions of the other person and in this case the manager should try to see things from the point of view of the newcomer.

It has to be recognized that induction training is necessarily conservatively biased and therefore there is a need both for up-dating and improvement training and for the general development of staff if innovative and positive librarianship is to take place.

Organizing specific training

By looking at a particular priority training need we can discuss the way training might be organized in an effective way. Imagine, therefore, the following situation:

'There has been an increase in activity by the trade unions, Nalgo and NUPE, in Wilbraham Metropolitan District Council and there have been a number of occasions when staff have had difficulties with the unions, for example, a district librarian had words with a porter who refused to mend a fuse because it was not his job, and an attempt to dismiss a member of staff failed when the union helped him with the appeal which was upheld. The chief librarian asks the training officer if he can do anything about improving staff performance when dealing with unions and matters of interest to them.'

Step 1: Establish needs.

(a) Discuss needs with staff in the different groups including trade union officials and library representatives.

(b) Analyse incidents where relationships between staff and the unions have been involved.

(c) Carry out a written survey of staff. If the staff is large the survey can be a sample one.

(d) In the long term a question can be incorporated into appraisal interviews.

Throughout this stage the investigation should emphasize future developments with implications for staff/union relationships and the problems which are likely to arise.

Step 2: Decide on the aim of the training. For example, to improve relationships with the unions by helping staff to become more aware of the situations and relations that cause problems and to help them to deal with such problems.

Step 3: Set specific objectives for each group of staff, decide on methods and trainers responsible. See Figure 7.4 for an example of this.

FIGURE 7.4. SETTING OBJECTIVES FOR EACH GROUP OF STAFF

Objectives	Staff (see list p. 175)	Method (see diagram p. 185)	Responsible Staff
Knowledge required of:			
1. The local authority's industrial relations policy, including the role of the unions	1,2, 4-12	2(a) 2(b) 2(e)	Chief Training Officer,* Local Authority Official
2. Channels of communication with the unions including negotiation and consultative procedures, e.g. shop stewards, committees, officers	All staff	2(a) 2(b) 2(c) 2(e)	Trade Union Officer, Shop stewards
3. Agreed conditions of employment: pay, allowances, grievance procedures, health and safety	All staff	2(a) -2(e)	Training Officer Health and Safety Officer
4. National industrial relations situation and relationship to Wilbraham	6,8	2(b) 2(e) 4	Trade Union Officer Trade Union Official (national)
Skills			
5. Communication skills especially in committees and with individuals	5,6,8	2(c) 2(d) 2(e) 3	Training Officer
Attitudes			
6. An attitude based upon an understanding of perception of each 'side' based upon information rather than prejudice	All staff	All methods used	All trainers

* Training Officer refers also to other staff with expertise

FIGURE 7.5. THE MAIN TRAINING AND DEVELOPMENT METHODS

Development of diffuse capabilities

20. Teamwork

8. Academic education

19. Delegation

7. Research

18. Visits to libraries

6. Professional education

5. Writing and publishing

17. Involvement with professional association

4. Reading professional literature

16. Appraisal

3. External courses

Implicit development

15. Consultancy

14. Job rotation

13. Job exchange

12. Staff meetings

11. Objectives approach to management

10. Projects

9. Working parties

Explicit development

2. In-house training programmes

(a) written instructions
(b) Lectures
(c) Case studies/ simulations
(d) Role-playing
(e) Seminar/discussion groups
(f) Audio-visuals
(g) Self-teaching packages

1. On-the-job training

Development of specific capabilities

Methods of training

The main methods used in training and development are displayed in Figure 7.5.

If we take training to mean the imparting of specific skills, knowledge and attitudes by direct methods usually involving a trainer, then the common methods are those shown in the diagram at 1 and 2(a)–(g). In the trade union example on p. 183 step three is concerned with methods. The intention is obvious – to use methods which achieve the aims and objectives in a cost-effective way – therefore rule one is to establish needs and decide on aims and objectives.

Secondly the trainer should be knowledgeable about those to be trained and in particular should be aware of their experience and existing knowledge of the training area in question. Thirdly the trainer should consider the various methods available. In some cases there will be published materials such as case studies, self-teaching packages and audio-visuals that can be used. Not a great deal of helpful material directly related to librarianship has been commercially published but trainers should regularly peruse the professional press for news of commercial and private publications, such as the tape-slides produced under the auspices of SCONUL, audio-visual introductions to library services and, with the advent of the computer, simulated bibliographical and information searches as well as management simulations. It is very likely that library schools are more knowledgeable than libraries about such materials as they are used a good deal in teaching. Most library schools will also be pleased to work on case studies and possibly audio-visuals, glad to use 'real' materials and situations as a basis. They can, at the same time, help to counter a common objection to case studies – that they are too artificial and lack depth of information. Collections of case studies in library management have been produced by Wills and Oldman[12] and by Hewitt[13] and can be used as a basis for drawing up simulations related to specific libraries.

The choice of training method should also be influenced by its potential to develop oral skills because they are so important in many library posts. Active methods such as case studies, simulations, role-playing and discussion groups will therefore have an additional advantage. They are, however, difficult to use successfully so that both the trainer and the trainees are satisfied they have learned from the experience. Helpful work has been done by Jean Ruddock[14] on small group work and by Jordan[15] and Jones[16] on task solving groups.

From our experience we can offer a few guidelines on group work. In particular participants should be adequately prepared, as training time is frequently wasted when information is given to groups which could easily have been read by participants beforehand. Groups should be clear what their task is and should normally not be more than six or seven in size. A chairman, familiar with, and competent in, interactive skills is essential and a blackboard or overhead projector must be available to enable participants, particularly the secretary, to summarize progress and arrive at decisions. Quick and helpful evaluations can be made after group meetings by use of Miles' reaction sheets[17] (see Figure 7.6). A number of libraries are using these sheets to initiate a short discussion after each meeting.

Role-playing is not only an active method but more than any other allows participants to enter into the perceptions of others. This is one reason

FIGURE 7.6. MILES' REACTION SHEETS

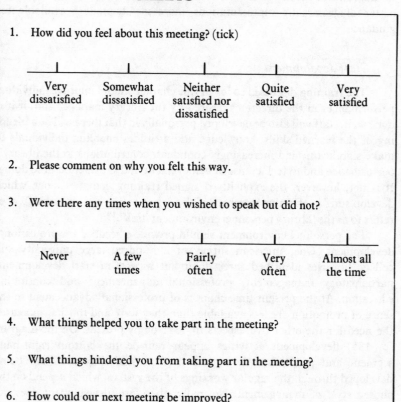

1. How did you feel about this meeting? (tick)

Very dissatisfied	Somewhat dissatisfied	Neither satisfied nor dissatisfied	Quite satisfied	Very satisfied

2. Please comment on why you felt this way.

3. Were there any times when you wished to speak but did not?

Never	A few times	Fairly often	Very often	Almost all the time

4. What things helped you to take part in the meeting?

5. What things hindered you from taking part in the meeting?

6. How could our next meeting be improved?

why it is preferable for trainees not to play themselves but others whose perceptions will be quite different. Such a policy also diminishes the threat which is present in role-play when those being observed perform 'poorly'. It is our experience that there needs to be a sympathetic and trusting rapport among participants and trainers before role-play can operate effectively but when it does it can be the most rewarding and enjoyable of methods.

On-the-job training, or 'sitting next to Nellie', as it is often disparagingly called, is valuable so long as Nellie can communicate well, explaining also the reasons she performs the way she does and how her routines are linked with others. Too much reliance is often placed on oral communication without accompanying written instruction which can be passed on to others to ensure a uniformity of procedures. Diagrammatic representation is potentially the most effective and has been employed, for instance, by Leicestershire with its algorithmic staff manual and by Manchester

Polytechnic in its Technical Services Division, but there is still a resistance to diagrams in favour of oral/written listing. For those wishing to provide better diagrammatic representations there is Chapman[18] available for guidance.

Staff development

The training discussed so far in this chapter should improve individual performances in the directions desired by the library manager and, if it is done well, staff will also be developed personally in that there will be a blending of the learned skills, knowledge and attitudes enabling individuals to make significant, and increasingly confident, contributions to the library's performance and to feel a sense of achievement and satisfaction in so doing. It is not, however, the explicitly designed training activities alone which develop staff as effective members of the organization but also what Weber refers to as the 'library personnel environment itself'.[19]

The personnel environment should provide a seedbed for professional development. One American survey of a hundred large university and college libraries identified three dominant aspects of staff development: participatory management, professional advancement and continuing education. At the present time chances of professional advancement in the sense of promotion are less available than they were and this has increased the need for the other two aspects to be strongly present. On the diagram (p. 185) development activities appear outside the bottom right-hand segment and predominantly on the implicit side since staff are being developed through the regular workings of the system, which depend on the chosen style of management. Normally, therefore, development does not involve a trainer concerned with passing on particular skills though it does not exclude support and advice from more experienced members of staff.

Staff development activities include ones which are not specifically related to the organization and its work. Academic education in subjects other than librarianship, for example, develops individuals and in some cases such education has direct relevance, the most obvious being where a subject specialist follows a course in the specialist subject. In times of economic restraint it is likely, however, that this form of staff development will be the one most likely to lose financial and other support yet it is at such times, when mobility and promotion are less available, that staff need to be helped in their efforts to avoid stagnation in their attitudes and ideas.

The extent to which librarians are involved in various continuing education activities is shown by Noragh Jones' 1977 survey[21] (see Figure 7.7). The librarians in the survey were also asked which activities they would like to be further involved in, if circumstances were favourable. Both these lists can be used to measure the continuing education involvement and needs of the staff of individual library systems.

FIGURE 7.7. CONTINUING EDUCATION ACTIVITIES RANKED BY DEGREE OF INVOLVEMENT

Public librarians		*Score*
1	Informal discussion with colleagues	226
2	Taking an active part in staff meetings	209
3	Giving talks to groups outside the profession	156
4	Writing staff aids for use in library	152
5	Visiting other libraries	151
6	Receiving in-service training	147
7	Writing guides, aids for use of readers	146
8	Reading librarianship literature	145
9	Attending conferences and meetings	142
10	Taking part in working parties in your library	129
11	Attending short courses	114
12	Studying for further qualifications	84
13	Carrying out research projects	70
14	Taking part in working parties with other bodies	61
15	Holding office in professional associations	58
16	Giving papers at meetings and conferences	49
17	Writing for publication	47
18	Taking an active part in institutional politics	33
19	Secondment to other libraries	28
20	Writing letters to the professional press	14

Academic librarians		
1	Informal discussion with colleagues	76
2	Taking an active part in staff meetings	72
3	Visiting other libraries	67
4	Writing guides, aids for use of readers	66
5	Writing discussion papers for use in library	62
6	Reading librarianship literature	60
7	Studying for further qualifications	57
8	Attending conferences and meetings	54
9	Receiving in-service training Attending short courses	44
10	Taking an active part in institutional politics	39
11	Taking part in working parties in your library	35
12	Carrying out research projects	29
13	Taking part in working parties with other bodies	28
14	Giving talks to groups outside the profession	25

15	Holding office in professional associations	17
16	Writing for publication	16
17	Giving papers at conferences and meetings	13
18	Writing letters to the professional press	9
19	Secondment to other libraries	5

NB Scores computed by allocating 3 for heavily involved, 2 for involved quite a bit, 1 for involved a little, and 0 for not involved.

1 Public librarians would like to make more visits to find out what is happening in other libraries.
2 Both academic and public librarians would like to take a greater part in working parties within their library systems, and would like to be more involved in short courses.
3 Academic librarians would favour more opportunity to develop closer contact with readers, through preparation of more readers' guides of various kinds.
4 Public librarians especially are concerned to have more opportunity to study for further qualifications. (This is the area where the greatest gap occurs between present involvement and would-be involvement.)
5 Both academic and public librarians would like to do more writing for publication and preparation of papers for meetings (but only to a limited extent).
6 Public librarians would like to do more professional reading.
7 Academic librarians are less involved in in-service training than public librarians and apparently do not want further involvement, whereas public librarians would favour even more.
8 Secondment to other libraries appears to be a rare occurrence, but both groups of librarians are strongly in favour of the idea.
9 Academic librarians are more strongly in favour of undertaking research projects than public librarians, who rank this activity consistently low in terms of present involvement, perceived importance, and wish to be further involved.

Work assignment

A small special library attached to a large firm of architects has a staff of two professionals and one non-professional. One of the professionals, second-in-charge, leaves and is replaced. A second assistant is also recruited to carry out work previously done by the general pool of typists plus some other work brought about by an increase in demand for the library's services. Training funds are very limited and it is difficult to spare staff for any length of time from their daily work.

As Librarian you are anxious that the library should respond to the changing needs of its community and, where possible, to anticipate them. Draw up a scheme of induction and training for the first six months for each new member of staff, whose job descriptions are shown below, and outline ways in which you would hope to develop them during the following twelve months.

Library assistant
Purpose of job:
To provide clerical support to the professional librarians and work with the other assistant in giving an efficient service to the firm.

Main tasks:
To type letters, memoranda, booklists, publicity leaflets and other items as requested by the professional librarians.

To staff the counter area, answer queries and pass certain ones to professional staff, maintain records of loans.

To send overdue reminders and reservation notifications to users.

To answer the telephone.

To maintain office files.

Relationships:
Directly responsible to the Librarian and, in his absence, to the second-in-charge. Equal in status to the other assistant with whom some tasks are shared.

Librarian: second-in-charge
Purpose of job:
To provide a library service relevant to the needs of the firm.

To enable the firm to be successful and profitable.

To work with, and support, the Librarian to the above end.

Main tasks:
To deputise for the Librarian in his absence.

To provide professional assistance from the enquiry desk.

To publicize the library services to the members of the firm.

To carry out literature searches and bibliographical enquiries on behalf of users.

To monitor developments in the firm through attendance at meetings, discussions with staff, etc. and design relevant library support.

To select and revise book, periodical and audio-visual collections.
To undertake various technical duties including cataloguing and classification.

Relationships:

Directly responsible to the Librarian. Responsible for the assistants in the Librarian's absence.

Postscript

It is often difficult for librarians to accept that concepts, which management writers have identified, apply to them and their libraries. This is most apparent where the concept's level of abstraction is high. Theories of motivation or management styles described in the early chapters, for example, are likely to present such problems but the theories should not be dismissed out of hand. Librarians, in general, are unused to analysing the organizations in which they work in any systematic way and in the past have often assumed and accepted that they are unlikely themselves to effect change in the wider organizations which employ them. As change is now taking place so rapidly, at least in the expectations individuals have of themselves as change agents, librarians have become more interested in organizational analysis though they may still regard themselves as being primarily concerned with the specific jobs they are undertaking – answering queries, selecting materials, providing services, etc.

Once interest is aroused a variety of reactions is likely from those reading this book for the first time. At the one extreme we have encountered those for whom management theory provides a new enlightenment, which they readily apply to all past and present experiences, while at the other there are those who find it completely irrelevant. Our belief is that the theory is often crude and difficult to apply without modification but nonetheless it provides a necessary starting point for an understanding of what is happening in the organization.

We hope that the reader will have appreciated how the theory informs the various techniques described in the book, and how this can help to analyse situations and suggest solutions to problems in individual libraries. Some librarians may deny, for example, that they carry out staff appraisal, and may even state their opposition to it, whereas undoubtedly appraisal of some sort is being practised in their library. We would hope that greater understanding of the theory and techniques of appraisal would lead to evaluation of existing practice and a move towards a more open system agreed by the staff.

Some librarians manage very well without being able to label or analyse what they are doing. They may never have read a management book in their lives but have worked mainly on instinct. Unfortunately instinct is not contagious, but once the underlying reasons for success achieved in an instinctive manner can be articulated they can be passed on to others. Most of what we have written has been derived from the work of people who have tried to apply management ideas to improve the management of libraries and other organizations. We have tried to pass on these ideas to librarians and students of librarianship so that each person does not have to start from scratch and depend simply on his or her instinct.

Others may say that most management is common sense and obvious. The trouble here is that common sense has to be recognized as such and it is those with common sense who are best able to do this for us. This tautology disguises the fact that common sense is generally arrived at through clear thinking and experience. The study of management ideas and their applications to a specific library is quite valuable in helping more people to the higher common sense. It is true that management writing can be circumlocutory and jargon-ridden. We hope that this book has avoided the worst of these faults and will not be used by our readers as an excuse to avoid thinking in management terms.

All librarians have views about what is important in library management and one common to chiefs is that it is the immediate political environment which has to be carefully nurtured if the library is to receive its fair share of resources. When this view is held to the exclusion of almost all others the criterion for library activities is whether they will please those who supply the resources. Such a view can stop desirable developments in personnel management. A widely held view is that it is not a good idea to reveal too much to influential persons outside the library who may misunderstand and misuse such information. It is therefore thought that the library is best served if flexibility of movement is retained by committing as little as possible to paper and communicating only what it is thought desirable to communicate. Aims and objectives, for example, would not be spelled out, job descriptions and personnel specifications would be vague or non-existent and appraisal would not be recorded. In these circumstances effective personnel management is difficult to achieve, since it is dependent on written records and upon wide communication. Our view is that the political environment has to be taken into account when making decisions but not to the exclusion of other important areas of the environment such as technological, educational and cultural aspects.

It is appropriate that we ended the book with a discussion of staff development in the last chapter because the development of individuals able to work effectively with others lies at the heart of good personnel management and it is the means by which the library is able to progress and achieve its aims. Describing jobs, selecting staff, appraising and training them are all stepping-stones in that direction. Individuals and organizations are complex and an understanding of individuals in organizations is even more complex. The last thing we would want is for the various techniques to be used as blunt instruments imposed upon staff in libraries. Rather we would ask for sensitive personnel management which is flexible enough to recognize and take into account those nuances which make each library different without jeopardizing the achievement of the objectives sought by each technique.

References

Chapter 1

1. N. Roberts. Graduates in academic libraries. *Journal of Librarianship,* 5 (2) April 1973, pp. 97–115.
2. G. C. K. Smith and J. L. Schofield. A general survey of senior and intermediate staff deployment in university libraries. *Journal of Librarianship,* 5 (2) April 1973, pp. 79–96.
3. R. Sergean, J. R. McKay and Cynthia M. Corkill. *The Sheffield Manpower Project: a survey of staffing requirements for librarianship and information work. Final report.* Sheffield, University of Sheffield Postgraduate School of Librarianship and Information Science, 1976.
4. Anthony Smith. *Goodbye Gutenberg.* London, OUP, 1980.
5. Ibid. p. 314
6. *U.K. On-line Users' Group Newsletter,* No 6, 1979, pp. 1–2.
7. *U.K. On-line Users' Group Newsletter,* No 7, 1979, p. 1.
8. Emma Bird. *Information technology in the office: the impact on women's jobs.* Manchester, Equal Opportunities Commission, 1980.
9. B. Dalby. Microprocessors – a marvel or a menace? *University of Bradford Newsheet,* Autumn 1980, pp. 12–14.
10. Kevin Hawkins. *A handbook of industrial relations practice.* London, Kogan Page, 1979, p. 15.
11. Ibid. p. 78.
12. Committee of Enquiry on Industrial Relations. *Report.* London, HMSO, 1977. (Bullock Report).
13. Jeremy McMullen. *Rights at work.* London, Pluto, 1978.
14. Greville Janner. *Janner's practical guide to the Employment Act 1980.* London, Hutchinson, 1980.
15. Department of Employment. *Industrial relations code of practice.* London, HMSO, 1976.
16. Advisory, Conciliation and Arbitration Service. *Disciplinary practice and procedures in employment.* London, HMSO, 1977.
17. Frank Walton. *Employee relations reference guide for chief officers and managers in local authorities.* London, Local Authorities Conditions of Service Advisory Board, Luton, Local Government Training Board, 1978, p. 28.
18. Department of Employment, *op.cit.*
19. T. Burns and G. M. Stalker. *The management of innovation,* London, Tavistock, 1961.

20. Equal Opportunities Commission. *Code of practice: equal opportunity policies, procedures and practices in employment: consultative draft.* 1981.
21. Institute of Personnel Management. Joint Standing Committee on Discrimination. *Towards fairer selection: a code for non-discrimination.* London, Institute of Personnel Management, 1978.
22. Advisory, Conciliation and Arbitration Service. *Code of practice: time off for trade union duties and activities.* London, HMSO, 1978.

Chapter 2

1. R. Sergean, J. R. McKay and Cynthia M. Corkill. *The Sheffield Manpower Project: a survey of staffing requirements for Librarianship and information work. Final report.* Sheffield, University of Sheffield Postgraduate School of Librarianship and Information Science, 1976, p. 293.
2. Ross Shimmon (ed.) *A reader in library management.* London, Bingley, 1976, p. 126.
3. N. Roberts. Graduates in academic libraries: a survey of past students of the Postgraduate School of Librarianship and Information Science, Sheffield University, 1964/65 – 1970/71. *Journal of Librarianship* **5** (2) April 1973, pp. 97–115.
4. Noragh Jones and Peter Jordan. 'One year later: a survey of students from the Leeds School of Librarianship.' *Research in Librarianship,* **28** (5) January 1975, pp. 113–123.
5. F. B. Gilbreth. *Primer of scientific management.* New York, Van Nostrand, 1912.
6. F. W. Taylor. 'The principles of scientific management.' *In* Victor H. Vroom and Edward L. Deci (eds.) *Management and motivation: selected readings.* Harmondsworth, Penguin Books, 1970, pp. 295–301.
7. N. Roberts. *Personnel in libraries and information units: a seminar for library managers.* London, British Library, 1978, (BLR&D Report 5449) p. 24.
8. Noragh Jones. *Continuing education for librarians.* Leeds, Leeds Polytechnic School of Librarianship, 1977, p. 213.
9. Richard E. Walton. 'How to counter alienation in the plant.' *Harvard Business Review Reprint Series,* No. 21168, 1973, pp. 101–112.
10. Elton Mayo. 'The Hawthorne investigations.' *In* D. S. Pugh, *et al. Writers on organizations.* Harmondsworth, Penguin Books, 2nd edn, 1971, pp. 126–130.
11. Abraham Maslow. *Motivation and personality.* New York, Harper & Row, 1970.

12. Roberts (1973), *op.cit.*

13. G. C. K. Smith and J. L. Schofield. A general survey of senior and intermediate staff deployment in university libraries. *Journal of Librarianship*, **5** (2) April 1973, pp. 79–96.

14. Jones and Jordan, *op.cit.*

15. K. H. Plate and Elizabeth W. Stone. 'Factors affecting librarians' job satisfaction.' *Library Quarterly*, **44** (2) April 1974, pp. 97–110.

16. Frederick Herzberg. 'How do you motivate employees?' *In* Dale S. Beach (ed.) *Managing people at work: readings in personnel.* New York, Macmillan & Co., 1971, p. 241.

17. Herzberg, *op.cit.* p. 250.

18. Douglas McGregor. *The human side of enterprise.* New York, McGraw-Hill, 1960.

19. Rensis Likert. *New patterns of management.* New York, McGraw-Hill, 1961, Chapter 14.

20. Likert, *op.cit.*, Chapter 9.

21. Robert R. Blake and Jane S. Mouton. *The managerial grid.* Houston, Texas, Gulf Publishing Co., 1964, p. 10.

22. Blake and Mouton, *op.cit.*, Chapter 7.

23. Victor H. Vroom. *Work and motivation.* New York, Wiley, 1964.

24. Fred Fiedler. *Theory of leadership effectiveness.* New York, McGraw-Hill, 1967.

25. Edgar H. Schein. *Organizational psychology.* Englewood Cliffs, N. J., Prentice-Hall, 2nd edn, 1970. p.70.

26. Plate and Stone, *op.cit.* p. 97.

27. B. G. Dutton. 'Staff management and staff participation.' *In* Ross Shimmon (ed.) *A reader in library management.* London, Bingley, 1976, pp. 132–133.

28. W. Ashworth. 'The administration of diffuse collections.' *Aslib Proceedings,* **24** (5) May 1972, p. 276. (Updated in *Organizing multisite libraries.* London, Library Association CTFE, 1976.)

29. Dutton, *op.cit.*, p. 140.

30. Roberts (1973), *op.cit.*

31. Smith and Schofield, *op.cit.*

32. Sergean, McKay and Corkill, *op.cit.*

33. Plate and Stone, *op.cit.*

34. Schein, *op.cit.*, p. 62.

35. Angela Bowey. 'Perceptions and attitudes to change: a pilot study.' *Personnel Review*, **9** (1) 1980, pp. 35–42.

36. Ken Jones. 'How to get the best out of meetings.' *New Library World*, **81** (956) February 1980, pp. 32–35.

Chapter 3

1. Hannah Gavron. *Captive wife*. London, Routledge, 1966.
2. E. M. Broome. 'Library manpower planning.' *Aslib Proceedings*, **25** (11) November 1973, pp. 400–414.
3. *Library Association Record*, **80** (11) November 1978, p. 573.
4. Library Advisory Councils for England and Wales. *A report on the supply and training of librarians*. London, HMSO, 1968. (Jessop Report) p. 18.
5. Department of Education and Science. *Census of staff in librarianship and information work in the UK, 1972*. London, HMSO, 1975.
6. Department of Education and Science. *Census of staff in librarianship and information work in the UK, 1976*. London, HMSO, 1978.
7. Library Association. Commission on the supply and demand for qualified librarians. *Report*. London, Library Association, 1977, (Barnes Report) p. 1.
8. Ibid. p. 44.
9. Ibid. p. 28.
10. N. Roberts. 'Graduates in academic libraries . . . 1964/65 – 1970/71.' *Journal of Librarianship*, **5** (2) April 1973, pp. 79–96.
11. G. C. K. Smith and J. L. Schofield. A general survey of senior and inter-mediate staff deployment in university libraries. *Journal of Librarianship*, **5** (2) April 1973, pp. 79–96.
12. Committee on Higher Education. *Higher education*. London, HMSO, 1963. (Robbins Report).
13. D. E. Davinson. Manpower planning. *New Library World*, **75** (890) August 1974, pp 161–162.
14. Library Association. Commission on the supply and demand for qualified librarians, *op.cit.*, p. 45.
15. R. Sergean. *Librarianship and information work: job characteristics and staffing needs*. London, British Library, 1976, (BLR&D Report 5321 HC).
16. R. Sergean, J. R. McKay and Cynthia Corkill. *The Sheffield Manpower Project: a survey of staffing requirements for librarianship and information work. Final report*. Sheffield, University of Sheffield Post-graduate School of Librarianship and Information Science, 1976.
17. N. Roberts (ed.) *Education, training and the use of staff*. Sheffield, University of Sheffield Postgraduate School of Librarianship and Information Science, 1977, (BLR&D Report 5394).
18. N. Roberts (ed.) *Personnel in libraries and information units: a seminar for library managers*. London, British Library, 1978, (BLR&D Report 5449).

19. Ian Winkworth. Library Association qualification structure and library staff situation. *Library Association Record*, **82** (4) April 1980, pp. 177–178.

20. LAMSAC. *The staffing of public libraries: a report of the research undertaken by the Local Authorities Management Services and Computer Committee for the Department of Education and Science.* London, HMSO, 1976. 3 vols.

21. Ibid. vol. 1, p. iii.

22. Ibid. Section 6 (i), vol. 1, pp. 232–234.

23. Ibid. Section 6 (i), vol. 1, p. 227.

24. Library Association. Working Party on Training. *Report.* London Library Association, 1977.

25. LAMSAC, *op.cit.*, vol. 1, p. 252.

26. Department of the Environment. *Local authority annual reports: code of practice.* London, HMSO, 1981.

27. Roberts (1978), *op.cit.*, p. 29.

28. Library Association. 'The effect of cuts in public expenditure on public libraries in England and Wales.' *Library Association Record*, **81** (9) September 1979, pp. 429–433.

29. Library Association. *Trade Union News*, 6, 1980.

30. Library Association (1979), *op.cit.*, p. 431.

31. Angela Bowey. *A guide to manpower planning.* London, Macmillan, 1974, Chapter 3.

32. Herbert Schur. *The education and training of information specialists in the 1970s.* Sheffield, University of Sheffield Postgraduate School of Librarianship and Information Science, 1972, p. 96.

33. LAMSAC, *op.cit.*, vol. 1, p. 173.

34. LAMSAC, *op.cit.*, vol. 1, pp. 172–173.

35. Nick Moore. *Manpower planning in libraries.* London, Library Association, 1980, p. 8.

Chapter 4

1. P. R. Plumbley. *Recruitment and selection.* London, Institute of Personnel Management, new edn rev., 1976, p. 19.

2. Noragh Jones. *Continuing education for librarians.* Leeds, Leeds Polytechnic School of Librarianship, 1977, p. 146.

3. N. Roberts. *Personnel in libraries and information units: a seminar for library managers.* London, British Library, 1978, p. 5.

4. Ian Winkworth. 'Library Association qualification structure and library staff situation.' *Library Association Record*, **82** (4) April 1980, pp. 177–178.

5. R. Sergean, J. R. McKay and Cynthia M. Corkill. *The Sheffield Manpower Project: a survey of staffing requirements for librarianship and information work. Final report.* Sheffield, University of Sheffield Postgraduate School of Librarianship and Information Science, 1976.

6. Institute of Information Scientists. Careers seminar held at the Leeds School of Librarianship, Spring 1980. Oral discussion.

7. J. Hinks. 'Leics. libraries: a team-based organizational structure.' *In* G. Holroyd (ed.) *Studies in library management.* Vol. 4. London, Bingley, 1977, pp. 67–84.

8. Association of Assistant Librarians Northern Division. *Team librarianship: papers given at the AAL Northern Division/LA Northern Branch Joint Annual Weekend School at Otterburn Hall, October 1978.* AAL Northern Division, 1979.

9. B. G. Dutton. 'Staff management and staff participation.' *In* Ross Shimmon (ed.) *A reader in library management.* London, Bingley, 1976, pp. 129–145.

10. Library Association. *Professional and non-professional duties in libraries.* London, Library Association, 2nd edn, 1974.

11. Joint National Council for Local Authorities' Administrative, Professional, Technical and Clerical Services. *Scheme of conditions of service.* London, NJC, [various dates]. Appendix H, sections 4, 6 (2).

12. L. Rothenberg. 'A job-task index for evaluating professional staff utilization in libraries.' *Library Quarterly,* **41,** October 1971, pp. 320–328.

13. Don Mason. *Information management.* London, Peter Peregrinus, 1978, Chapter 6.

14. Ibid. p. 94.

15. Quoted in Plumbley, *op.cit.,* pp. 23–25.

16. Plumbley, *op.cit.,* p. 24.

17. Alec Rodger. *The seven point plan.* London, National Institute of Industrial Psychology, 3rd edn, 1970.

18. J. M. Fraser, *Employment interviewing.* London, Macdonald and Evans, 5th edn, 1978.

19. Sergean, McKay and Corkill, *op.cit.*

20. Jones, *op.cit.*

21. Rodger, *op.cit.,* p. 13.

Chapter 5

1. B. J. Edwards. 'Application forms.' *In* Bernard Ungerson (ed.) *Recruitment handbook.* Epping, Gower Press, 2nd edn, 1975, pp. 76–94.

2. Equal Opportunities Commission. *Code of practice: equal opportunity policies, procedures and practices in employment: consultative draft.* Manchester, Equal Opportunities Commission, 1981.

3. James Walker, Clive Fletcher and Leith Taylor. 'Performance appraisal: an open or shut case?' *Personnel Review,* **6** (1) Winter 1977, pp. 38–42.

4. Peter John Jordan. 'Staff selection in public libraries.' *Library Management News,* 9 August 1979, pp. 27–32.

5. Raymond L. Gorden. *Interviewing: strategy, techniques and tactics.* Homewood, Illinois, Dorsey Press, 1969.

6. Derek Peter Torrington and John Chapman. *Personnel management.* Englewood Cliffs, Prentice Hall, 1979.

7. T. M. Higham. 'Choosing the method of recruitment.' *In* Bernard Ungerson (ed.) *Recruitment handbook.* Epping, Gower Press, 2nd edn, 1975, pp. 35–51.

8. Richard A. Frear. *The evaluation interview.* New York, McGraw-Hill, 1973.

9. Frear, *op.cit.*

10. John Munro Fraser. *Introduction to personnel management.* London, Nelson, 1971.

11. Neil Rackham and Terry Morgan. *Behaviour analysis in training.* London, McGraw-Hill, 1977.

12. Peter John Jordan. *Managing a public library team.* Sudbury, Branch and Mobile Libraries Group of the Library Association, 1979.

13. Bernard Ungerson (ed.) *Recruitment handbook.* Epping, Gower Press, 2nd edn, 1975, p. 8.

14. Frank Sneath, Manab Thakur and Bruce Medjuck. *Testing people at work.* London, Institute of Personnel Management, 1976.

15. Kenneth Maxwell Miller (ed.) *Psychological testing in personnel assessment.* Epping, Gower Press, 1975.

16. Sneath, *op.cit.*

17. Oscar Krisen Buros (ed.) *The eighth mental measurements yearbook.* Highland Park, Gryphon Press, 1978.

18. Peter John Jordan. Staff selection in public libraries. *Library Management News,* 9 August 1979, pp. 27–32.

19. Nicola Kingston. *Selecting managers: a survey of current practice in 200 companies.* London, British Institute of Management, 1977.

20. J. P. Guilford. Traits of creativity. *In* P. E. Vernon (ed.) *Creativity: selected readings.* Harmondsworth, Penguin, 1970, pp. 167–188.

21. Clyde Kluckhohn and Henry A. Murray. *Personality in nature, society and culture.* New York, Knopf, 2nd edn, 1953.

22. Paul Kline. 'Personality threats.' *New Society,* **24** (552) 3 May 1973, pp. 241–42.

23. Kline. *op.cit.*

Chapter 6

1. Gerald Anthony Randell *et al. Staff appraisal.* London, Institute of Personnel Management, rev. edn 1974.
2. R. J. Forbes and E. M. Anaya. 'Appraiser and appraised.' *Management Today,* January 1980, pp. 33–34, 39.
3. James Walker, Clive Fletcher and Leith Taylor. Performance appraisal: an open or shut case? *Personnel Review,* **6** (1) Winter 1977, pp. 38–42.
4. *Camden Newsletter,* **58** August/September 1976, p. 1.
5. Michael Messenger. 'Professional staff assessment: the Shropshire pattern.' *Library Association Record,* **77** (1) January 1975, pp. 2–4.
6. Clive Fletcher. 'Management/subordinate communication and leadership style: a field study of their relationships to perceived outcomes of appraisal interviews.' *Personnel Review,* **7** (1) Winter 1978, pp. 59–62.
7. Robert C. Hilton. 'Performance evaluation of library personnel.' *Special Libraries,* **69** (11) November 1978, pp. 429–434.
8. Anne M. Turner. 'Why *do* department heads take longer coffee breaks? A public library evaluates itself.' *American Libraries,* **9** (4) April 1978, pp. 213–215.
9. 'Action exchange.' *American Libraries,* **8** (8) September 1977, p. 421.
10. Roland Person. 'Library faculty evaluation: an idea whose time continues to come.' *Journal of Academic Librarianship,* **5** (3) July 1979, pp. 142–47.
11. Action exchange *op.cit.*
12. David Peele. 'Some aspects of staff evaluation in the UK and the USA.' *Library Association Record,* **74** (4) April 1972, pp. 69–71.
13. Walker, *op.cit.*
14. Person, *op.cit.*
15. American Library Association. Subcommittee on personnel organization and procedure of the A.L.A. board on personnel administration. *Personnel organization and procedure: a manual suggested for use in public libraries.* Chicago, American Library Association, 1952.
16. Messenger, *op.cit.*
17. David Peele. 'Performance ratings and librarians' rights.' *American Libraries,* **1** (6) June 1970, pp. 595–605.
18. Kaye H. Rowe. 'An appraisal of appraisals.' *Journal of Management Studies,* **1** (1) March 1964, pp. 1–25.
19. John W. Ellison and Deborah B. Lazeration. 'Personnel accountability form for academic reference librarians: a model.' *Reference Quarterly* **16** (2) Winter 1976, pp. 142–48.
20. Peter John Jordan. *Managing a public library team.* Sudbury, Branch and Mobile Libraries Group of the Library Association, 1979.

21. Michael Rutherford Williams. *Performance appraisal in management.* London, Heinemann, 1972.
22. Edgar Anstey, Clive Fletcher and James Walker. *Staff appraisal and development.* London, Allen and Unwin, 1976.
23. Peter Honey. *Face to face: a practical guide to interactive skills.* London, Institute of Personnel Management, 1976.
24. Dave Barker. *T. A. and training: the theory and use of transactional analysis in organisations.* Farnborough, Gower Press, 1980.
25. Barker, *op.cit.*

Chapter 7

1. T. H. Boydell. *A guide to the identification of training needs.* London, British Association for Commercial and Industrial Education, 1973.
2. David Lewis. 'In-service training in the polytechnic library.' *New Library World,* **74** (875) May 1973, p. 104.
3. Leicestershire Libraries and Information Services. *The effective use of team time.* Leicester, Leicestershire Libraries and Information Services, 1977.
4. Library Association. *Training in libraries.* London, Library Association, 1977.
5. Ronald J. Edwards. *In-service training in British Libraries: its development and present practice.* London, Library Association, 1976.
6. Local Government Training Board. *Training and development of training officers.* London, Local Government Training Board, 1974.
7. Library Association. Library Education Group. *Directory of library training officers in the U.K. 1976–77.* London, Library Association. 1977.
8. Edwards, *op.cit.*, p. 149.
9. Peter Smith. *The design of learning spaces.* London, Council for Educational Technology for the United Kingdom, 1974.
10. P. Robertson. Systematic induction. *In* Library Association. *Guidelines for training in libraries.* London, Library Association, 1980, p. A2.
11. Robertson, Ibid. pp. A1–36.
12. Gordon Wills and Christine Oldman (eds) *Developing the librarian as a manager.* Bradford, MCB Books, 1975.
13. Roy Hewitt. *Library management case studies.* London, Crosby Lockwood, 1969.
14. Jean Ruddock. *Learning through small group discussion: a study of seminar work in higher education.* Guildford, Society for Research into Higher Education, 1978.
15. Peter Jordan. *Managing a public library team.* Sudbury, Branch and Mobile Libraries Group of the Library Association, 1979.

16. Ken Jones. 'How to get the best out of meetings'. *New Library World,* **81** (956) February 1980, pp. 32–5.

17. M. B. Miles. *Learning to work in groups.* New York, Columbia University, Teachers College Press, 1959.

18. Edward Chapman, Paul L. St. Pierre, and John Lubans. *Library systems analysis guidelines.* New York, Wiley-Interscience, 1970.

19. David C. Weber. The dynamics of the library environment for professional staff growth. *College and Research Libraries,* **35** (4) July 1974, pp. 259–67.

20. Amelia Breiting, Marcia Dorey and Deidre Sockbeson. 'Staff development in college and university libraries.' *Special Libraries,* **67** (7) July 1976, pp. 305–10.

21. Noragh Jones. 'Continuing education for librarians.' *Journal of Librarianship,* **10** (1) January 1978, pp. 39–55.

Bibliography

American Library Association. Subcommittee on personnel organization and procedure of the ALA board on personnel administration. *Personnel organization and procedure: a manual suggested for use in public libraries.* Chicago, American Library Association, 1952.

Advisory, Conciliation and Arbitration Service. *Code of practice: time off for trade union duties and activities.* London, HMSO, 1978.
Disciplinary practice and procedures in employment. London, HMSO, 1977.

Anstey, E., Fletcher, C. and Walker, J. *Staff appraisal and development.* London, Allen and Unwin, 1976.

Argyle, M. *Social psychology of work.* Harmondsworth, Penguin Books, new edn, 1974.

Ashworth, W. *Organizing multi-site libraries.* London, Library Association CTFE Section, 1976.

Association of Assistant Librarians Northern Division. *Team librarianship: papers given at the AAL Northern Division/LA Northern Branch Joint Annual Weekend School at Otterburn Hall, October 1978.* AAL Northern Division, 1979.

Barker, D. *T. A. and training: the theory and use of transactional analysis in organisations.* Farnborough, Gower Press, 1980.

Beach, D. S. (ed.) *Managing people at work: readings in personnel.* New York, Macmillan, 1971.

Bird, E. *Information technology in the office: the impact on women's jobs.* Manchester, Equal Opportunities Commission, 1980.

Blake, R. R. and Mouton, J. S. *The managerial grid.* Houston, Texas, Gulf Publishing Co., 1964.

Bowey, A. *A guide to manpower planning.* London, Macmillan, 1974.

Boydell, T. H. *A guide to the identification of training needs.* London, British Association for Commercial and Industrial Education, 1973.

Burns, T. and Stalker, G. M. *The management of innovation.* London, Tavistock, 1961.

Buros, O. K. (ed.) *The eighth mental measurements yearbook.* Highland Park, Gryphon Press, 1978.

Chapman, E., St. Pierre, P. L. and Lubans, J. *Library systems analysis guidelines.* New York, Wiley-Interscience, 1970.

Committee on Higher Education. *Higher education.* London, HMSO, 1963. (Robbins Report).

Department of Education and Science. *Census of staff in librarianship and information work in the UK, 1972.* London, HMSO, 1975.
Census of staff in librarianship and information work in the UK, 1976. London, HMSO, 1978.

Department of Employment. *Industrial relations code of practice.* London, HMSO, 1976.

Department of the Environment. *Local authority annual reports: code of practice.* London, HMSO, 1981

Department of Trade. *Report of the committee of inquiry on industrial democracy.* London, HMSO, 1977. (Bullock Report.)

Dutton, B. G. 'Staff management and staff participation.' *In* Ross Shimmon (ed.) *A reader in library management.* London, Bingley, 1976, pp. 129-145.

Edwards, B. J. 'Application forms.' *In* Ungerson, Bernard (ed.) *Recruitment handbook.* Epping, Gower Press, 2nd edn, 1975, pp. 76-94.

Edwards, R. J. *In-service training in British libraries: its development and present practice.* London, Library Association, 1976.

Equal Opportunities Commission. *Code of practice: equal opportunity policies, procedures and practices in employment: consultative draft.* Manchester, Equal Opportunities Commission, 1981.

Evans, G. E. *Management techniques for librarians.* New York, Academic Press, 1976.

Fiedler, F. *Theory of leadership effectiveness.* New York, McGraw-Hill, 1967.

Finnigan, J. *The right people in the right jobs.* London, Business Books, 1973.

Fraser, J. M. *Employment interviewing.* London, Macdonald and Evans, 5th edn, 1978.

Fraser, J. M. *Introduction to personnel management.* London, Nelson, 1971.

Frear, R. A. *The evaluation interview.* New York, McGraw-Hill, 1973.

Gavron, H. *Captive wife.* London, Routledge, 1966.

Gellerman, S. W. *Behavioural science in management.* Harmondsworth, Penguin Books, 1974.

Gilbreth, F. B. *Primer of scientific management.* New York, Van Nostrand, 1912.

Gode, W. *Training your staff.* London, The Industrial Society, 1972.

Gorden, R. L. *Interviewing: strategy, techniques and tactics.* Homewood, Illinois, Dorsey Press, 1969.

Guilford, J. P. 'Traits of creativity.' *In* Vernon, P. E. (ed.) *Creativity: selected readings.* Harmondsworth, Penguin, 1970, pp. 167-188.

Hawkins, K. *A handbook of industrial relations practice*. London, Kogan Page, 1979.

The management of industrial relations. Harmondsworth, Penguin, 1978.

Health and Safety Commission. *Health and Safety at Work etc. Act 1974: the Act outlined*. London, Health and Safety Commission, 1975.

Henderson, J. *A guide to the Employment Act 1980*. London, Industrial Society, 1980.

Herzberg, F. 'How do you motivate employees?' *In* Dale S. Beach (ed.) *Managing people at work: readings in personnel*. New York, Macmillan, 1971.

Hewitt, R. *Library management case studies*. London, Crosby Lockwood, 1969.

Higham, T. M. 'Choosing the method of recruitment.' *In* Ungerson, Bernard (ed.) *Recruitment handbook*. Epping, Gower Press, 2nd edn, 1975, pp. 35-51.

Hinks, J. 'Leics. libraries: a team-based organizational structure.' *In* G. Holroyd (ed.) *Studies in library management*. Vol. 4. London, Bingley, 1977, pp. 67-84.

Honey, P. *Face to face: a practical guide to interactive skills*. London, Institute of Personnel Management, 1976.

Institute of Personnel Management. Joint Standing Committee on Discrimination. *Towards fairer selection: a code for non-discrimination*. London, Institute of Personnel Management, 1978.

Janner, G. *Janner's practical guide to the Employment Act 1980*. London, Hutchinson, 1980.

Jones, N. *Continuing education for librarians*. Leeds, Leeds Polytechnic School of Librarianship, 1977.

Jordan, P. J. *Managing a public library team*. Sudbury, Branch and Mobile Libraries Group of the Library Association, 1979.

Kingston, *Selecting managers: a survey of current practice in 200 companies*. London, British Institute of Management, 1977.

Kluckhohn, C. and Murray, H. A. *Personality in nature, society and culture*. New York, Knopf, 2nd edn, 1953.

LAMSAC. *The staffing of public libraries*. London, HMSO, 1976. 3 vols.

Lawshe, C. H. and Balma, M. L. *Principles of personnel testing*. New York, McGraw-Hill, 2nd edn, 1966.

Leicestershire Libraries and Information Services. *The effective use of team time*. Leicester, Leicestershire Libraries and Information Services, 1977.

Library Advisory Councils for England and Wales. *A report on the supply and training of librarians*. London, HMSO, 1968. (Jessop Report.)

Library Association. *Draft code of professional ethics: a discussion document*. London, Library Association, 1980.
Guidelines for training in libraries. London, Library Association, 1980.
Professional and non-professional duties in libraries. London, Library Association, 2nd edn, 1974.
Training in libraries. London, Library Association, 1977.
Commission on the supply of and demand for qualified librarians. *Report*. London, Library Association, 1977. (Barnes Report.)
Library Education Group. *Directory of library training officers in U.K. 1976-77*. London, Library Association, 1977.
Likert, R. *New patterns of management*. New York, McGraw-Hill, 1961.
Local Government Training Board. *Training and development of training officers*. London, Local Government Training Board, 1974.

McGregor, D. *The human side of enterprise*. New York, McGraw-Hill, 1960.
McMullen, J. *Rights at work*. London, Pluto, 1978.
Marsh, P. R. *White-collar unions in libraries*. Sheffield, University of Sheffield Postgraduate School of Librarianship and Information Science, 1980.
Maslow, A. *Motivation and personality*. New York, Harper & Row, 1970.
Mason, D. *Information management*. London, Peter Peregrinus, 1978.
Mayo, E. 'The Hawthorne investigations.' *In* D. S. Pugh, *et al. Writers on organizations*. Harmondsworth, Penguin Books, 2nd edn, 1971, pp. 126-130.
Miles, M. B. *Learning to work in groups*. New York, Columbia University, Teachers College Press, 1959.
Miller, K. M. (ed.) *Psychological testing in personnel assessment*. Epping, Gower Press, 1975.
Miner, J. B. *Personnel psychology*. London, Collier-Macmillan, 1969.
Moore, N. *Manpower planning in libraries*. London, Library Association, 1980.

National Joint Council for Local Authorities' Administrative, Professional, Technical and Clerical Services. *Scheme of conditions of service*. London, NJC, [various dates].

Plumbley, P. R. *Recruitment and selection*. London, Institute of Personnel Management, new edn, 1974.

Rackham, N. and Morgan, T. *Behaviour analysis in training*. London, McGraw-Hill, 1977.
Randell, G. A. *et al. Staff appraisal*. London, Institute of Personnel Management, rev. edn, 1974.

Roberts, N. (ed.) *Education, training and the use of staff.* Sheffield, University of Sheffield Postgraduate School of Librarianship and Information Science, 1977. (BLR&D Report 5394.)
Personnel in libraries and information units. London, British Library, 1978. (BLR&D Report 5449.)

Robertson, P. 'Systematic induction.' *In* Library Association. *Guidelines for training in libraries.* London, Library Association, 1980, pp. A1-36.

Rodger, A. *The seven-point plan.* London, National Institute of Industrial Psychology, 3rd edn, 1970.

Ruddock, J. *Learning through small group discussion: a study of seminar work in higher education.* Guildford, Society for Research into Higher Education, 1978.

Savage, A. W. *Personnel management.* London, Library Association, 1977.

Schein, E. H. *Organizational psychology.* Englewood Cliffs, N. J., Prentice-Hall, 2nd edn, 1970.

Schur, H. *The education and training of information specialists in the 1970s.* Sheffield, University of Sheffield Postgraduate School of Librarianship and Information Science, 1972.

Sergean, R. *Librarianship and information work: job characteristics and staffing needs.* London, British Library, 1976. (BLR&D Report 5321 HC.)

Sergean, R., McKay, J. R. and Corkill, C. M. *The Sheffield Manpower Project: a survey of staffing requirements for librarianship and information work.* Sheffield, University of Sheffield Postgraduate School of Librarianship and Information Science, 1976.

Shimmon, R. (ed.) *A reader in library management.* London, Bingley, 1976.

Sidney, E. and Brown, M. *The skills of interviewing.* London, Tavistock, 1961.

Sidney, E., Brown, M. and Argyle, M. *Skills with people: a guide for managers.* London, Hutchinson, 1973.

Smart, C. *Industrial relations in Britain: a guide to sources of information.* London, CPI, 1980.

Smith, A. *Goodbye Gutenberg.* London, OUP, 1980.

Smith, P. *The designer of learning spaces.* London, Council for Educational Technology for the United Kingdom, 1974.

Sneath, F., Thakur, M. and Medjuck, B. *Testing people at work.* London, Institute of Personnel Management, 1976.

Snell, M. R. 'Recruitment of minorities.' *In* Ungerson, Bernard (ed.) *Recruitment handbook.* Epping, Gower Press, 2nd edn, 1975.

Staff of TUCRIC, Leeds. 'Hazards of VDUs.' *Librarians for Social Change,* Summer 1979.

Stewart, J. D. *The responsive local authority.* London, Charles Knight, 1974.

Taylor, F. W. 'The principles of scientific management.' *In* Victor H. Vroom and Edward L. Deci (eds.) *Management and motivations: selected readings.* Harmondsworth, Penguin Book, 1970, pp. 295-301.

Thomason, G. *A textbook of personnel management.* London, Institute of Personnel Management, 1978.

Torrington, D. and Chapman, J. *Personnel management.* Englewood Cliffs, N.J., Prentice-Hall, 1979.

Ungerson, B. (ed.) *Recruitment handbook.* Epping, Gower Press, 2nd edn, 1975.

Vernon, P. E. (ed.) *Creativity: selected readings.* Harmondsworth, Penguin Books, 1970.

Vroom, V. H. *Work and motivation.* New York, Wiley, 1964.

Vroom, V. H. and Deci, E. L. (eds.) *Management and motivation: selected readings.* Harmondsworth, Penguin Books, 1970.

Walton, F. *Employee relations reference guide for chief officers and managers in local authorities.* London, Local Authorities Conditions of Service Advisory Board, Luton, Local Government Training Board, 1978.

Williams, M. R. *Performance appraisal in management.* London, Heinemann, 1972.

Wills, G. and Oldman, C. (eds) *Developing the librarian as a manager,* Bradford, MCB Books, 1975.

Wilson, T. D. 'Organization development in library management.' *In* Holroyd, G. (ed) *Studies in library management,* vol 4. London, Bingley, 1977, pp. 45-66.

Wrigglesworth, F. and Earl, B. *A guide to the Health and Safety at Work Act.* London, Industrial Society, 1974.

Periodical Articles

'Action exchange.' *American Libraries,* **8** (8) September 1977, p. 421.

Ashworth, W. 'The administration of diffuse collections.' *Aslib Proceedings,* **24** (5) May 1972, pp. 274-283.

Bowey, A. 'Perceptions and attitudes to change: a pilot study.' *Personnel Review,* **9** (1) January 1980.

Breiting, A., Dorey, M. and Sockbeson, D. 'Staff development in college and university libraries.' *Special Libraries,* **67** (7) July 1976, pp. 305-10

Broome, E. M. 'Library manpower planning.' *Aslib Proceedings,* **25** (11) November 1973.

Camden Newsletter, **58** August/September 1976, p. 1.

Creth, S. 'Conducting an effective employment interview.' *Journal of Academic Librarianship,* **4** (5) November 1978, pp. 356-60.

Dalby, B. 'Microprocessors – a marvel or a menace?' *University of Bradford Newsheet*, Autumn 1980, pp. 12-14.

Davinson, D. E. 'Manpower planning.' *New Library World*, **75** (890) August 1974, pp. 161-162.

D'Elia, G. P. 'The determinants of job satisfaction among beginner librarians.' *Library Quarterly*, **49** (3) 1979, pp. 283-302.

Ellison, J. W. and Lazeration, D. B. 'Personnel accountability form for academic reference librarians: a model.' *Reference Quarterley*, **16** (2) Winter 1976, pp. 142-48.

Fletcher, C. 'Management/subordinate communication and leadership style: a field study of their relationships to perceived outcomes of appraisal interviews.' *Personnel Review*, 7 (1) Winter 1978, pp. 59-62.

Forbes, R. J. and Anaya, E. M. 'Appraiser and appraised.' *Management Today*, January 1980, pp. 33-34, 39.

Haslam, D. 'Noblesse oblige: NALGO's debt to librarians.' *Library Association Record*, **79** (5) May 1977, pp. 251-55.

Hilton, R. C. 'Performance evaluation of library personnel.' *Special Libraries*, **69** (11) November 1978, pp. 429-434.

Jones, K. 'How to get the best out of meetings.' *New Library World*, **81** (956) February 1980, pp. 32-5.

Jones, N. 'Continuing education for librarians.' *Journal of Librarianship*, **10** (1) January 1978, pp. 39-55.

Jones, N. and Jordan, P. 'One year later: a survey of students from the Leeds School of Librarianship.' *Research in Librarianship*, **28** (5) January 1975, pp. 113-123.

Jordan, P. 'Staff selection in public libraries.' *Library Management News*, 9 August 1979, pp. 27-32.

Kline, P. 'Personality threats.' *New Society*, **24** (552) 3 May 1973, pp. 241-42.

Lewis, D. 'In-service training in the polytechnic library.' *New Library World*, **74** (875) May 1973, p. 104.

Library Association. 'The effects of cuts in public expenditure on public libraries in England and Wales.' *Library Association Record*, **81** (9) September 1979, pp. 429-433.

Lumsden, C. A. 'Communication within the organization: organization development, team making and informal meetings.' *Aslib Proceedings*, **27** (8) August 1975, pp. 327-338.

Maidment, W. R. 'Trade unionism in public libraries.' *Journal of Librarianship*, **8** (3) July 1976, 143-52.

Meredith, G. P. 'The changing role of the training officer in local government.' *Local Government Studies*, (7) February 1974, pp. 53-57.

Messenger, M. 'Professional staff assessment: the Shropshire pattern.' *Library Association Record*, **77** (1) January 1975, pp. 2-4.

Peele, D. 'Fear in the library.' *Journal of Academic Librarianship*, **4** (5) November 1978, pp. 361-65.

'Performance ratings and librarians' rights.' *American Libraries*, **1** (6) June 1970, pp. 595-605.

'Some aspects of staff evaluation in the UK and USA.' *Library Association Record*, **74** (4) April 1972, pp. 69-71.

Person, R. 'Library faculty evaluation: an idea whose time has yet to come.' *Journal of Academic Librarianship*, **5** (3) July 1979, pp. 142-47.

Plate, K. H. and Stone, E. 'Factors affecting librarians' job satisfaction.' *Library Quarterly*, **44** (2) April 1974, pp. 97-110.

Roberts, N. 'Graduates in academic libraries.' *Journal of Librarianship*, **5** (2) April 1973, pp. 97-115.

Rothenberg, L. 'A job-task index for evaluating professional staff utilization in libraries.' *Library Quarterly*, **41** (3) October 1971, pp. 320-328.

Rowe, K. H. 'An appraisal of appraisals.' *Journal of Management Studies*, **1** (1) March 1964, pp. 1-25.

Simpson, N. A. 'Training in context.' *In* Library Association. *Proceedings of the public libraries conference, Aberdeen 1974*. London, Library Association, 1974, pp. 27-33.

Smith, G. C. K. and Schofield, J. L. 'A general survey of senior and intermediate staff deployment in university libraries.' *Journal of Librarianship*, **5** (2) April 1973, pp. 79-96.

The Staff Development Committee. 'Developing a model for continuing education and personnel development in libraries.' *Library Trends*, **20** (1) July 1971 pp. 92-6.

Staff of TUCRIC, Leeds. 'Hazards of VDUs.' *Librarians for Social Change*, (20) Summer 1979, pp. 6-9.

Turner, A. M. 'Why *do* department heads take longer coffee breaks? A public library evaluates itself.' *American Libraries*, **9** (4) April 1978, pp. 213-215.

UK On-line Users Group Newsletter, Nos 6 and 7, 1979.

Walker, J., Fletcher, C. and Taylor, L. 'Performance appraisal: an open or shut case?' *Personnel Review*, **6** (1) Winter 1977, pp. 38-42.

Walton, R. E. 'How to counter alienation in the plant.' *Harvard Business Review Reprint Series*, No. 21168, 1973, pp. 101-112.

Weber, D. C. 'The dynamics of the library environment for professional staff growth.' *College and Research Libraries*, **35** (4) July 1974, pp. 259-67.

Winkworth, I. 'LA qualification structure and library staff situation.' *Library Association Record*, **82** (4) April 1980, pp. 177-178.

Index